JOCK STEIN: THE CELTIC YEARS

First published in Great Britain in 1998 by
MAINSTREAM PUBLISHING COMPANY (EDINBURGH) LTD
7 Albany Street
Edinburgh EH1 3UG

This edition 1999

Reprinted 2000

ISBN 1 84018 241 5

A catalogue record for this book is available from the British Library

Printed and bound in Finland by WSOY

Contents

For the home teams:

Pauline, Robin and Dana
Rosemary, Alison, Susan and Andrew

Acknowledgements

The authors would like to acknowledge the help received from the following in the compilation of this work: Charlie Gallagher, Billy McNeill, Bobby Murdoch, Ronnie Simpson; Sean Fallon, Jimmy Farrell, Alex Ferguson, Kevin Kelly, Bob Crampsey, Kevin Macarra, Archie Macpherson, Ken Robertson; Peter Burns (S.J.), Frank Glencross, Robin Marwick, Bobby Reid and Pat Woods.

In the past, the following have been interviewed and the memories and notes from those meetings have been of great value: Bertie Auld, Steve Chalmers, Willie Fernie, Dr John Fitzsimons, Tom Grant, Cyril Horne, Sir Robert Kelly, Jim Kennedy, Matt Lynch, Willie Mathieson, John McAlindon, Jimmy McGrory, Gerry McNee, John McPhail, Paul McStay, Willie Ormond, Desmond White – and, of course, Jock Stein.

The authors are very grateful to Tom Leonard for permission to reproduce his poem 'Fireworks'.

Foreword

I am proud to say that I knew Jock Stein as a football manager, as a colleague and as a friend.

Our paths had crossed when I first started playing for Dunfermline Athletic shortly after Jock Stein left for Hibernian. Jock's presence still permeated East End Park. All the players there, particularly the young ones – Willie and Tom Callaghan, John Lunn, Jackie Sinclair and the Lanarkshire boys Jim Herriot and George Miller – looked up to him as a coach and manager.

I played against Celtic in late December 1964 and scored the winning goal in a 2–1 win but the atmosphere at Celtic Park was dreadful, a very small crowd and a typical winter's day in Glasgow: dreich. In April 1965 when Dunfermline played Celtic in the Scottish Cup final, things had changed, as all the players at Dunfermline knew they would. Jock Stein, now in charge at Celtic Park, had overhauled the players' attitude and they had a great belief in themselves. They already had a better team shape and understanding, and I felt there was an inevitability about the outcome – a 3–2 victory for Celtic which ended their long trophy drought.

I should say that I was not selected for that Dunfermline team, although I was their top scorer; I've often told Big Billy McNeill that he had an easier afternoon than he expected with me out of the side!

Jock Stein's sides had certain criteria, the characteristics of all the great British teams in history: they always tried to win games, they never gave in and they were always fit and mentally tough. And those Celtic sides had tremendous players, men who performed with style and skill.

Jock Stein revolutionised football in Scotland as a tracksuit manager. Every manager since has been influenced by him: his training methods, his tactics and his strong principles. At Dunfermline they were still speaking about his tactics-talks on the chalk board, a practice they had never experienced before. He also was the first manager to hold press conferences in the modern sense – although, like most present-day managers, I have mixed feelings about that.

And, now that I am an experienced manager myself, I can appreciate just how difficult it is to achieve such success. I would like to think that I have always worked hard – as did Jock Stein; and that I also am willing to travel in order to learn more about this game of football. In 1970, only a year after I was playing for Rangers against Celtic in a Scottish Cup final, I went to Milan hoping to see Celtic win the European Cup for Scotland; I can remember getting soaked like the rest of the supporters.

I also remember fondly the number of times that my wife and I used to meet Jock and Jean Stein and Sean and Myra Fallon at the Beechwood Restaurant near Hampden Park for a meal and to have a good night's blether. He was always pleasant and cheerful, a good companion; he was always generous with his praise and advice; he was the greatest manager in British football, a legend . . . and I was young and inexperienced then.

Men like Jock will live for ever in the memory.

Alex Ferguson,
Manchester,
May 1998

Prologue

In January 1965 Celtic Football Club was in a mess.

On the playing field, a young team, always filled with potential but permanently disappointing, was producing mediocre football. They were not performing as a unit and, as individuals, were becoming increasingly drained of confidence. The talk in the dressing-room was not of winning trophies or honours but of probable transfers: the captain, Billy McNeill, totally frustrated at the continuing lack of success, had already decided that he would be leaving at the end of the season; Tottenham Hotspur were favoured to capture him. Bobby Murdoch, too often played out of position, was considering emigrating to Australia. Jimmy Johnstone had become so fed up with football that he asked to be dropped. Bobby Lennox, yet another whose potential had not developed as it should have, had been the subject of recent inquiries from Falkirk.

During the course of the downward spiral of yet another disappointing season, attendances at Celtic Park had started to dwindle alarmingly. Strangely enough, the crowds at away fixtures were more acceptable: 16,000 at Rugby Park to see Kilmarnock beat Celtic 5–2 on 28 October 1964, but only 12,000 at Parkhead three days later to watch Celtic defeat Airdrie 2–1; 13,500 at Celtic Park on 2 January to witness a 1–1 draw with Clyde, but 18,000 at Tannadice on 9 January to see Dundee United win by 3–1. Perhaps the terminal decline of a once-great club had a greater fascination for outsiders than for Celtic's own followers. A thoroughly disillusioned Celtic following was disappearing, and what remained was the basic bedrock numbering some 15,000, a pathetic remnant of what used to be called 'The Faithful'.

Perhaps the most depressing match of all was at Celtic Park on 16

January 1965, when Hearts visited Glasgow. The day was miserable with overcast skies, and the rain persisted from midday onwards. The crowd was a respectable 23,000, but the more honest Celtic supporters would have to agree that the Hearts' followers outshouted their own, and seemed to outnumber them – and at Celtic Park! The evidence could be seen in the Jungle which, on a rainy, windswept day, was little better than an old cattle shed, when the Edinburgh fans actually dared to enter that so-called covered enclosure. They were not exactly made welcome, but there was no outright hostility as the visitors attempted to escape the rain soaking them on the exposed Rangers' end of the ground. Even in the Jungle the spectators risked getting wet, as water cascaded down through the rusty, leaky roof.

Johnny Hamilton scored for Hearts very early in the contest and, although Gemmell equalised in 28 minutes, Hamilton added a second for the Edinburgh side, a lead which they maintained comfortably until the end. By completing a league double over Celtic, Hearts were able to maintain their run of good form and challenge for the title. Celtic remained mired in sixth place with little interest in the championship.

That match represented the nadir of Celtic's season – and perhaps their fortunes.

It was a bit too much to bear from those supporters who were prepared to stick it out to the bitter end. Torrents of abuse were being hurled from all parts of the ground, not at Hearts, nor at the referee, but at some Celtic players, and very clearly at the directors' box. The main target of the insults was the chairman of the club, Bob Kelly.

A stockbroker's clerk, he had inherited or controlled a sizeable portion of the shares owned by the Kelly family and had assumed the chairmanship back in 1947. At that time, Celtic were a struggling club, and nothing much had changed over the years, although there had been memorable moments of almost miraculous flashes of form in otherwise drab seasons. Nobody questioned Kelly's zeal or commitment, but the chairman was a man who ran the show with no real football qualifications apart from having watched Celtic for decades (from the directors' box), and having inherited shares passed down from his father, James Kelly, Celtic's first captain. His arrogance in determining every aspect of Celtic's policy bordered on the pathological. He was loathed by many of the fiercely loyal supporters, nostalgic for a glorious past but without any comfort in the present and with absolutely no hope in the future.

Jimmy McGrory, a magnificent player for Celtic back in the late 1920s and 1930s, had been appointed manager in 1945, but he had made little impact. Like other managers of the immediate post-war era, he ran things from his office and rarely ventured near the players at training sessions. Preparation for matches was left to the trainer, or was entrusted to a few key players strong-willed enough to take the initiative. Apart from Rangers – who were prepared to buy their way out of trouble, and who always had a coterie of determined players – Scottish football was similarly haphazard. Occasionally, splendid sides would evolve, like the glorious Hibernian team of the late 1940s and 1950s, and the Hearts side of a little later. But nothing like that was developing at Celtic Park.

Since 1957, when Celtic had inflicted a stunning 7–1 victory over Rangers in the League Cup final, the club had stagnated. This period, which lasted for virtually seven seasons, has (with hindsight) often been referred to as 'the youth policy' – but it should never have been designated as 'a policy' because there was no planning, no method and no prospects. The maladministration of the club amounted to dereliction of duty by the board of directors. Frustratingly, many of the young men who played for Celtic at that time were highly promising and later developed into exceptional players, but at Celtic Park the important matches during this time were fated to end in disaster, often self-inflicted through bizarre team selections. Bob Kelly, the man responsible, was rightly criticised for this and the subsequent lack of success unacceptable in a club of Celtic's reputation. Those who blamed him for Celtic's ills had a valid point, but the chairman, apparently immune to criticism and secure in his position at Celtic Park, seemed prepared to sit things out indefinitely.

Infuriatingly self-righteous, Kelly may have claimed to be unaffected by the abuse, some of it unavoidably personal, which was being hurled at him, but he was also a man looking for an honourable escape from the stress of running Celtic. He had no wish to be remembered as the least successful chairman in the club's history and, now in his early 60s, he was becoming physically drained, and getting more and more discouraged as the trophy drought continued.

As custodians of 'a family club', Celtic's directors always took a keen interest in the gate-receipts, and they could see at a glance that the club was declining financially. The Scottish Cup remained the only chance of a reprieve – and of a major trophy that season – but the draw had decreed that Celtic would be travelling to Love Street to face a St Mirren side that had inflicted two heavy and embarrassing defeats on them at the semi-final stage in recent years. An early dismissal from the Scottish Cup would be ruinous.

Within the boardroom, too, there were notes of dissent. James Farrell, a Glasgow lawyer and a long-time associate of the directors, had only recently been appointed as a board member. A Celtic supporter since childhood, he could see what the club needed and, in his view, the appointment of a new manager was a priority. As a new director he had to be careful about voicing his opinions forcefully, but others were clearly thinking along the same lines.

Kelly was also becoming concerned about the emotional and physical well-being of his manager, Jimmy McGrory. He had always admired McGrory as an exceptionally decent human being but he had to admit that the former player's tenure as manager (which virtually paralleled his own reign as chairman) had not been successful by Celtic standards. Jimmy McGrory would soon be 61 and, blaming himself in part for Celtic's repeated failures, he recognised that anxiety was beginning to affect his health.

In the background was the rumbling of discontent from several keen Celtic supporters who were also astute businessmen and lawyers. It was rumoured, not without reason, that some of these men were preparing a bid to take over the moribund club . . .

Bob Kelly was rightly worried.

★

It was at that time that the chairman received a phone call from Jock Stein, Hibernian's manager and a former Celtic captain and coach, ostensibly asking Kelly for some advice. The pair arranged to meet for lunch in Glasgow's North British Hotel, just off George Square, to discuss Stein's problem.

Stein had been allowed to leave Celtic Park in March 1960, relinquishing his position as second-team coach to take over as Dunfermline's manager. Before leaving, Stein – who had always been ambitious[1] – had determined after meeting Bob Kelly that he should not consider Celtic as one of his future managerial options, the chairman having made it plain that Stein, nominally a Protestant, would not have been acceptable to some in Celtic's support. Jock Stein was in absolutely no doubt about that and, as a West of Scotland man, accepted the reality of the situation. When Stein left Celtic, it was with Kelly's good wishes but nothing more.

Dunfermline Athletic were deep in relegation trouble at the time, and nobody expected Stein, an untried manager, to revive them in the closing six matches of the season. However, his new career got off to a meteoric start against his old club on 19 March when Dunfermline scored within fifteen seconds of the start and went on to collect both points with a scrappy 3–2 win. By winning all six of those remaining fixtures in 1959–60, Dunfermline managed to avoid relegation. In 1960–61 they had improved enough to win the Scottish Cup by beating Celtic in a replay; in 1961–62 the unfashionable Fifers enjoyed a sensational run in Europe, and finished fourth in the First Division. Throughout the same period, Celtic were largely standing still.

In April 1964 Hibernian, a larger club than Dunfermline Athletic, approached Jock Stein. Stein's first reaction was to contact Bob Kelly, nominally to seek his advice but, in reality, to remind Celtic of his existence. A natural politician, Stein would never admit that these contacts with the chairman were calculated to keep him in the picture at Celtic Park but, significantly, he never denied them. Having once again made his availability known to Celtic – and been rejected for his pains – Stein eventually accepted the vacant post of Hibernian manager.

The Edinburgh club, celebrated in the immediate post-war seasons as the best footballing side in Scotland with three championships to prove it, had declined since those days. It was Stein's task to restore some of that lustre to Easter Road, and he was fortunate that the Summer Cup of 1964, a competition which the Old Firm had declined to enter, was there for the taking. By the turn of the year, Hibernian – recently flirting with relegation – had improved enough to be in serious contention for the championship and well tipped for the Scottish Cup.

Such achievements with Dunfermline and Hibs were drawing attention to Jock Stein as a young and effective manager. Wolverhampton Wanderers, another famous club in decline, had approached him, and this was the matter he said was concerning him when he telephoned Bob Kelly. Listening to Stein outlining his predicament, Kelly advised against accepting any offer from Wolverhampton, pointing out that the Midlands club recently had sacked its long-time manager, the legendary Stan Cullis, in acrimonious circumstances.

As the conversation went on, Bob Kelly began to realise that Jock Stein might well be the answer to Celtic's travails and at some point during lunch, the chairman finally took the bait. How would Stein feel about taking over at Celtic Park? This was exactly what the wily Stein had been praying for.

Why had it taken Kelly so long to realise what most football followers in Scotland had already recognised? The major stumbling-block – at least, for some directors and fans – was the matter of religion. Like many other non-Catholics, he had played for Celtic – although in Stein's case he had done so despite the misgivings of some of his friends and relatives. Like those others, he had been accepted by Celtic players and supporters as the team's captain without too many qualms. Appointed as the second-team coach after his enforced retirement as a player, he had experienced little difficulty in communicating with the youngsters in his charge, and had been considered a success in that role. Cyril Horne, the long-time correspondent for the *Glasgow Herald* and a confidant of Stein from the latter's days as a player, told one of the authors several years ago that Stein had been reprimanded by Kelly for recommending too many Catholic youngsters as Celtic prospects. According to Stein, the chairman had told him in blunt terms that any lad, regardless of religion, was eligible to play for Celtic if he were good enough.

Still, there were people who anticipated difficulties for Jock Stein in his public and private life as Celtic's first non-Catholic manager. Upon hearing of his appointment one prominent journalist was reported as saying: 'Well, he's going to have to learn to whistle "The Sash" and hum "The Soldiers' Song" at the same time from now on.' Jock Stein himself was totally familiar with the nuances of the sectarian divide in Scottish society, but he was confident that he could overcome the difficulties. Apart from his growing reputation as a manager, Stein had another great thing in his favour. He was untainted by the sectarianism which surrounded him in Lanarkshire, and he despised the worst manifestations of it. In fact, his wife, Jean, came from a Catholic background. As far as humanly possible, he was open-minded and tolerant, capable of judging all people (players, officials, journalists and supporters) strictly on merit.

He knew the Celtic supporters better than the club's chairman did, and was aware of what they needed in the person of a manager: a good man who deserved respect, a strong man to stand up to a dictatorial chairman and a leader who could deliver some success on the football pitch. He had enough self-confidence to believe that he was capable of answering those needs.

On the eve of his appointment the mood among Celtic's support was so apathetic that only 14,000 bothered to turn up at Parkhead for the visit of Aberdeen. It was 30 January, the day of Winston Churchill's state funeral, televised nationally. The players, however, seemed to have heard something to their liking – or sensed the probability of change – as they trounced the Dons by 8–0, John Hughes leading the way with five goals. For those fans within Celtic Park that day the atmosphere had become charged with electricity. They realised instinctively that something was 'on' and, throughout Scottish football, rumours began to circulate about changes at Celtic Park.

In London's Westminster Abbey at much the same hour, the invited guests and dignitaries – and millions watching on television – were listening to a moving rendition of one of the wartime leader's favourite poems:

> *And not by eastern windows only*
> *When daylight comes, comes in the light.*
> *In front, the sun comes slow, how slowly*
> *But westward, look, the land is bright!*

In retrospect, the same words were just as apt for Celtic Park that day, as Jock Stein was preparing to switch his workplace from Edinburgh to Glasgow.

Even before he took over officially, Jock Stein had had to face an unexpected test. At one meeting with Kelly, after having shaken hands on the appointment, Stein was preparing to discuss the general and specific terms of his employment, when the chairman momentarily left him gobsmacked.

It was an open secret that Bob Kelly had always intended Sean Fallon to succeed Jimmy McGrory as Celtic's manager. Kelly was reluctant to abandon his plans for Fallon and the proposal that he put to Stein was breathtaking in its simplicity, if not stupidity. The chairman, having gone so long without seeing the need for a manager, was now suggesting to Stein that Celtic would be better off with two. Stein listened carefully as Kelly outlined his proposal: Jock Stein and Sean Fallon would operate as joint-managers of Celtic; Stein would largely be in control of the football squad, its training and coaching – the other details could be worked out later.

Stein may have been desperate to become Celtic's manager, but never on those impractical terms. He was deeply disturbed at the implications inherent in the proposal, but he was street-smart – he knew that Celtic needed him, and sensed that they could not afford to lose him at the last minute. He asked for time to consider the proposal, and Kelly agreed to that request. Shortly afterwards, Stein made an appointment with Desmond White, the club's secretary and also a senior director. White assured him that Celtic wanted him as their manager, and advised him to hold out for sole control.

Given Kelly's reputation for pigheadedness, it was a calculated gamble. At this point it might be worth while to speculate on what might have happened to Celtic had the offer to Jock Stein been withdrawn.

Almost certainly, the position would have reverted to Sean Fallon, who had been acting as Celtic's manager (and coach) for the past couple of seasons although Jimmy McGrory remained nominally in charge. As the official manager, Fallon's position would have been strengthened and the chain of command would have been more streamlined, but would things have improved very much? The training and the coaching would have remained largely the same – and with the same disappointing results. Bob Kelly would have continued to make too many of the important football decisions – and with the same consequences. Billy McNeill, for one, has little doubt about the prospects: 'Celtic might well have won a trophy every couple of seasons, most likely the Scottish Cup, and the directors would have been happy enough with that.'

By that time, Billy McNeill would have left Celtic for England and several others would have been plying their trade for other Scottish clubs. Other players, Bobby Murdoch and Jimmy Johnstone among them, would not have developed fully as professionals and might have drifted out of the game.

In the event, Kelly was backed into a corner, and admitted defeat – on his own terms. With commendable loyalty he arranged adequate consolations for Sean Fallon and Jimmy McGrory: Fallon was appointed as Stein's assistant-manager, and McGrory was given the newly created role of public relations officer.

Sean Fallon was fully justified in feeling disappointment in being passed over for promotion, having waited patiently for so long and having worked so hard without gaining too much recognition. The Irishman sought out a meeting with Jock Stein, and the two former team-mates very quickly reached an amicable understanding: Stein was coming to Celtic as manager with complete responsibility for football matters, and Fallon would assist him in every way possible.

That meeting took place in Edinburgh, at Easter Road, where Fallon had intended to watch a reserve game before returning home. However, in the course of the conversation, Jock Stein happened to mention that Tommy Docherty, Chelsea's manager, had visited him earlier that day and had remarked that he would be meeting a youngster that evening at the North British Hotel. Sean Fallon was aware that Docherty was interested in a 16-year-old from Paisley who had been watched by Celtic. Acting on intuition, Fallon changed his plans about the Easter Road match and hurried over to the hotel where he contacted the boy (and his father). Within an hour or so, the teenager had been persuaded by the earnest Irishman to join Celtic. His name? David Hay.

Sean Fallon, that most loyal of Celtic men, had no trouble in accepting the understanding that he had reached with Stein – and, to his infinite credit, he remained totally true to the new manager throughout his years at Celtic Park, modestly retreating from the limelight as much as possible. In fact, Fallon's steadiness and other attributes at times complemented Stein's and he proved a most worthy assistant, his contribution at times being undervalued – although, significantly enough, not by the players.

Sean Fallon also deserves credit for steering Celtic through a difficult interregnum as the players waited for Jock Stein to become available on or about 8 March 1965. The astonishing 8–0 victory over Aberdeen at Parkhead at the end of January may well have been put down to a positive reaction to the hints about the change in manager, but a more difficult task lay in wait a week later with a visit to Love Street on Scottish Cup business on 6 February and 28,300 crowded into the ground to see the match. At half-time after an evenly fought battle the score was 0–0, but Stevie Chalmers put Celtic in front only four minutes into the second half. Celtic took command of the situation but their two other goals, both from Lennox, came late in the match.

Thanks to inconsistency earlier in the season, Celtic's remaining league fixtures were meaningless, but provided an opportunity for the side to prepare for the Scottish Cup ties. Still, Celtic's form was impressive: a 5–1 rout of St Mirren a week after the cup tie and a 2–0 win over Kilmarnock at Celtic Park on 27 February. Kilmarnock were formidable opposition; in fact, the Ayrshire side, managed by ex-Ranger Willie Waddell, would go on to win the league championship with a dramatic win at Tynecastle in their last match of the season.

Having edged Queen's Park at Hampden Park on 20 February in their first Scottish Cup clash with the Spiders since 1928, Celtic qualified to face Kilmarnock in the quarter-final on 6 March. It was a critical match for Celtic as the success of the whole season hinged on it. It proved an enthralling game for the crowd of 47,000 at Celtic Park who were left in suspense until the final whistle confirmed a 3–2 win for Celtic. Even greater suspense was in evidence at Easter Road as Hibernian, with Jock Stein in charge for the last time, faced Rangers for a place in the semi-final. In the very last minute of a bruising battle, Hibernian scored to knock Rangers out of the Cup by 2–1. A great day for Celtic!

Sean Fallon had performed admirably in his difficult role: since the news of Stein's appointment he had led Celtic to three successive league wins; he had steered the team to the Scottish Cup semi-final with victories over St Mirren, Queen's Park and Kilmarnock; and he had landed a promising youngster in David Hay. He stepped down with Celtic perfectly safe in seventh place in the league table and with a place in the Scottish Cup semi-final. Not too bad a performance from a caretaker.

Having decided that it was time to replace McGrory, the chairman had wasted little time in imparting the news to the manager. According to a reliable source, the conversation took place while McGrory was preparing the pay-envelopes for his players – the clearest indication of the duties expected of Celtic's manager at that time. Perhaps Jimmy McGrory was relieved to be free of responsibilities which, increasingly, were proving to be too much for him. However, despite the security in retaining much the same salary in his less stressful position, he did feel some twinges of resentment at the much greater sum offered to Jock Stein upon his appointment.

Stein knew Celtic as a 'family club' and raised no objections to working with Sean Fallon and Jimmy McGrory, both of whom he liked, trusted and respected. He realised the awkwardness of McGrory's new position and went out of his way to ease McGrory into his new role by deference to his own former manager. Bob Kelly was particularly impressed with Stein's habit of referring to Jimmy McGrory as 'Boss', especially in front of impressionable players.

Jock Stein was unfailingly polite and respectful towards his chairman, knowing instinctively that the most important relationship within a football club is the rapport and mutual trust between manager and chairman. But he was determined that he would succeed or fail on his own terms as a 'football man' and, for Stein to succeed at Celtic Park, it might have to be at the expense of the chairman's considerable ego. Kelly himself gave an early indication that he had realised the sea-change in Celtic's fortunes when he reported back to his fellow-directors after his first meeting with Stein. Jim Farrell, with a lawyer's total recall, remembers the exact words: 'Gentlemen, I think I've found a manager . . . but he'll make life hard for us.'

Farrell also confided to the authors his recollections of the traditional Thursday night board meetings prior to Stein's arrival: 'Desmond

[White] would read the minutes, somebody would approve them, the correspondence would be read out, the Chairman [Bob Kelly] would allocate some responsibilities along the lines of "X, could you speak to him about that?" or "Y, write to them and see what can be done?" . . . This took about ten minutes at the most, and then the Chairman would relax, sit back, and say, "About Saturday's game, does everybody agree with me that it's time we brought in young Z to add some speed to the forwards?" And the conversation would go on for a couple of hours about football and players and teams and referees.'

The real issue would be over the right of the manager to select the team, a right which Stein had demanded from the outset, and which he had been promised. This area had always been a bone of contention at Celtic Park since the start of Kelly's chairmanship. Stein could remember vividly an incident in 1956 when Bobby Evans was informed of the team by Jimmy McGrory on the morning of the Scottish Cup final and, as captain, started to make plans for the match against Hearts. A few hours later, he had to lead out a vastly different side at Hampden Park at the whim of the chairman. Needless to say, the Cup was lost – thrown away – as were others due to unrealistic team selections.

Stein's first six weeks in charge at Celtic Park were a model of professionalism. He had very quickly established a rapport with his board of directors and most significantly with its prickly chairman; he had eased Jimmy McGrory out of the firing-line smoothly, allowing the former manager to keep his dignity intact; and he had set in operation a good working relationship with his assistant, Sean Fallon.

It was perfectly clear what Stein had to do: he had to guide Celtic through the tail-end of another disappointing season while making plans for the future. He had to assess every player on the books and gauge his attitude and potential. He had to become accustomed to being the manager of a truly big club and learn how to cope with the pressures of that position.

Every manager rules his players with some degree of fear – the fear that they will be dropped from the side and eventually released. Stein was more than capable of utilising this fear and, by making it known that no player's situation was entirely secure, he obtained better performances from those Celtic players used to a more *laissez-faire* approach.

The players were fully conscious of the manager's intentions and watched carefully for any indication of his leanings. Either by accident or design, Stein remarked casually that he had noticed that Charlie Gallagher and Bertie Auld rarely played well when both were fielded in the same team, suggesting that the inside-forwards were too similar in style, although vastly different in temperament and attitude.

Other players were equally apprehensive about the new man's expectations of them, sensing that in the remaining six weeks of the season they would be playing for a place in the following year's Celtic. Stein assured them that they would all be given a fair chance to prove they deserved to be retained, and went out of his way to speak to Ronnie Simpson with whom he had had a poor relationship at Easter Road. Simpson, upon hearing that Stein was coming to Celtic Park, is said to have gone home and informed his wife that they would be on the move again. At any rate, the veteran Simpson – who had played against Stein as a player – listened glumly to the manager, nodded agreement without comment . . . and carried on training with the reserves, not too hopeful about his prospects.

Jock Stein knew before taking over at Celtic Park which players were indispensable and which ones were suspect. At one meeting of the directors, the manager was invited to give his long-term plans for the team, and he presented a list of those players who, he felt, could be released or put on the transfer-list. Such decisive actions on the part of a manager caused some consternation among the directors and perhaps rightly because the latter column reportedly included the names of Jimmy Johnstone and John Hughes.

At the time, Stein's thinking was correct: neither Johnstone nor Hughes had lived up to the expectations aroused by their potential; both players had been discouraged at the lack of success, and both were notoriously inconsistent. On their day, they could be worldbeaters – or flops. It would be hard to imagine the Celtic of the next few seasons without Johnstone in particular, but Cyril Horne of the *Glasgow Herald* insisted that 'Jimmy Johnstone was at such a low ebb early in 1965 that it was probable that he would revert to junior football again – and sink without a trace'.

Stein was putting pressure on his squad, challenging them to show him what they could do, and they started to respond. Despite the weariness brought on by a long, and so far fruitless, season the players showed a renewed enthusiasm for training, welcoming the new manager's hands-on approach.

From the first day in charge he showed the players a new concept in football managership. Billy McNeill remembers clearly the impact of the manager on the training-ground, when he turned up wearing a tracksuit: 'I never saw Mr McGrory in a tracksuit; I don't suppose he owned one. But Jock Stein was rarely out of it at training.'

But, consciously, Jock Stein was utilising the remaining league fixtures to give some members of his squad another chance to prove themselves – and to protect himself from any possible charge of dictatorial management.

His method was seen most obviously in the case of Jim Kennedy. The rugged defender was a popular figure at Parkhead, and had been a stalwart for many seasons, earning representative honours with Scotland. A regular in Celtic's team at the start of the season, he had played for his country against Wales and Finland as recently as October 1964 and against Northern Ireland in November. Since then his form had tailed off, and Stein knew that the veteran was starting his inevitable decline; accordingly, he was selected for only three matches in the run-in – against Dundee at Dens Park on 20 March, against Hibernian at Celtic Park on the 22nd, and finally against Thistle at home on 17 April. Stein's suspicions were well founded: Celtic drew 3–3 against Dundee and lost to Hibernian (4–2) and Thistle (2–1) while Kennedy struggled.

Other players were given the opportunity to earn a place in the line-up for the Scottish Cup ties, including Hugh Maxwell, a surprise signing from Falkirk for £15,000 in mid-November. But he was unimpressive in the defeat by Hibernian, and in a 5–1 drubbing from Dunfermline in the last league match of the season.[2]

Tommy Gemmell was another all too aware that the new manager was looking closely at his players and he laid his plans accordingly. Gemmell had heard through the grapevine that Stein was partial to the idea of the attacking full-back, and so Gemmell spent much of the first half of one league match foraging down the left wing in search of goals, and neglecting his defensive duties. At half-time, Stein took him aside and growled menacingly at him – and promptly replaced him for the next (unimportant) fixture.

One criticism frequently levelled at Jock Stein is that he was – relatively speaking – a poor judge of goalkeepers. But, to his credit, Stein realised very quickly that John Fallon, the current goalkeeper, was one player who responded better to a vote of confidence. Accordingly, Fallon, although criticised in past seasons for lapses, was selected for every game until the end of the season.

The league fixtures could now be used for tinkering or even experimentation but not the semi-final of the Scottish Cup against Motherwell at Hampden Park on 27 March. The Lanarkshire side had frequently played well against Celtic, particularly in the Scottish Cup, and they made things difficult for the favourites in this match. Twice they led, goals coming from the alert and mobile Joe McBride, who tormented Billy McNeill on the ground – and even in the air. Bertie Auld twice equalised for a stuttering Celtic, his second goal coming from the penalty spot in 60 minutes, while a couple of his younger colleagues turned away, unable to watch. The match finished 2–2 and Celtic were in complete command during the closing stages, Jimmy Johnstone being unlucky to have his close-range effort chalked off in a dubious offside decision.

Stein made only one change for the replay, held at Hampden on 31 March before a crowd of 58,959: Jimmy Johnstone, out of touch four days earlier, was dropped in favour of the more reliable Stevie Chalmers. Motherwell's chance had gone, as Celtic overpowered them in an emphatic 3–0 victory. This time McNeill, helped by John Clark, was in complete control of Joe McBride.

Celtic's league results had been mixed, to say the least. The pessimists among the support feared the worst; the optimists hoped that the manager was consciously adjusting his squad and evaluating them. Stein's first game in charge was on 10 March, an evening fixture at Broomfield against Airdrie on the day that he took over. The players responded with a sparkling performance to win by 6–0, Bertie Auld leading the way with five goals. The same team was selected for Stein's first home game – against St Johnstone on 13 March – but gave a tepid display and went down by 1–0.

Jock Stein was given a rousing reception as he took his place on the bench but he sat stoically throughout a miserable 90 minutes, commenting in a matter-of-fact tone to the BBC interviewer afterwards: 'I see now why I've been brought here.' That same inconsistency marked Celtic's play as the season drew to a close: a loss by 4–2 to Hibernian at Celtic Park was followed shortly afterwards by a 4–0 win for Celtic at Easter Road; Celtic's last-ever fixture against Third Lanark ended in a 1–0 win, but the next home match against Partick Thistle was lost by 2-1; and the most ominous result was a 6–2 pounding at the hands of lowly Falkirk at Brockville.

Stein said very little in public during this time and it was suggested that he was not too perturbed by the league results. For one thing, it gave him valid reasons for dropping some players for the more important Scottish Cup programme; he could argue convincingly to the likes of Kennedy, Maxwell, Cushley, O'Neill, Brogan and even Jimmy Johnstone that the team performed more effectively without them.

For the Scottish Cup final on 24 April 1965 he chose this side to face

Dunfermline Athletic: Fallon, Young, Gemmell, Murdoch, McNeill, Clark, Chalmers, Gallagher, Hughes, Lennox and Auld.

There was no place for Jim Kennedy although the romantics noted that he had been forced to withdraw at the last minute from the 1961 final, which had also been against Dunfermline; Stein had a match to win and sentiment would not be allowed to interfere with his plans. Some time before the final, Jock Stein faced a test of his authority when his line-up was questioned by the chairman. Having already told his players at Seamill who would be in the team – and explained his thinking to them, and the tactics to be used – Stein as a courtesy informed the chairman. Kelly immediately spotted that Bobby Murdoch was listed as wing-half, and queried the manager's decision, growling at Stein that Murdoch was an inside-forward. Stein ended the discussion with the firm but polite statement: 'You'll see on Saturday what he is.'

As a matter of fact, Bobby Murdoch had played several times as a wing-half, both under Jimmy McGrory and Jock Stein, notably in the Scottish Cup semi-final against Motherwell, but only a week before the Cup final he had a shocker against Partick Thistle. Stein had already decided that Murdoch was a wing-half or a midfield player, and would not be swayed from his evaluation even though the player had been inconsistent of late.

The final was destined to go down in Celtic folklore: twice they were a goal down to the resolute Fifers, and twice they fought back to equalise through goals by Bertie Auld. Just before half-time Dunfermline had shocked Celtic with a spectacular goal following a free-kick, and the mood at Hampden Park among the Celtic support was funereal. Jim Farrell remembers going up the steps towards the directors' lounge, and nodding gloomily to Mrs Stein. She smiled at him and said: 'It's not over yet. Maybe I should say a wee prayer to St Anthony.'[3]

As the match entered the closing stages, the excitement was reaching a peak. Celtic had equalised shortly after the interval, and had been threatening Dunfermline's goal since then. Lennox burst through on the left, and won yet another corner in 81 minutes. Charlie Gallagher considered his options carefully and then flighted the ball perfectly across the face of the goal. Billy McNeill, unusually for him at that stage in his career, had come upfield and eluded his marker.

The moment is etched in Celtic's history in a dramatic photograph which shows McNeill connecting with the ball about five yards out; the camera-angle shows McNeill rising above the goalkeeper's outstretched arms and he is framed head and shoulders above the vast Hampden terracings. A split-second later that same terracing – and most of Hampden Park, with 108,800 spectators inside – erupted with joy as Celtic took the lead at 3–2.

Bobby Murdoch remembers clearly the agony of the remaining nine minutes: 'I thought the final whistle would never come.' Like every other Celtic supporter, Murdoch was tortured by the thought of the prize being snatched away at the last moment; a victim of repeated failure, he could take nothing for granted until Hugh Phillips blew the final whistle. He had no way of knowing as he watched Billy McNeill hold up the Scottish Cup how spectacular the future success would be, or how sustained.

A curious episode unfolded in the joyous hubbub of the Celtic dressing-room afterwards. Charlie Gallagher, always a quiet man, was sitting down admiring his medal, when Bertie Auld approached him and insisted on borrowing it. Auld, as cocky as ever, marched up to Jock Stein and held out the medals, one in each hand: 'You said that Charlie and I couldnae play in the same team. What aboot these medals, eh?' Stein apparently smiled knowingly and declined to answer.

The glory days had begun at Celtic Park . . .

Notes

1. As a player with Celtic, Jock Stein had not been shy about volunteering his presence at quiz nights and other supporters' functions. Some organisers would have preferred a more famous player, but invariably they were delighted with Stein's perceptive contributions.

2. Jim Kennedy's last game for Celtic was that match against Partick Thistle as he moved on to Morton, and Hugh Maxwell was transferred to St Johnstone for £10,000 in the close season.

3. Theologically, Mrs Stein was perfectly correct: St Anthony is the patron saint of the lost. Had she said 'St Jude' (the patron saint of hopeless cases), Mr Farrell would have had cause to be more worried.

The Genius

Chapter 1

Paradise at Last

After the trials and tribulations of a biblical span of 'seven lean years', Celtic had at last tasted the heady wine of success – and it was good. Things seemed to be turning their way, and much of it was due to the almost tangible confidence and self-belief emanating from the new manager. Celtic now had a leader envied by other clubs and organisations, the SFA quickly recognising his talents by requesting his services as Scotland's part-time manager at the same time as he was fulfilling his full-time responsibilities at Parkhead. This interest on the part of the SFA was to be a constant anxiety for Celtic in the years ahead: Scotland needed a manager, and Jock Stein, a patriotic Scot, was naturally interested in the position – and the ambitious Stein knew his own worth in the sport. The SFA's trust in Celtic's manager was fully justified by Scotland's early results with him in charge: a draw in Poland (1–1) and a win in Finland (2–1).

That was highly commendable but the supporters were becoming excited at what was happening at Celtic Park.

For several seasons Celtic had lacked a consistent goalscorer, and Stein remedied that situation swiftly. Early in June he snapped up Motherwell's Joe McBride, a proven striker known to be 'Celtic-daft'. Back in March, McBride had bothered the Celtic defence in the Scottish Cup semi-final and his two goals for Motherwell earned the Lanarkshire side a lucrative replay. For several seasons Celtic had been rumoured to be on the verge of signing him as McBride performed honourably with lesser clubs – and as a model professional had always played well against Celtic.

Joe McBride had scored goals wherever or whenever he played, but he was more than a penalty-box poacher; he worked hard, distributed the ball well, and had a refreshing and positive approach. When playing with Kilmarnock as a youngster in a league match against a powerful Rangers side, he skinned an Ibrox defender; the veteran growled at young Joe, and threatened him: 'Dae that agane, an' Ah'll break yur legs.' Young McBride laughed, as he skipped away: 'Ye'll have tae catch me first, auld yin.' This was the attitude that Celtic wanted, and Stein sensed that McBride would fit in perfectly at Parkhead. However, Joe had played senior football for a long time and Stein wondered if the striker still had the fitness for life at Celtic Park. Accordingly, as the season drew to its close, Stein had Joe McBride watched on four different occasions and, when satisfied, he put in a bid at a mere £22,000. The capture of McBride for that sum would earn the new manager a reputation for larceny.

Jock Stein was a natural at public relations, proving himself adept at keeping the press happy. He seemed able to distance himself from the ghetto mentality so characteristic of Celtic Park in the preceding seasons. Several journalists he liked and respected, men like John Rafferty and Cyril Horne, and they were given insights into his thinking and philosophy. Others he did not care for, but he knew they had a job to do. Accordingly, he would always give every journalist some quote or angle to a story. In the summer of 1965 news about Celtic – positive, complimentary stories – flooded the sports pages. Only later did the grateful members of the Fourth Estate realise that one of Stein's primary aims was to knock Rangers off the back pages of Scotland's newspapers.

Nowhere was this more evident than in Stein's skilful handling of the 'Brazilian invasion'. Four young Brazilian players, represented by the first of the football agents, turned up in Glasgow and were given training facilities at Celtic Park. Brazil had been world champions since 1958, and the word 'Brazilian' implied football genius. Stein was well aware of this, and used the situation for Celtic's benefit. A couple of the players, Marco di Sousa and Ayrton Inacio, made it into Celtic's reserve team, and a crowd of 7,000 turned up at Celtic Park and paid good money to watch them perform. They played well enough, and one of them scored a spectacular goal, but in hindsight it seems that Stein did not seriously consider them as contenders for a place in Celtic's first-team squad. There would have been complications with work permits and Stein, never noted for his liking of foreign players in Scotland, was not enamoured with their agent's financial demands. The episode proved to be a major propaganda coup, however.

The club had taken the bold and innovative step of becoming part of the media itself by launching *The Celtic View* on 11 August 1965, the eve of the new season. Celtic's Board of Directors issued a statement in the first issue that they wished to 'emphasise that we have no intention of competing with the press, with whom we are on excellent terms'.

The idea was first promoted by Jack McGinn, then working in the circulation department of Beaverbrook Papers. As a Celtic follower he felt that his team were under-represented in the sports coverage of the national papers, and that a platform could be provided for the club to present an unfettered viewpoint on matters affecting it, as well as proving a direct conduit to the supporters. The decision to proceed with a newspaper had been taken in March at the first board meeting attended by Jock Stein and, when he learned of the date of its initial publication, he assured the editor that he would have a photograph of the Celtic side with the Scottish Cup for its front page. It was the first club newspaper of its kind in Britain, and for some years proved to be light years ahead of any rivals.[1] However, Stein very quickly saw the possibilities of using *The Celtic View* as a means of educating the fans to the world of modern football – and to remove the club from the frequent accusations of paranoia in dealing with the media.

Another major coup was achieved when Celtic staged an Open Day for the benefit of the press and the journalists were given an opportunity to see a specially staged Celtic training session. They were impressed at the enthusiasm shown by the players, by the pace and energy of the workouts and the drills, and by the superb fitness of the Celtic squad on the eve of the season. They filled their reports with words such as 'impressive', 'awesome' and 'terrifying'. One photograph showed the Celtic players somersaulting through a hoop, an exercise designed to promote flexibility, but the more cynically humorous among the hacks wondered how many penalties Celtic would get in the coming season. Pat Woods, Celtic's most eminent historian, remembers watching those sessions: 'It was enthralling . . . Jock Stein was always in the centre – like a ringmaster, cracking his whip. A lot of banter and jokes among the hard, physical work . . . the mood was always upbeat.'

The training programme, devised by Neil Mochan,[2] had been another ingredient. Few teams could match Celtic's level of fitness, and that fitness was used as a tactical weapon; the opposition would be harassed by a Celtic onslaught in the first half, and might be able to cope with it but, when Celtic upped the pace in the closing stages of a contest, they often had no answer. From the start of his tenure at Celtic Park, Stein had called for more and more speed, and the training was geared to quickness of movement and thought. Joe McBride, a well-travelled player with Kilmarnock, Wolverhampton Wanderers, Luton Town, Partick Thistle and Motherwell, once claimed that he could hardly wait to get to the training-ground in the mornings: 'It was great. Before the season we worked on general fitness and stamina. Every day during the season there would be something new and different – something designed to sharpen us up. As players, we could see right away the purpose of the exercise.'

Jock Stein arranged a series of pre-season friendlies: a 1–1 draw with Motherwell on the Isle of Man and a thumping of Shamrock Rovers in Dublin, but the only major test was a visit to Roker Park to face Sunderland. The Wearside club were now managed by Ian McColl, an ex-Ranger and former Scotland manager, and he had recently signed Jim Baxter, so frequently the scourge of Celtic in his Ibrox days. Celtic administered a 5–0 thrashing to the shellshocked home side, and left the pitch to a standing ovation from both sets of supporters. Although delighted with the performance of his men, Stein pointed out that the English club were still a week or so behind the Parkhead men in their training programme.

Immediately after the match there were outbreaks of hooliganism in the streets surrounding Roker Park, and the Celtic supporters bore most of the responsibility although many claimed to have been carried away by the satisfaction of a famous victory. Jock Stein refused to buy that feeble excuse. He asked *The Celtic View* to condemn the fans' misbehaviour in the strongest terms, and spoke out against it himself. He was determined to stamp it out.

The opening League Cup tie at Dundee United was lost by 2–1 but once again there were outbreaks of loutish behaviour and 12 Celtic supporters later appeared at Dundee Police Court, each being fined £220 for breach of the peace. Stein was bitterly disappointed with the behaviour of the fans, and he warned them: 'If Celtic do well on the field, it will not be worth it if their supporters cannot or will not behave decently.' His message was refreshingly clear: hooliganism was always unacceptable, and losing a football match was no excuse nor was winning one. Faced with a manager who spoke so frankly, the fans were impressed, and an obvious attempt was made by the club's supporters to live up to their leader's expectations.

The opening fixture in the league programme was also scheduled for Tannadice, on 25 August 1965, a Wednesday night, and the United fans in the 18,000 crowd were exuberant and confident before the kick-off. In the second minute Celtic silenced them with a shot from Charlie Gallagher that struck the bar and left it quivering for some minutes afterwards. The visitors' domination was complete, and John Divers opened the scoring in 15 minutes. Billy McNeill, who had struggled in the past against United's Danish centre Finn Dossing, was clearly the master this time, while the other Scandinavian, Orjan Persson, on their left wing found life equally hard against the determined Ian Young. Joe McBride scored a typical close-in goal shortly after the restart, and Young calmly converted a penalty-kick for a third goal as Dundee United's discipline went. Tommy Gemmell was joining in the attack – a sight that was to become familiar in the future – and scored with a powerful shot from the edge of the penalty area. The Tannadice side's humiliation was complete near the end when Persson was ordered off for aiming a kick at Gemmell.

This performance was highly encouraging, suggesting that Celtic could learn from past mistakes and remedy the situation, a feeling confirmed with the League Cup matches against the other Dundee side. The Dens Parkers had visited Glasgow on 21 August and spoiled Joe McBride's competitive début with their 2–0 win; however, in the vital return fixture on 4 September Celtic ran out convincing winners by 3–1 and this match, made memorable by an individual goal from John Hughes (when he swept past Scotland full-back Alec Hamilton, and cut inside before unleashing an unstoppable drive past the goalkeeper from fully 25 yards out), guaranteed Celtic first place in the section and advancement to the quarter-finals.

Celtic's next championship fixture was a home match against Clyde. As has so often been the case between these two close neighbours, the result was a scrappy game. Only after Young scored with a penalty in the 72nd minute, with Gemmell making it two shortly after, did the supporters relax. Near the end, however, slack play in Celtic's rearguard allowed Clyde to pull one back, and the last few minutes were tense and frustrating for the fans. For the second game in a row both full-backs had scored, and the supporters pondered the changes in Celtic's tactics.

The first Old Firm clash of the season was always going to be critical, everybody at Parkhead knowing that a win at Ibrox over Rangers was the only result that could satisfy the supporters' lust for success. The attendance was more than 76,000 with many locked out at the Celtic end. Great things were now expected of this side but the game proved another massive disappointment as Rangers scraped through by 2–1. Excuses were being offered freely, if unconvincingly: Billy McNeill had suffered a leg injury which handicapped him throughout the second half; John Hughes, despite scoring from a penalty, had had one of his off-days; Joe McBride, who surely would have taken advantage of chances created late on, had missed the fixture through injury. Jock Stein made reassuring sounds about it being a match worth only two points, the same as one against Stirling Albion, but the supporters were still in despair.

It became a habit for Jock Stein to play down the importance of the fixtures against Rangers but his public utterances were at total variance with the emphasis he placed on these encounters in dealing with his players. Following the Scottish Cup triumph against Dunfermline, Celtic had faced Rangers in an unimportant Glasgow Cup fixture; Stein demanded success in that match and got it with a 2–1 win. The manager knew how important it was to establish a psychological edge over the ancient rivals – and his players were left in no doubt about it.

After the league result at Ibrox the manager decided to make changes. John Divers had played poorly there and Stein knew that his inside-forward – despite his football intelligence and years of honest toil in difficult times – had played his last game for Celtic. More and more, the manager was demanding a different style from his players. In an interview with John Rafferty of *The Scotsman* a week or so prior to the Ibrox match, Stein had explained the new approach prevalent in Scottish football: players are faster, and they release the ball sooner; no one has time to delay, even though players are more skilled with the ball than ever before. John Divers was the first notable Celtic casualty of the new approach.

Another change was imminent. Stein was not totally happy with John Fallon in goal, and he replaced him with the Irishman Jack Kennedy for the midweek League Cup tie against Raith Rovers. He also decided on Ronnie Simpson to play against Aberdeen in the next league match. For Stein, the goalkeeper was an individualist, an alien form in a team sport, a player to be tolerated on occasion but never fully trusted. Still, three goalkeepers in three matches within one week was exceptional even by Stein's standards.

The decision to restore Ronnie Simpson to Celtic's goal was a strange one, given the two men's relationship at Easter Road, and Stein could be thought lucky in that Simpson embarked on a remarkable Indian Summer to his long career – and that Celtic got more than three seasons of exemplary and inspirational goalkeeping from him. Simpson had started out near the end of the Second World War with Queen's Park as the youngest keeper in Britain, and was touted as Rangers' next custodian. In fact, his father Jimmy Simpson, himself a Rangers defensive stalwart in pre-war days, was released from his part-time job at Ibrox when he could not persuade his son to join the club.[3] As an amateur, young Ronnie played for Great Britain in the Olympic Games held at London in 1948. He turned professional with Third Lanark in 1950, and moved on to Newcastle United in 1951, where he won FA Cup medals in 1952 and 1955. When he was given the time, Simpson was a stylist; under pressure from close-in shots or deflections, he was happy to block the ball with any part of his body: arms, legs or feet. In England he was nicknamed 'The Cat' because of his quickness and agility and, when he was transferred on a free to Hibernian, the Newcastle fans complained that he had been allowed to go far too soon.

At Easter Road, Stein clearly considered Simpson to be nearing the end of his career; after all, he had been a playing contemporary of the manager back in the 1940s and '50s. He was persuaded by Sean Fallon to allow him to leave Hibs for Celtic for a fee of £2,000 in September 1964, and was quite surprised to find him still at Parkhead as a player when he himself joined Celtic in March 1965, seven months later. Given Stein's distrust of goalkeepers, it was not surprising that changes would be made but Simpson was astonished to be given a chance in the first team again a month away from his 35th birthday. Perhaps Stein was trying to make a point with John Fallon, the regular goalkeeper; perhaps he had been impressed with Simpson's attitude at training. Whatever the reason, Ronnie Simpson's comeback was a bonus for Celtic.

Celtic might as well have played without a goalkeeper that afternoon, in fact, as they crushed the visitors by 7–1. Goals were now coming easily, as they went on to beat Hearts 5–2 with the Edinburgh side's late counters being a consolation prize for turning up; and, in an old-fashioned thriller at Brockville, Celtic edged Falkirk by 4–3. Aberdeen, Hearts and Falkirk were respectable sides but their defences had no answer to the cantrips of Jimmy Johnstone and the speed of Bobby Lennox. In fact, the speed of the whole side was breathtaking and marked the first real indication that the pre-season training sessions prior to the season were now paying off.

One player who had impressed the manager with his improved attitude was the red-headed winger Jimmy Johnstone. Before Stein's arrival at Parkhead, Johnstone had drifted in and out of the first team despite his great natural ability. Johnstone recalls the half-time at one reserve game at Celtic Park against Hibernian when he found himself in the toilet alongside his manager. Stein broke the awkward silence with words that made Jimmy Johnstone think about his future in football: 'What are you doing here tonight? You could be – and you should be – playing for the first team!'

At that time, Jock Stein was quite prepared to transfer the player, but what he saw on the training-ground was winning him over. Stein, always an astute observer, could see that Johnstone was a good trainer, and was listening perhaps for the first time in his unsettled career. He could see a young man who lived for football, and who might have been devastated without it. He approved of the way in which he could pick himself up after a heavy challenge – and some of the practice sessions could be ferocious at times – and, above all, he could see that, when Jimmy Johnstone had the ball, nobody in Celtic's first-team squad could dispossess him. With all that talent, and that courage – and an improved attitude – it might be worth persevering with Johnstone, and Stein determined to do so regardless of the problems such a decision entailed. An approach for the player by Tottenham Hotspur in mid-September may have been the final factor in Stein's decision to hold on to Johnstone.

The most important match of the season so far was fought out at Hampden Park on 23 October. The occasion was the League Cup final, and the opponents were Rangers. Celtic had qualified for the final by beating Hibernian 4–0 in a semi-final replay at Ibrox on the Monday night but, as the jubilant players celebrated noisily in the showers, they were suddenly silenced by the approach of an angry Jock Stein. He gestured furiously, and asked the chastened players: 'Do you want to win on Saturday? Tonight was fine but it means nothing if you don't win on Saturday against Rangers.' One by one his men nodded their agreement.

Some of Stein's players had become convinced, years later, that the manager's anger could be turned on and off at will, but nobody was prepared to risk finding out for himself if Stein was pretending. More than one Celtic player has confided to the authors that Jock Stein's physical presence was intimidating, and has admitted fear about the prospect that a confrontation with the burly manager might just possibly turn violent.[4] On several occasions over the years, the manager – two red spots of anger glowing in his cheeks – actually threw a player bodily across the room, and such displays of rage had the desired effect on everybody present.

No one among his players was left in any doubt for a second of the value the manager attached to beating the Ibrox side in the League Cup final. The very first minute set the tone for a savage battle in which five players – a large number for 1965 – would be booked as the referee,

Hugh Phillips, struggled to maintain order. Ian Young, Celtic's right-back, hacked down Willie Johnston, Rangers' dangerous left-winger – and was lucky not to be ordered off, the referee clearly giving him the benefit of the doubt about a mistimed tackle so early in the match.

But a very important point had been made by this Celtic side: they would no longer be intimidated by any Rangers team while Stein was their manager. Far too many times in the past seven years, young Celtic players had been knocked off their stride and eventually cowed by more physical Rangers teams. Not so now. Celtic would prefer to play football but, if a contest turned unduly physical, they could handle themselves. Young, in particular, had listened to his manager's last-minute instructions: 'When you make a tackle early in the game, just let him know that you are there!'

They went on to win this League Cup final by 2–1, both goals being scored by John Hughes from the penalty spot in the first half as Rangers had no answer to Celtic's new-found determination when allied to traditional skill. Hughes had been in devastating form on the left wing where Stein had more and more frequently opted to play him, his thinking being that a man of his power and running needed more space. The luckless Kai Johansen, delegated to mark him, was left floundering time after time in Hughes's wake.

The newspapers would make much of the physical element in the contest, and the more partisan of Celtic's supporters pointed out that a similar result in favour of Rangers might have produced the comment that 'it's a man's game, after all'. However, nothing could excuse the scenes at the end of the match when Rangers' fans in their scores invaded the pitch in an attempt to stop the triumphant Celtic players from showing the trophy to their supporters at the opposite end of Hampden. Fortunately, the Celtic following decided to remain in their places rather than becoming involved in a worsening situation. The sequel was that laps of honour – or even half-laps – were banned at the conclusion of cup finals for a number of years.

The more knowledgeable among the sports writers had to reassess Celtic's recovery under Jock Stein after the following midweek fixture. Dundee at Dens Park had always been a reliable barometer of Celtic's fortunes, and Celtic settled down immediately despite the euphoria generated by the League Cup breakthrough. By half-time they were comfortably in control thanks to goals from Lennox and McBride and were able to cope with a late rally after Andy Penman pulled one back near the end. The next Saturday's thrashing of Stirling Albion by 6–1 at Celtic Park was followed by a hiccup against that most unpredictable of sides, Partick Thistle, who came to Parkhead and gained a 1–1 draw courtesy of a late goal from Jim Conway – a 'failed' Kelly Kid of the 1950s.[5]

Once again Celtic struck a purple patch of form: an excellent performance bringing a 4–1 win at Perth against St Johnstone, a routine demolition of Hamilton Academical by 5–0 at Parkhead, and a narrow 2–1 win over Kilmarnock, also at Celtic Park, on 27 November. The Ayrshire side were highly competent, as befitted the reigning Scottish champions. Celtic ground out their 2–1 win, coming from behind on a hard, frosty pitch and got through with a dubious penalty late in the game.

Stein had always preached the advantages of a strong squad, and it would be tested with the absence of the captain Billy McNeill, out with a leg injury for several weeks. Into his place against Kilmarnock had come the rugged John Cushley, who coped well with the champions' dangerous counter-attacks. Accordingly, Cushley was retained against Hibernian and starred in another fine 2–0 victory. John Cushley was a rarity among Scottish players of that era in that he was a university graduate, with a degree in Modern Languages from Glasgow University, and he could be counted on to give a professional performance, not showy and flashy but solid. Whenever called upon, Cushley proved a mature and dependable deputy for the team's captain, and he might be considered unlucky that his career at Celtic Park coincided with that of McNeill. Some felt – admittedly with the considerable advantage of hindsight – that Cushley and McNeill would have proved a very effective partnership of twin central defenders.

Celtic went to East End Park on 18 December for a critical match. Dunfermline were currently in third place in the league table behind Rangers and Celtic and faced the prospect of playing the Old Firm on successive Saturdays. It was an engrossing, tense, end-to-end affair, Cushley being outstanding in seeing off the Pars' determined opening onslaught. At half-time there had been no scoring although Celtic had assumed command of the midfield where Bobby Murdoch was starting to feed Johnstone and Hughes with a stream of precise passes.

After 62 minutes Celtic took the lead with an opportunist goal by Chalmers, who neatly avoided the offside trap set for him, and the striker followed that up with a second shortly afterwards while the home side's defence was still disorganised and reeling. For the rest of the contest Celtic played cautiously, content to hold on to that hard-earned 2–0 lead. As the Celtic supporters streamed towards their buses and trains, an uncertain rumour started to spread that Rangers had been held to a draw (2–2) at Shawfield by Clyde. In the mid-1960s radio coverage was neither as comprehensive nor as reliable as nowadays and it was dangerous to believe such rumours – but this one proved true. The realisation began to dawn that, if Celtic won their game in hand (against St Mirren), the Parkhead men would top the league table.

There was no possibility of complacency among the squad members. Simpson had been in exceptional form, in complete command of the penalty area, and had made two astonishing saves at East End Park to deny Dunfermline Athletic – but Jock Stein nevertheless invited a Danish goalkeeper, Bent Martin from Aarhus, to Parkhead for an extended trial period.

On Christmas Day, Celtic entertained Morton at Parkhead. As if sensing that events were working out perfectly, Celtic raced to an incredible lead of 7–0 by half-time and eventually won by a charitable 8–1 scoreline. So long a Celtic stalwart, poor Jim Kennedy, like the rest of his struggling and humiliated Greenock side, could not cope with the rampant home side. Perhaps Rangers were dispirited upon hearing the half-time score, as they surrendered 3–2 to Dunfermline at home.

Everybody at Celtic Park could be satisfied as 1965 drew to an end. After years of stagnation a new spirit of optimism pervaded the ground. Celtic were now in first place in the championship; the Scottish Cup had been won dramatically in April; the League Cup had joined it on the sideboard; and Celtic had reached the quarter-finals of the European Cup-Winners' Cup by defeating Go Ahead Deventer and Aarhus. At Deventer, Celtic put on a remarkable display to win by 6–0 and entertained the home crowd so much that they were applauded throughout the entire second half. Jock Stein saw clearly in this match that Jimmy Johnstone in an impish mood could unsettle the most organised of European defences.

At New Year the weather turned cold throughout Scotland and Celtic took the precaution, in time-honoured Parkhead custom, of protecting the pitch with 14 tons of straw and also by spreading sand over the surface. The referee, Tom 'Tiny' Wharton, passed the field as playable, but both teams spent several minutes examining the surface before deciding on their footgear. Rangers opted for the regular boots, but Celtic took the gamble of playing in sandshoes – or 'trainers' as they would be called today. Before the match the Celtic fans were in full voice, optimistic about the outcome and boosted by the decision to fulfil the fixture while the team were in such rampant form; after a minute's play those same fans were standing in utter silence as Rangers went ahead when the ball broke to an unmarked Davie Wilson who scored.

The rest of the first half was dominated by Celtic, but they were unable to break down a determined Rangers rearguard. The pounding endured throughout those 45 minutes took immediate effect on the Ibrox side when Celtic resumed the pressure after the restart. Within a few minutes Stevie Chalmers had equalised, after Gemmell had dashed up field and swung over a cross from the bye-line; McBride alertly stepped over the ball and the defenders were caught out, leaving Chalmers to finish the move from only six yards out.

A rout was on, and the Celtic supporters savoured every moment. Chalmers was again left unmarked at a corner-kick, and headed the ball cleanly into the net. Charlie Gallagher, working hard in the role now being described as 'midfield', drove a ferocious shot into the Rangers net off the crossbar. And Bobby Murdoch scored a memorable goal. He shouted for the ball and McBride squared it to him instinctively, but Mr Wharton, a referee of aldermanic proportions, was in the way; nimbly, the referee skipped over the ball and Murdoch lashed it home from 25 yards.

Murdoch punched the air with delight, perhaps remembering that in the corresponding fixture at Ibrox a year previously he had missed a late penalty for Celtic. At that time, Murdoch was a struggling inside-forward, and a repeated target for abuse from the terracing. Changed days too for Steve Chalmers, another frequent scapegoat for the supporters' frustration in previous seasons. In the last minute he slipped into the box again and scored after a low shot had rebounded off the post for that treasured rarity, a hat-trick in an Old Firm match.

Only one anxiety was consuming the Celtic followers as the match drew to a close. Fog was descending across Parkhead, and visibility was fading rapidly; the fans in the Celtic end could scarcely see their Ibrox counterparts leave the ground early in their thousands as the match proceeded. Those who claim to detect a conspiracy in every refereeing decision were convinced that the fixture would be abandoned before the end, and the result nullified.

The sheer extent of Celtic's triumph over their closest rivals – and not only the score but the manner of it – took the breath away. Celtic looked certainties for the championship at that stage. The team would surely go from strength to strength and Rangers would not recover from such a thrashing. John Rafferty, writing in *The Scotsman*, had little doubt that the league race was over: '[Celtic] humiliated them, exposed the threadbare patches on their famed blue garb, laid bare the dreadful performances of those who were once so rich in pride and skill. In short, Celtic, romping on the way up, passed them [Rangers] on the road down.' (4 January 1966)

Celtic staggered through the reaction to such a victory by scraping through against Dundee United at Parkhead on 8 January with a goal from Charlie Gallagher in 57 minutes. The crowd was a highly pleasing 36,000 – a massive increase on the numbers in recent seasons and an indication that the supporters were aware that Celtic were now operating on a different level. Gallagher, destined to live in Celtic's folklore only as the taker of important corner-kicks, was a vastly underrated player; he could hold the ball when required, he could pass accurately and he was an excellent striker of the ball. Despite that, he never established the type of rapport with the fans that lesser players could. Perhaps unfairly associated with the lean days of the early 1960s, he contributed much to Celtic's squad in the mid-1960s.

The first blow to Celtic's confidence came at Pittodrie on 15 January, following a famous victory over Dynamo Kiev in Glasgow in midweek. It appeared that Celtic supporters formed the majority of the 20,000 crowd, as the spectators arrived to see a pitch from which tons of snow had been removed, although patches remained in some areas. In the early 1960s, in the days before the rigid segregation of fans, the supporters could decide at the last moment where they wanted to stand on the terracing. It would have taken about the first five minutes of the match for many among the Celtic following to make their way to the Merkland Road end of the ground – and those spectators got an excellent view of Joe McBride rising high to head home the opening goal in six minutes. Celtic continued to dominate the course of the match, until Cushley was slack with a passback and Joergen Ravn nipped in to slip the ball past Simpson in 24 minutes. Aberdeen went on to record an impressive 3–1 victory over the championship contenders.

It was the first defeat since 18 September, but Stein did not seem too perturbed. He offered his congratulations to the Aberdeen manager, Eddie Turnbull, who acknowledged them with his customary dourness while the players embraced each other on the pitch – as it had been yet another sporting encounter in a long tradition of Celtic–Aberdeen fixtures. At the railway station Stein consoled the supporters waiting to board the 5.15 train to Glasgow: 'Don't worry too much. Aberdeen are a good side. It had to happen some time.' He could take some consolation in the fact that Celtic remained in first place in the title race, and that some of his players had had an off-day. He appeared confident that it would not happen again for a long time . . .

An unconvincing win in a dull home game against Motherwell followed, but then Celtic started to pay the price that success demands.

After a tremendous 3–0 win over Dynamo Kiev on 12 January, Celtic had to face the ordeal of a long journey to Georgia and settle for a 1–1 draw to ensure their progress into the semi-final of the Cup-Winners' Cup, but it had been no routine fixture. First of all, the match had to be switched to Tbilisi in order to avoid the rigours of a Russian winter. Celtic agreed to play there, and then the Soviets insisted that the routing of Celtic's chartered flight with Aer Lingus should be through Moscow. This was unacceptable as it meant added hours on to the flight, and there were fears that the fixture might have to be postponed while UEFA sorted out the problem.

The return trip to Glasgow was a nightmare, virtually an odyssey which involved stops, scheduled and otherwise, hostile and friendly, at Moscow and Stockholm; technical problems with the aircraft and a catering mix-up at Tbilisi; lengthy formalities and paperwork in Moscow, compounded by a Russian refusal to let anybody leave the plane for several hours, a refusal enforced by grim-faced armed guards at the exit doors of the aircraft; a risky take-off in sub-zero weather from a runway only recently cleared of snow; and a rerouting due to bad weather to Stockholm. Following more problems with the plane, amid worsening weather, another Aer Lingus aircraft had to be rerouted from Brussels to complete the journey home. A weary Celtic party, with little sleep for 40 hours, finally arrived at Glasgow Airport late on the Friday night, and they were due to face Hearts at Tynecastle the following day. Celtic had kept the Scottish League informed about the developments, but did not officially ask for a postponement of the Tynecastle match. Perhaps they had grounds for expecting that one might be offered by the authorities.

For once, Stein made matters worse by insisting that the players board a bus and head for Celtic Park for an hour's training session – to the frustration of the players' families and friends who had gathered at the airport to take them home. Even the propaganda value of the exercise was largely lost as the Saturday-morning newspapers had already been printed. A brisk 30-minute session on the Saturday morning might have been a better idea.

Perhaps there had been some disagreement between Jock Stein and the chairman Bob Kelly prior to and during this trip: the Russians had objected to Celtic's choice of airline, Aer Lingus, as they had no diplomatic relations with Ireland, but Kelly had refused to budge, thus endangering the fixture. Much to Stein's chagrin, the airline had been less than impressive in returning the party to Glasgow in good time. In addition to that, Jim Craig, Celtic's right-back, had been ordered off, along with his immediate opponent, for fighting and Kelly was furious at the indiscipline. He went so far as to demand that Craig apologise for his lapse, and Stein, always aware of the chairman's prickly temper, felt it prudent to 'rest' Craig for the Hearts game.

At Tynecastle before a crowd of 45,965, Celtic went down 3–2 to a Hearts side reduced to ten men from early in the first half, and a side which had also played a gruelling midweek European match, against Real Saragozza. John Cushley, one Celtic player clearly affected by jet-lag, was given a roasting by Hearts' centre-forward, Willie Wallace, who scored twice, a fact not lost on Celtic's manager.

The gap between Celtic and Rangers was narrowing dangerously and Stein was fully aware that his squad was still relatively young and unused to competing for championships and trophies. At Dunfermline his sides had learned to compete meaningfully without major success in the league, but the manager knew better than most the quantum leap involved in winning the championship. Against Falkirk, Celtic resembled their early season selves and won 6–0, with Billy McNeill restored at centre-half, but a visit to Stirling for a routine fixture against the struggling local side on 26 February brought the situation into crisis mode.

Celtic had frequently laboured against Stirling Albion in the pre-Stein days, but nobody expected much trouble this time. But Stirling survived early scares and took the lead against the run of play in 37 minutes. The Celtic fans waited for their favourites to raise their game and crush the home side. For the third successive away game Celtic were in trouble, having all sorts of problems with the notorious slope at Annfield. They applied constant pressure to Stirling's goal, were desperately unlucky with the final pass or shot, eventually going down 1–0 in what could be described as a major upset. Stirling's manager, Sammy Baird, an ex-Ranger and always a target of the Celtic fans' vitriol, must have enjoyed reading his paper that evening which showed that Celtic and Rangers were now level on points, but that the Ibrox men had a superior goal average *and* a game in hand.

Stein was furious about the Stirling result against a team doomed to relegation but his first task was to restore dented morale. At Celtic Park the next day, when his players turned up for treatment for various knocks, he was positive and cheerful as he reassured his players that Rangers too were feeling the strain.

The memory of a recent visit to Dens Park and the methodical elimination of Dundee from the Scottish Cup helped the mood of the players, and a convincing league victory over the same side at Celtic

Park by 5–0 only two days after the defeat at Stirling restored morale.

On 9 March 72,000 crammed into Parkhead to watch Celtic defeat Hearts 3–1 in a Scottish Cup replay, and as the delighted fans were leaving the ground the rumour started to spread that Rangers had lost by 3–2 to Falkirk at Brockville. Parkhead erupted as the news was confirmed, and Janefield Street echoed to the songs of victory.

March was a highly successful month as Celtic continued to apply pressure on their rivals and Rangers' title challenge started to unravel. On 12 March Celtic defeated St Johnstone by 3–2 at Parkhead where a late goal from the Saints caused a few flutters among the faithful; Rangers dropped another point by drawing at home against Hearts. On 19 March Celtic were toying with Hamilton, leading by 7–1, but the fans were only half-watching as they listened to the news on the radio that Rangers were dropping another point in a draw with Kilmarnock at Rugby Park. On 21 March, a Monday, Celtic visited Firhill and, playing without Bobby Murdoch, struggled to scrape a scarcely deserved 2–2 draw with Partick Thistle thanks to a late equaliser from Bertie Auld; but on that same night Rangers lost by 1–0 to Dundee United at Tannadice.

The Celtic fans were ecstatic at the escape – and at regaining the lead in the championship. In fact, they readily forgave Bill Shankly, the legendary manager of Liverpool, who attended the match at Firhill and proclaimed: 'I would be more worried about facing Partick Thistle [than Celtic] in the Cup-Winners' Cup.'

April was destined to be a nerve-wracking month for Celtic, and the pile-up of fixtures looked ominous for a squad unused to competing on so many fronts simultaneously. They faced seven critical matches within 17 days in three competitions: the league championship, the Scottish Cup and the European Cup-Winners' Cup!

It was a time which tested the resources, mental and physical, of every member of the squad at Parkhead. Celtic had not won a league championship since 1953–54 and not one of their players could call on past experience to cope with the demands of the present. Added to the emotional strain was the cumulative effect of injuries over the course of a long season. Several of the players were nursing knocks, while some faced the risk of suspension due to cautions picked up throughout the various campaigns.

The first leg of the Cup-Winner's Cup semi-final against Liverpool at Celtic Park was a highly emotional night, and Celtic could count themselves unlucky to win by only 1–0, the goal scored from close in by Bobby Lennox. Perhaps worse from the viewpoint of the challenge for the league was the fact that the match was played on a Thursday night and Celtic were due to travel to Easter Road on the Saturday. They managed a 0–0 draw against Hibernian but their play lacked sparkle. 'Tired' and 'jaded' were the words heard in the press-box. Rangers, still in contention for the championship, defeated Morton by 5–0 at Cappielow to apply even more pressure. The Ibrox men had pulled level with Celtic at the top; Celtic, however, had three matches left and Rangers only two.

To the despair of the supporters, Celtic's goalscoring touch deserted them at this critical stage of the season. At Anfield, where the visiting Celtic supporters outshouted and outsang the Kop, in a magnificent cup tie played on a heavy pitch, Celtic survived tremendous pressure for an hour before giving up two goals (one a deflection) to the English side. And then, for the first time in the contest, Celtic went on the attack but were frustrated by a referee's mistake. Lennox raced through the middle from a head flick by McBride to score an equaliser in the last minute of play, but the referee (or his linesman) decided that he had been offside. Poor Lennox was again a victim of his own acceleration, the linesman thinking that a man so far clear of opponents had to have started from an offside position, but Joe McBride had the best view of all: 'I could see Bobby about ten yards behind me. I got a wee touch to the ball, and I saw him flying past me . . . It was never offside.'

A furious Jock Stein scarcely nodded to his friend Bill Shankly in the tunnel as he stomped back to the dressing-room; Liverpool's manager, sympathising with Stein and wisely avoiding communication, remembers him saying only one word: 'Referees!'

It was scarcely a consolation when the Belgian official, after seeing film footage of the incident, admitted that he was wrong. A bad day was made worse by the sickening outbreak of violence among the Celtic supporters at Anfield when the goal was disallowed. Fights broke out, and bottles rained down from the packed terracing and the epic contest ended amid chaos.

No time remained to regroup after the bitter disappointment of Liverpool as Celtic were due to face Rangers in the Scottish Cup final only four days later. A tense, fraught match ended up in a 0–0 draw before 126,552 equally tense spectators, and had to be replayed in the middle of the following week. The result was a 1–0 win for Rangers although, for much of the match, Celtic outplayed their oldest rivals and dominated the game. However, the forwards were not given the time to steady themselves before shooting as Rangers' heroes were all in defence. After Kai Johansen had scored with a snap shot from the edge of the area, Celtic piled on the pressure but were unable to break through for the one goal which surely would have led to an avalanche. All too soon the whistle went, and Celtic, so free-scoring earlier in the season, had now played four successive matches without a single goal.

The team bus on the short journey to Greenock – to face a Morton side with one last chance of avoiding relegation – must have contained a few men with frayed nerves. Celtic were now level with Rangers, and the two sides had almost identical goal averages. One result could change the picture and decide the championship. After playing Morton, Celtic knew they had to face Dunfermline at Parkhead and then Motherwell at Fir Park; Rangers had to visit East End Park to face Dunfermline and close their season with a home fixture against Clyde. Adding another factor to the equation was the fact that Dunfermline were still very much in contention for a place in next season's European competition – and they had to face both members of the Old Firm.

At Greenock, Jock Stein had to cajole a performance out of his nervous players. Despite his own private misgivings and doubts he exuded an air of confidence and calm. His message to the players was simple: he asked for patience, and wanted absolute concentration on this match, knowing that should be enough to see off Morton. What thoughts must have been going through his mind when Morton were rightly awarded a penalty in 30 minutes! But Neilsen drove the ball high over the crossbar to the clear relief of every Celtic player. One minute before the interval Jimmy Johnstone – who had earlier conceded the penalty-kick – put Celtic in front when his cross/shot was deflected past Sorensen by a defender. Near the end of the second half Johnstone outstripped the defence to cross for Bobby Lennox to head past the goalkeeper. The joy and the relief at getting back to winning ways was muted by the news that Rangers, boosted by their unexpected Cup triumph, had won by 2–1 at Dunfermline.

Dunfermline then visited Celtic Park on the Wednesday night. The 30th minute was critical: Alex Ferguson, who would later manage Aberdeen and Manchester United, scored to give the Pars the lead . . . and at the same moment Rangers took the lead at Ibrox against Clyde. Celtic fought back and won by 2–1 with the same pair of Johnstone and Lennox scoring the vital goals, but the last ten minutes were played out with 30,000 Celtic fans, all too aware of Rangers' 4–0 lead over Clyde, whistling anxiously for time-up. That whistle was the prelude to a field invasion as some joyous Celtic supporters started to celebrate a shade prematurely the winning of the championship for the first time in 11 years.

The league race was over, although a heavy defeat at Motherwell on the Saturday could have given Rangers the title on goal average, but there was little danger of that happening. Celtic wanted to win the flag outright and always looked in control against Motherwell. Their trim little ground was packed – and some spectators, perched on the tin roof of the enclosure throughout, waited patiently for the final whistle and the celebrations to begin. A bonus was awarded when Bobby Lennox scored from close range in the last minute to settle the outcome of the championship with a margin of two points. It was, as one journalist described it with a Churchillian flourish, 'a goal scored in the last minute of the last game on the last day of the season'.

Notes

1. The 'Letters to the Editor' section was lively and controversial initially in those early days before the publication became more 'establishment' and deserving of the nickname *Pravda*, a derogatory reference to the official newspaper of the Soviet Union.
2. Neil Mochan, an outstanding striker for Celtic in the 1950s and '60s, had been appointed as trainer/coach in mid-July on Jock Stein's recommendation. Stein, who had played alongside Mochan in the double-winning team of 1953–54, always appreciated his value as a key member of the backroom staff.
3. Simpson remembers arriving at Celtic Park to be greeted by Jimmy McGrory, who pointed to his own broken nose and said: 'Your father did this – with his elbow.' He obviously harboured no ill-feelings – and, in fact, Simpson's own father, upon learning that his son was about to join Celtic, told Ronnie that Jimmy McGrory would treat him with every respect.
4. Billy McNeill remembers as a teenager one of Stein's little 'mind-games' as a coach. Stein would stand on one side of the massage table with the player on the other. Both had to keep one hand behind their backs, and then: 'We would skelp each other. He had hands like shovels! Even years later, when you were a grown man and an international player, you would remember those hands.'
5. The young and successful Manchester United side of the 1950s was nicknamed 'the Busby Babes'; misguided Scottish sports-writers of the early 1960s referred to the hapless Celtic sides as 'the Kelly Kids'.

Chapter 2

Glory, Glory, Glory

During the summer of 1966 the World Cup was held in England, and the TV screens were filled with the exploits of the football teams of those nations who had qualified for it – and, in particular, the host nation. Accordingly, Scots watched the BBC coverage with highly ambivalent emotions as England went on to win the Jules Rimet Trophy at Wembley. Had they realised just how many reruns of that triumph would be shown over the next few decades, most Scots would have happily settled for a German victory in the final.

Scotland had failed to qualify for the competition, a fair reflection of the country's global status. Scottish football was considered a backwater in 1966, and few anticipated how quickly Jock Stein and his Celtic team would change that perception in the near future.

A working relationship had been forged between Kelly and Stein to the ultimate benefit of the club. Despite the occasional clash of two determined and stubborn Lanarkshire men, there was a genuine and growing bond between the manager and the chairman. While frequently disagreeing with him on purely football concerns, Stein admired the strong will of Kelly on matters of principle; Kelly could see almost on a weekly basis the maturing of Stein into a great manager.

The chairman could scarcely argue with results, nor could he quibble with the methods used to gain those results. Jock Stein had effected a sea-change in Celtic's level of performance and consistency. The idealistic Kelly was most impressed with another aspect of the manager's style; not only was Stein outspoken in his campaign to stamp out hooliganism among the supporters but he was also largely successful in his efforts.

Realising that the reputation of his club, as well as the performance of its team, was in good hands, Kelly gradually took more of a back seat and left the day-to-day running of Celtic to Stein. He was content, it appears, to take much of the credit for bringing Jock Stein back to Celtic Park and noticeably slow to deny the growing myth that the return was part of long-range planning on the chairman's part. The shambles of the early 1960s were being conveniently ignored.

It was a highly successful first season, Celtic's best in decades, but it was considered by Stein to be no more than the springboard to even greater exploits. He wanted Celtic to take a long tour, criss-crossing the United States and Canada. But this was no mere jaunt nor was it a reward for 1965–66. In the first place, he had arranged some stern tests – matches against Bayern Munich, Bologna and Tottenham Hotspur – in addition to more casual fixtures against local sides. The trip was a success in every way: on the field Celtic emerged undefeated in all matches. In 1966 such an experience would have been beyond the dreams of professional footballers, and the *esprit de corps* grew among the young players, uprooted as they were from prosaic, everyday life in Scotland. The more skilful of the golfers, among them Steve Chalmers and Ronnie Simpson, helped the manager's game with somewhat mixed results. With considerable irony they reported to *The Celtic View* that the manager's swing resembled that of the flamboyant Doug Saunders – a reference to the American golfer's short, swift and choppy backswing; in private, they compared it to that of the Grim Reaper.

It was a working holiday and an opportunity for the manager to experiment with new formations, one feature being the reintroduction of Bertie Auld in the middle of the pitch alongside Bobby Murdoch. This grouping had been tried out before, in the Scottish Cup semi-final against Dunfermline at Ibrox, for example, and had proved effective there. Now it was being given an extended outing against a variety of opposition.

This switch gave Celtic a midfield comparable to any in Europe as the two players combined their talents in perfect harmony. Exceptional passers of the ball, they could change the tempo of a match at will; Sean Fallon, an astute observer, pointed out that 'Bobby [Murdoch] and Bertie [Auld] could take two or three opposing players out of the game with one pass.' Both were determined, able to impose their will even in the most difficult of contests, and both were highly skilled. Competitive and talented, they were winners.

Throughout his first season Stein had tinkered and experimented with his full-backs. He had inherited Ian Young and Tommy Gemmell from the previous régime, and had Jim Craig and Willie O'Neill as back-ups, and he had even played Billy McNeill there on occasion in the previous campaign. As a serious student of the game, the manager was already starting to think that full-backs with the capacity and strength to overlap would be one way to break down the stubborn, well-organised defences Celtic would encounter in Europe.

That meant that Gemmell was assured of a place despite some deficiencies in his defensive duties. The extroverted Gemmell had impressed Stein with his speed and aggression and, although he had not scored many goals so far, the power of his shooting was not overlooked by the manager. O'Neill was a more traditional full-back, always steady in defence but not inclined to contribute too much to attack; he was unlucky in that although he was the most technically sound of the four players, he was also the slowest.

The tour did solve Stein's dilemma temporarily. Jim Craig did not travel to America as he was studying for his finals in dentistry at Glasgow University while Ian Young did go, but he returned early in order to be married.[1] Throughout the tour, Gemmell and O'Neill were Celtic's recognised full-backs and they formed an outstanding partnership. Bill Shankly, a master of hyperbole, may have said something about football being more important than life or death, and Jock Stein, a master of understatement, may have said that football was only a game. But Stein was every bit as singleminded and as pragmatic as his fellow-manager. In Stein's mind, Craig and Young had removed themselves from the equation while Gemmell and O'Neill had shown themselves to be full-time professionals by being available. Accordingly, Ian Young made only two first-team appearances for Celtic (one in the Glasgow Cup) next season, while Jim Craig, apart from an unimportant League Cup tie and two championship outings in November, was forced to wait until January 1967 before regaining a regular place.

Rangers were smarting and chafing under Celtic's success in 1965-66 and were determined to do something about it. Near the end of the previous season they had appointed a full-time public relations officer in the person of Willie Allison, although the more cynical football follower wondered at the necessity as Allison had been performing the same function in his capacity as a *Sunday Mail* reporter. However, it was recognition that Celtic under Stein had succeeded in getting the headlines week in and week out.

Rangers had also strengthened their playing squad by signing two sound midfield players: Alex Smith from Dunfermline Athletic and Dave Smith from Aberdeen. Both had been excellent performers for their provincial clubs, but it remained to be seen how they could cope with the pressure of playing for a member of the Old Firm.

Celtic were expected to do well at the start of the new campaign, with their fitness honed to an exceptional degree after the tour. Ironically, the two results that sent shockwaves resonating through Scottish football were not in the league championship but in seemingly unimportant encounters: a friendly against Manchester United at Celtic Park and a Glasgow Cup tie at Ibrox against Rangers.

Manchester United turned up at a sun-drenched Parkhead with a star-studded line-up. On display were Nobby Stiles and Bobby Charlton who had starred so recently for England in the World Cup. Also featured were Scottish internationals Pat Crerand and Denis Law as well as the Irish genius George Best. They were swept aside by a Celtic side playing at its very best, and the 4–1 scoreline flattered the visitors.

At Ibrox, the competition might have been the somewhat diminished Glasgow Cup, but both Rangers and Celtic knew the importance of this opening match in terms of morale. Once again Celtic dominated an Old Firm contest, but this time the score reflected what was happening on the pitch. Billy McNeill opened the scoring early on and Bobby Lennox scored a memorable hat-trick in what ended up as a most satisfying 4–0 rout. The pace of Lennox was a sore torment for John Greig in this match, as it would continue to be in subsequent Old Firm clashes. Bobby Lennox had added the priceless gift of anticipation to his natural speed and energy and had emerged as splendid striker.

Jimmy Farrell recalls that Stein approached this fixture in a determined mood as he had been vastly disappointed at the outcome of the previous season's Cup final. Stein showed Farrell (and the Celtic players) that he had a rare insight into the psychology of opposing players. Stein's reasoning went like this: Johansen was not noted as a scorer, but had netted a memorable goal for Rangers at Hampden; playing at Ibrox, and urged on by the home support, the full-back might well be tempted to try to repeat his feat; Bobby Lennox was instructed not to pursue his marker if he ventured upfield. The gambit worked perfectly: Johansen, to the roars of the Ibrox crowd, dashed forward to be dispossessed frequently by well-primed Celtic defenders, and Bobby Lennox, given yards of a start in the counter-attack, had a field-day. It was a perfect 'sting operation' planned by a master of the art.

The opening league fixture was at Shawfield on 10 September 1966 against a competent Clyde side who, under their young manager Davie White, would eventually finish third in the league. Celtic were simply too strong and skilful for their neighbours, though, and ran out comfortable winners by 3–0, a fine preparation for the following week's Old Firm clash at Parkhead.

Astonishingly, this most fiercely contested of all sporting rivalries was over within the opening four minutes. By that time Celtic were two goals up against a Rangers side panicking in defence at the speed of the Celtic forwards. Auld netted in the first minute of play, alertly slipping the ball past Ritchie after Joe McBride had completely miskicked in front of an open goal; Murdoch added a second goal only three minutes later, intelligently lobbing the ball over a Rangers defensive wall after his first shot had been blocked. One Rangers' fan was said to have commented that the only hope for the Ibrox men lay in getting Ian Paisley over from Belfast to referee the second half.

The Celtic fans, still savouring that 4–0 win at Ibrox on 22 August, were in a state of delirium and started to anticipate a flood of goals. They were surprised – and perhaps disappointed – at developments. Celtic's play was composed and mature, the midfield and defenders too fast for their rivals, and thus thwarted any concentrated Rangers attack. Celtic permitted Rangers a great deal of possession, but only in the least dangerous areas of the field. The days of watching the arrogant Jim Baxter and the intelligent Ian McMillan taking charge of the midfield were over and the Celtic followers started to relax and enjoy the spectacle.

Once again a visit to Tayside was going to act as a barometer for the season after an Old Firm clash. Dundee had not yet started their later decline and offered a fair test for any visitors at Dens Park. Again Celtic played well enough to win, and again they won by the same 2–1 score as in the previous season. The kick-off was delayed because of the dangerous build-up of fans outside the ground; play was stopped momentarily due to the spillage of spectators from an overcrowded terracing, and another hold-up occurred when one of the linesmen took ill and had to be replaced. Still, Celtic kept calm even after Penman opened the scoring for Dundee; Lennox equalised almost immediately, and Chalmers scored the winning goal near the end. The decider came at a time when ordinary sides would have settled for a draw away from home, but it was becoming clear that Stein's Celtic were capable of scrambling a result when not playing particularly well. It would prove a useful trait in winning championships.

St Johnstone, another club which had bothered Celtic in the recent past, came to Parkhead on 1 October and were roundly defeated by 6–1 on a wet pitch. Three men – Jimmy Johnstone, Bobby Lennox and Joe

McBride – each scored twice in the rout. The following week brought a visit to Easter Road, a ground which would become associated with great things during Stein's tenure at Celtic Park. The weather had improved and both teams concentrated on football on an excellent surface. Celtic led by 2–1 after 15 minutes, but Hibernian clawed themselves back into the contest and were rewarded with a softish penalty shortly before half-time. Joe Davis calmly slotted the ball past Simpson, and the feeling was that Hibs were lucky to be on equal terms at the break. No side could afford to relax for a split second against Celtic, however, and within a few minutes the Glasgow team were leading comfortably by 4–2. Joe McBride was the sharpshooter-in-chief, leading the way with a first half hat-trick by finishing off superb outfield play. Near the end, Celtic were in full command as McBride scored a fifth goal – and his own fourth – while the team entertained the crowd with splendid football inspired by a virtuoso performance from Bertie Auld.

The crowds were back: 65,000 for the Rangers match; 28,500 at Dens Park; 24,000 for the St Johnstone fixture played in a downpour; 43,265 jammed into Easter Road; and a remarkable 41,000 at Parkhead to see Celtic take on unfashionable Airdrie. It was not just to share in the thrill of winning matches; it was to witness the evolution of a remarkable side taking place week by week. Celtic coasted to another victory, this time by 3–0, with the goals coming in a ten-minute burst as Airdrie's resistance crumbled .

Ayr United could not cope with Celtic's pace and imagination either, going down by 5–1 on Monday, 24 October. Before the match the crowd and players observed a heartfelt minute's silence for the victims of the Aberfan mining disaster on Friday when a coal bing had engulfed a school in Glamorgan, killing more than a hundred children. The enormity of this calamity seemed to affect everybody and, after Lennox scored in only two minutes, the contest lapsed into a quiet, eerie occasion until Ayr United equalised just before half-time. Celtic were jolted by this action, and perhaps roasted by their manager during the interval; at any rate, they upped the pace in the second half and ran out comfortable winners.

By the time Celtic faced Stirling Albion in a routine fixture on 2 November at Parkhead, the first trophy of the season was already decorating the sideboard in the directors' lounge.

Once again Rangers provided stern opposition in the League Cup final, and few would have denied the Light Blues the right to a replay as they outplayed Celtic after Lennox had given the holders the lead in

18 minutes. That one moment revealed the essential difference between the sides: Auld gathered the ball on the left flank of midfield and held it before sending over a long cross beyond the back post; the front-runner McBride realised instantly that his angle of attack was unpromising and headed the ball back and across the goalmouth. Anticipating this, Bobby Lennox sprinted into the open space to clip the ball past Rangers' goalkeeper.

One particular player deserved credit for his performance, the generally unsung Willie O'Neill. He had made his début as a teenager in the disastrous Scottish Cup final against Dunfermline in 1961 after Kennedy had gone down with appendicitis, but had never been able to break through as a regular. In this final he was outstanding although faced with Rangers' tricky winger Willie Henderson, and his greatest moment came when he raced back to clear a prodded shot from Alex Smith off the goal-line. It was O'Neill's best day in football and the other Celtic players made a fuss of him after the whistle, realising how much the medal meant. Willie O'Neill was highly popular, a sociable type always ready to add to the collective morale of the squad with his sense of humour and good nature.

It would have been easy to relax their standards in the bread-and-butter of the league programme, especially when facing lowly Stirling Albion at Parkhead but Celtic were prepared for their visitors, scoring seven times; as an indication of their more human qualities, however, they conceded three goals themselves.

St Mirren's visit to Parkhead on the following Saturday did much to shake Celtic out of any overconfidence. It did not appear to be a challenging match although the home side would be without the towering presence of Billy McNeill at the centre of defence. Stein decided not to play Cushley in his captain's place as had been done successfully on occasions in the past two seasons. Instead, he moved Tommy Gemmell into the centre and brought Jim Craig into the side at right-back. The thinking behind the move was clear: Craig had been challenging for a berth in the side since the start of the season but had been unable to dislodge either Gemmell or O'Neill, and Stein sensed that his reserve needed some outings in the side again.

Although Tommy Gemmell, his replacement, put Celtic ahead early in the second half, McNeill was badly missed for his leadership qualities. Treacy equalised for the Buddies seven minutes later as Celtic's makeshift defence, bereft of McNeill's organisational talents, failed to clear with any conviction. Celtic charged forward for the winning goal, but their play was a disappointing throwback to the desperation of past seasons. A cool head was needed, but Auld was having a poor day and Bobby Murdoch was ordered off for a silly offence.

It made one thing abundantly clear. Celtic, without Billy McNeill, were not the same effective team. McNeill was Celtic's captain in every sense of the word, making sure that Stein's wishes were carried out on the pitch. A natural leader, he could bark at players and snap them out of inattention, and he could encourage others when they were drooping. Bob Crampsey, a keen observer of Celtic at this time, pointed out that McNeill was obviously Celtic's captain; had any stranger been allowed into Celtic's dressing-room, he would have known within seconds without being told which man was the captain. McNeill had presence and natural authority and he needed all that because this emerging Celtic side contained quite a few independent, strong-willed characters.

On 7 November Celtic were due to face Partick Thistle in the Glasgow Cup final, and although it was considered a relatively minor tournament it still represented a dramatic occasion. Celtic went on to win the handsome trophy with a 4–0 trouncing of the Maryhill Magyars, their second within nine days.

After sloppy displays at home against Stirling and St Mirren, Stein was able to make the point that every match was of equal importance and that there could be no letting up in the struggle to retain the championship. An ex-miner, a journeyman player, and now a football manager: nobody could ever accuse Jock Stein of being in tune with transcendental meditation but his players soon became accustomed to his mantra-like utterances as time after time he repeated the phrase: 'Two points are two points.'

It was beginning to be a struggle as Rangers were improving. In fact, their 'improvement' could be charted in their results against Celtic: 0–4 at Ibrox in the Glasgow Cup, 0–2 at Parkhead in the league, and 0–1 at Hampden in the League Cup final. In the latter contest many felt that Rangers had been the better side, and had been unlucky to have had a goal disallowed. On the day that Celtic dropped the first point in the draw with St Mirren, Rangers thrashed Motherwell by 5–1.

Two difficult fixtures were looming in November: successive away matches at Brockville and East End Park. Falkirk could be awkward playing at home, as the young Celtic sides of the early '60s had discovered, but this Celtic team was different. They assumed command from the start and kept control throughout to finish 3–0 winners.

The match against Dunfermline Athletic was the most enthralling encounter of the 1966-67 league campaign. Dunfermline were a formidable side, and had not declined too much since their heady days under Stein's management. It was an old-time thriller, more like a Scottish Cup tie than a league match. Without ever being in control of the contest, the home side led three times by two clear goals: 2–0, 3–1, and 4–2. At half-time the score was 3–2 for Dunfermline and, when Ferguson snatched a fourth shortly after the restart, the outcome seemed certain.

And then came a Celtic revival of epic proportions. Dunfermline's defence may have been solid and adequate against most teams, but it simply had no answer as Celtic surged into attack. Bobby Murdoch and Bertie Auld were inspirational figures as they seized control of the midfield and released their forwards. Jimmy Johnstone was a will-o'-the-wisp as he twisted and turned past lunging defenders, while Bobby Lennox thrust at the heart of the home defence with quicksilver runs. In 60 minutes Auld pulled one goal back, and the more perceptive (if there were any in the ground at the time) pointed out that Auld tended to score only when a goal was vital for Celtic. Ten minutes later, with Celtic in full cry and Dunfermline reeling, McBride equalised.

The battle raged on and Dunfermline, calling on reserves of raw courage, fought back. In fact, the Pars scored in a goalmouth scramble and had the goal disallowed for some reason that was not readily apparent. Approaching the whistle, Celtic redoubled their efforts and in the 88th minute were awarded a penalty-kick; Joe McBride was designated to take it, and he smashed the ball into the net for a famous and breathtaking victory by 5–4. It had been an afternoon for dungarees rather than designer gear.

Hearts came to Celtic Park on 26 November, and left suitably chastened by a 3–0 defeat, although Celtic took some time to add an insurance goal after a Hearts defender had given them the lead with a spectacular own-goal. McBride scored the third in the last minute with another penalty. The clash with Hearts had an added ingredient in that stories were starting to spread that Willie Wallace, Hearts' centre-forward, was available as he was unhappy at Tynecastle. The rumour mill was turning out stories of interest from both Celtic and Rangers.

Once again Celtic paid the price of success on the continent as the team dropped another point unexpectedly at Rugby Park against Kilmarnock. This match came only days after a superb performance against Nantes in France which produced a 3–1 away win. It was difficult to be motivated after that on a cold December day in Ayrshire, and a disappointing match ended in a 0–0 draw. However, the punters leaving the ground were cheered with the news that Rangers had been defeated 3–2 by Dunfermline at East End Park.

Another mammoth crowd of 40,000 swarmed into Celtic Park on 10 December to see Willie Wallace make his début against Motherwell. It was a crowd buzzing with excitement as Celtic had eliminated Nantes from the European Cup with another 3–1 victory in midweek and had qualified for the quarter-finals of that most prestigious tournament. In fact, Celtic had made an excellent start in the European Cup with four successive victories, against Zurich by 2–0 at Parkhead and 3–0 in Switzerland, and by 3–1 against Nantes in Glasgow and in France. The newspapers were full of 'the details' of how Jock Stein had filched Wallace from Rangers. According to these accounts, Stein had waited until Rangers were away in Germany on Cup-Winners' Cup business before making Hearts an attractive offer, estimated at £30,000, with little time for refusal. The wily Stein had also let it be known that he was equally interested in another striker, an Anglo-Scot named Gibson, in order to put more pressure on Hearts to sell quickly. The fans were intrigued by the audacity suggested by the newspaper reports.

To his credit, Wallace behaved like a model professional, refusing to state that he had always supported Celtic as a boy and other such nonsense. He signed on for Celtic, trained hard, took his place in the team and played as conscientiously as he had done for Stenhousemuir, Raith Rovers and Hearts. In other words, he was the type of level-headed professional that Jock Stein wanted at Celtic Park.

Before the Motherwell match some Celtic fans unfurled a huge banner which seemed to extol the values of the *Sunday Post*, as it read simply: 'Oor Wullie'. They were highly relieved that Wallace would not be playing against Celtic again. As a Heart he had inflicted much pain on Celtic defences in the past, and the thought of such a dangerous forward playing for Rangers against Celtic was frightening. Undoubtedly, Celtic's central-defenders McNeill and Clark (and Cushley) were equally thankful they would not have to mark him again.

Stein had wanted to strengthen his squad with another striker, and one who could take some of the weight off the others was an ideal choice. However, a long-term injury problem with Joe McBride would alter any such provisional plans.

Shortly before the fixture with Motherwell, Joe was forced to call off, and his place was taken by Steve Chalmers, who fitted in perfectly and led Celtic to a 4–2 win by scoring a hat-trick. McBride, a prolific scorer that season, had been experiencing twinges in his knee for some time, and subsequent visits to various specialists in Scotland had produced no specific answer. In the 1960s – before the development of keyhole surgery – a knee operation was a serious matter for a football player as recuperation was lengthy and there was no guarantee of the joint regaining its former strength and flexibility. Accordingly, any decision regarding the condition would continue to be deferred while the medical men disagreed among themselves.

Wallace scored twice in his next game, against Partick Thistle at Celtic Park on 17 December as Celtic routed the visitors by 6–2. His first was a close-in header, but the second – a glorious half-volley from 20 yards out – ignited Parkhead for some minutes afterwards. A feature of the performance was the unselfish way that three potential rivals for two positions (Chalmers, McBride and Wallace) interacted with one another: they read the others' intentions in a flash, interchanged positions, ran intelligently off the ball, and worked hard for each other. There was no hint of rivalry or jealousy as they revelled in the goals scored – by Wallace (2), Chalmers (2), McBride and Murdoch. In a recent (1997) television documentary about the three great Scottish managers, Matt Busby, Bill Shankly, and Jock Stein, the journalist Hugh McIlvanney made much of the fact that all three came from a mining background in industrial Scotland. It was suggested that the same rough-hewn qualities of teamship essential down the mineshaft were valuable on the football pitch. Stein, for one, was able to instil such virtues in his players and they could be sure that he was quick to spot extra effort even if it did not result in goals.

However, time was running out for McBride, Scotland's leading goalscorer with 37 competitive goals. In the second-last fixture of 1966, against Aberdeen at Pittodrie on Christmas Eve, McBride had to leave the pitch as his knee finally gave way. He did not play again that season but he still finished the country's leading marksman. He missed out on the glory of the European Cup and the Scottish Cup and his chagrin is apparent to this day. The loss of the popular McBride was a grievous one for Celtic, and it marked the end of his career as a Celtic regular as he never fully regained the level of sharpness that had earned him the reputation as Celtic's most effective striker since Jimmy McGrory.

It had been assumed generally that the manager had bought Wallace to replace Steve Chalmers eventually but, while Joe McBride's career started to decline, Chalmers embarked on a glorious Indian summer to his. Bobby Murdoch acknowledges that Stein knew more about strikers than goalkeepers: 'A brilliant judge – and most of them were wee. But they were all hard: Joe [McBride] and Willie [Wallace] were ferocious fighters and could take care of themselves in the penalty area.'

Celtic ended 1966 shakily, as the visit to Pittodrie ended in a 1–1 draw and a Hogmanay call at Tannadice resulted in a 3–2 loss to Dundee United. Celtic had looked in control of the situation, enjoying a 2–1 lead with 15 minutes to play, but defensive lapses allowed Dundee United to pull off an upset. Ronnie Simpson, normally a model of concentration, seemed at fault for both late goals although some supporters blamed Willie O'Neill since both goals originated on United's right wing.

One minor matter was settled with the loss. A highly popular programme on BBC featured Raymond Burr as Perry Mason, a highly skilled defence lawyer. Even among Celtic supporters this was one Mason to be identified with. In court he pitted his wits time after time against the District Attorney, a glum-faced man named Ham(ilton) Burger; time after time Perry Mason would confound the odds and win his case. The fact that Perry always won likened him to Celtic – as did a passing resemblance of Raymond Burr to Jock Stein. The question that people began to ask was 'Who will lose first – Perry Mason or Celtic?'.

A minor consolation could be derived from the fact that Rangers had dropped a point to Dundee at Ibrox and remained two behind Celtic at the top of the league table. Rangers were aware that Celtic's form had been shaky – at least, by Celtic's standards – and that a win for them at Ibrox in the traditional New Year fixture might swing things in their favour. They had valid grounds for optimism because 1966–67 was one of their better seasons. In the European Cup-Winners' Cup they were making splendid progress against strong opposition (and they would reach the final, losing only after extra-time). They may well have been included in the top sides in Europe that season, but one fact remained like a cancer, gnawing away at their vitals: they were only second best in Glasgow.

Unfortunately for the Ibrox club, the New Year match on 3 January was called off in mid-morning because of frost – although other games went ahead. The Celtic players returned to Parkhead and staged a practice match but it remained a bitter disappointment for many fans who had travelled far to find the match off.

Celtic resumed the league campaign with a resounding victory over Dundee at Parkhead on 7 January where a crowd of 37,000 saw Jim Craig restored to the side at right-back. A good result (5–1) and one enhanced with the postponing of the Aberdeen–Rangers fixture at Pittodrie. Four days later Clyde surrendered by the same 5–1 scoreline although this time the goals came in the second half; with Celtic leading by 2–1 after Gallagher's goal in 54 minutes, three more goals came within four minutes from Chalmers (72), Gemmell (74) and Lennox (75).

The visit to Muirton Park to take on St Johnstone was a significant one for the 19,000 spectators and for Celtic historians because, for the first time, the side which would represent the club later in the season at Lisbon in the European Cup final was chosen as a unit. It took them some time to settle as the interval score was 0–0, but Jimmy Johnstone opened the scoring in 63 minutes and Celtic pulled ahead to win by 4–0. For the record, the team lined up as Simpson, Craig, Gemmell, Murdoch, McNeill, Clark, Johnstone, Wallace, Chalmers, Auld and Lennox.

During this season almost everything fell into place for Celtic – but not exactly by chance although they had only gradually evolved into a remarkable team. Some factors might be noted. Bobby Murdoch and Bertie Auld worked in tandem in midfield, and they were the most intelligent and hard-working midfielders in Scotland. With Auld moving back into midfield, John Clark – once a normal left-half – found himself stationed alongside Billy McNeill in the centre of defence and that also was an inspired pairing: McNeill dominated his area in the air, but sometimes could be tricked on the ground; Clark developed a sixth sense of when McNeill was in trouble and mopped up any danger with magisterial calm.

Jimmy Johnstone was now approaching his best, and he was simply unique – a player unable to be contained no matter what methods, fair or foul, were employed to halt him. Bobby Murdoch recalls one tactics talk that involved Jimmy Johnstone. Stein explained in general terms what he expected from the opposition and what he wanted from Celtic. He went on to give more specific instructions to some players, but did not mention Johnstone. The little winger was in a nervous mood and intercepted the manager as he was leaving the dressing-room: 'Whit aboot me, Boss? Whit aboot me?' Stein paused for a second and gave him a pat on the cheek: 'You? You just do whatever the —— you want.'

The excellent form continued with a comfortable 2–0 win over Hibernian at Parkhead although there were murmurings of discontent from the Jungle as Celtic eased up after going ahead. A 2–0 win over Hibs was no longer enough, but a week later Celtic strolled through a Scottish Cup tie against Arbroath. Nobody complained that day as the news spread through the ground that Rangers had been knocked out of the competition in sensational manner by humble Berwick Rangers.

The kick-off at Berwick had been brought forward, and the result had been confirmed well before the Celtic–Arbroath tie was completed; the atmosphere inside Celtic Park changed to one of carnival as the fans (and players) rejoiced. Any defeat for Rangers marks a good day for Celtic supporters, but this shock result virtually meant that the greatest danger in the Scottish Cup had been removed at the first hurdle. However, it also meant that Rangers would be more free to concentrate on the league championship. For Celtic it would mean even more care in the bread-and-butter fixtures . . .

During February, Celtic completed three more away assignments: at Airdrie, Ayr and Stirling. A comfortable 3–0 win at Broomfield was followed by a 5–0 rout at Somerset Park, a visit marked by a hat-trick for Steve Chalmers in a fixture that started at noon to avoid a possible clash with Rangers' match at Kilmarnock. Those victories left Celtic in good spirit but other distractions were looming: Celtic had advanced to the quarter-finals of the Scottish Cup, and had reached the same stage in the European Cup. A home tie against Queen's Park on 11 March did not seem too threatening, but a midweek expedition on 1 March to an obscure place called Novi Sad to play a side called Vojvodina could be construed as a diversion.

In comparison with Yugoslavia, Stirling is next door to Glasgow; the natives, however, were not friendly. Once more Stirling Albion, still managed by Sammy Baird, turned out in an orange strip – an act of provocation, according to some Celtic zealots. The ground itself, Annfield, on a summer's day might be considered one of the more picturesque in Scotland; in late February, with rain drenching the spectators on exposed terracings, it was miserable.

Albion scored first through Peebles, and held the lead until half-time despite Celtic pressure. When John Hughes equalised early in the second half, it looked as if Celtic were going to open the floodgates and swamp the home side. 'Flooding' and 'swamping' were appropriate metaphors because puddles were forming in hollows on the pitch; the linesman on the stand side caused momentary relief by skidding and falling on his backside; and the rain refused to stop. Stirling kept fighting for every ball with ferocious tackling and, as one or two Celtic players began to retaliate in kind, vendettas sprang up culminating in Rogerson of Stirling Albion being ordered off. Celtic poured forward to settle the match, and very near the end Billy McNeill rose in his inimitable way to power home a corner-kick. The joy of the Celtic following turned to rage when the referee disallowed the goal, presumably on the grounds that McNeill had pushed a defender on his way to the ball. It was a harsh decision, considering the conditions underfoot, but the referee was adamant.

Celtic played sensibly in Yugoslavia and retained enough of an attacking threat to make the home side – a virile, physical side who were also technically skilled – unwilling to risk all-out attack. In fact, Celtic looked as if they had gained their primary aim of a draw – until a casual passback by Gemmell took John Clark by surprise, and was translated into a simple goal. Celtic had no doubts about the magnitude of the task awaiting them in Glasgow against this redoubtable outfit.

After the disaster at Berwick, Rangers had recovered to have a good February and Celtic's advantage at the top of the table was only two points. In the previous season at much the same time, Celtic had to catch up on Rangers; now, they were being asked to stay in front. The postponed match against Rangers at Ibrox still loomed as a championship decider.

March was another testing month but nothing was allowed to stop Celtic's progress. The Parkhead side warmed up for the key match against the Yugoslavs with a demolition job by 5–0 over St Mirren on 4 March. On the following Wednesday they faced Vojvodina in the quarter-final of the European Cup in what proved to be the most tense and dramatic of all European ties before a packed Celtic Park. Jock Stein, relishing more and more the opportunity to pit his wits against continental opposition, advised his players time after time that the tie was only half-over and that patience would be rewarded, but at the interval he must have been anxious. The first half had been disjointed with Celtic attacking throughout but showing no signs of achieving a breakthrough; the Yugoslav defenders were coping efficiently and their goalkeeper, the giant figure of Pantelic, was indulging in annoying actions and gestures in his goalmouth whenever the Celtic attacks broke down.

Perhaps the behaviour of the goalkeeper indicated an inner tension – and one picked up by somebody on the Celtic staff – because it was clear that the Celtic attackers were starting to crowd him at corner-kicks and the tall goalkeeper would not be allowed to leave his goal-line unchallenged to dominate the area. Steve Chalmers was on the spot in 58 minutes when the keeper mishandled a cross/shot from Gemmell, but a play-off match, scheduled for Rotterdam, looked inevitable until Celtic got yet another corner-kick, this time on the right.

Charlie Gallagher raced over to take it but hesitated after placing the ball within the arc: the most obvious move was another short kick to

Johnstone, but Gallagher knew that this corner represented Celtic's last chance. While the crowd howled for him to hurry, Gallagher waited until he saw that Billy McNeill had started to move upfield. The move was straight out of the practice sessions: if Billy McNeill was in the opponents' penalty area, he did not want to be fighting his own players for the ball; accordingly, two Celtic players started to sprint out towards Gallagher and took their defenders with them. Stevie Chalmers remained inside the six-yard box and positioned himself so that the goalkeeper would have to go round him, giving McNeill a few more feet of space. Everything now depended on the corner-kick, and Gallagher delivered the perfect ball, just outside the six-yard line, just out of reach of the goalkeeper, a high ball firmly struck that could be reached only by a tall player, or one with exceptional timing in the air. And McNeill's header crashed into the roof of the net while Parkhead exploded with joy and pent-up relief.

Dunfermline came to Celtic Park on 18 March and Celtic played without Jimmy Johnstone. During the previous week's cup tie against Queen's Park the little redhead, frustrated by the attentions of an amateur defender, took the law into his own hands. The referee missed the incident, but Jock Stein and many spectators saw it. The result was that Johnstone was given a club suspension for seven days. Celtic struggled at times against Dunfermline, and displayed some nervousness in the closing minutes after Alex Ferguson had scored his second goal of the day to make the score 3–2 for Celtic.

On the Monday night Celtic routed Falkirk by 5–0, again at Parkhead, to set up the two away fixtures at Tynecastle and Firhill, grounds filled with danger. On 25 March Celtic played Hearts in the rain, but this time it proved a day of triumph. From the start, the Hearts supporters booed and catcalled Willie Wallace for deserting them, but the player had the last laugh. Late in the first half Bertie Auld lived up to his reputation as the scorer of crucial goals by giving Celtic the lead at the interval. Hearts were fighting desperately for the equaliser but Celtic broke away after 62 minutes and were awarded a free-kick some 20 yards out; Wallace placed the ball carefully, surveyed the defensive wall and blasted a ferocious shot straight through it. Tommy Gemmell added a third goal with a penalty-kick five minutes from the end. The only drawback in a splendid result was an injury to Bobby Murdoch who had to be replaced by Lennox.

Murdoch was to miss the next two matches, against Thistle and Motherwell, but the Celtic juggernaut rolled on. At Firhill, Lennox opened the scoring in 41 minutes, and that was Celtic's hundredth goal of the season; in the second half, after the home side had dared to equalise, Celtic pulled further and further ahead to win 4–1.

Injury to key players was not going to affect this Celtic side, nor was the cumulative fatigue of a long season – one lengthened by the pre-season tour of the United States. The excitement of chasing every trophy open to them was a major factor; Celtic's players were filled with the energy produced by surges of adrenaline.

John Hughes came back into the side for a spell and justified his selection by scoring goals against Ayr United, Stirling, St Mirren and Falkirk. Hughes had always been something of an enigma. He was powerfully built and a strong runner; for a big man he had a delicate touch – and there was no more thrilling sight in Scottish football than John Hughes in full flight at the top of his form. The down side was that, on his bad days, Hughes looked hopeless. He had been switched out to the left wing where he seemed to thrive on the greater space and freedom allowed him, but Stein valued consistency as a virtue. Talent and potential had to be displayed every week regardless of the mood of the player, the nature of the opponents or the playing conditions. Like Joe McBride – who was excluded from Lisbon through serious injury – Hughes in 1967 was another 'nearly' man. He would participate in every competition: 19 league matches, five European Cup ties, four Scottish Cup ties and four League Cup ties. But he played in only one final – against Rangers on 29 October 1966 – and was substituted by Chalmers before the end.

The situation was tense – and it was a situation made worse by the recollection that in 1965–66 Celtic had been in exactly the same position. Both Rangers and Celtic had five league matches left to play, and both had three home fixtures. Both sides were involved in European semi-finals, with Rangers facing Slavia Sofia and Celtic taking on Dukla Prague. Celtic had a two-point lead in the championship, but had to face a visit to Ibrox Park and a head-to-head clash with Rangers; in addition, Celtic were still heavily involved in the Scottish Cup.

On 1 April Celtic faced Clyde in the Scottish Cup semi-final at Hampden Park, Aberdeen played Dundee United at Dens Park in the other and Rangers took advantage of the schedule to play Dunfermline Athletic at Ibrox. The football that day was dull and uninspiring: Celtic and Clyde staggered to a 0–0 draw, Aberdeen got through thanks to an own-goal and Rangers went down to a 1–0 defeat, being unable to pierce a stout Pars defence. It is amazing to recall how many times the Fifers were involved in key matches against the Old Firm – and how many times they were able to thwart Rangers. The news of the upset at Ibrox was celebrated loudly and joyously by the Celtic supporters waiting in the long queues at Mount Florida railway station. Six points from five league games would now do it for Celtic.

Two of those points came at Fir Park the following Saturday in a competent, professional performance. Wallace scored first and Gemmell settled the match by blasting home a penalty-kick in his patented manner. Rangers, meanwhile, had edged Stirling Albion by 1–0. Celtic's next league match was against Aberdeen on 19 April, a Wednesday night – a Scottish Cup final rehearsal and one postponed because of the European Cup semi-final and the Scotland–England international. A win in this encounter would have done much to bring the championship to Celtic Park, but Aberdeen played in an ultra-defensive manner and Celtic could not break down their stubborn defence, being held to a 0–0 draw. Once again, late-season nerves were a factor and the result caused a slight *frisson* of apprehension about the forthcoming final.

The Scottish Cup final was another great occasion for Celtic – and Jock Stein. Although it was late in the season (29 April), Stein decided that Celtic would produce something new in tactics: Chalmers, always an intelligent, unselfish runner off the ball, would be played wider on the right instead of through the middle as expected. Wallace would be the main striker up front while Lennox would patrol the left flank. One Celtic forward, Jimmy Johnstone, would be given a free rein alongside Wallace. Aberdeen, who had to travel to Hampden Park without their manager Eddie Turnbull after he had taken ill on the morning of the match, had no answer to Celtic's switch; their left-back had prepared all week for containing Jimmy Johnstone on Celtic's right wing and he did not know whether to follow Johnstone or stay wide and cover Chalmers. The confusion spread rapidly throughout the Aberdeen defence, and two goals scored by Willie Wallace on either side of half-time gave Celtic an easy victory before an appreciative crowd of 126,102.

Rangers were finding the run-in for the championship tense as well. On the day that Celtic won the Scottish Cup for the 19th time, the challengers dropped another point by drawing with Dundee. It seemed the icing on the cake: the League Cup and the Scottish Cup already at Celtic Park might soon to be joined by the League Championship trophy – and Celtic were through to the final of the European Cup in Lisbon.

Amazingly, Celtic contrived to lose the next league fixture, against

Dundee United at Parkhead, and in much the same circumstances and by the same score (3–2) as at Tannadice on New Year's Eve. Dundee United were able to claim for posterity that they had beaten Celtic both home and away in the Parkhead club's greatest-ever season. This meant that the championship might be decided officially at Ibrox on 6 May in the fixture postponed from New Year. Celtic had a considerable advantage in that they still had a one-point lead, and a better goal average – and, most importantly of all, they still had another match left, against Kilmarnock at Parkhead. Rangers had to win well, and then hope for the Ayrshire side to upset Celtic.

The rain poured down at Ibrox for hours before the match, and persisted throughout. The match was curiously symmetrical: each side scored a brilliant goal at the Rangers end of the ground, long-range shots from Sandy Jardine and Jimmy Johnstone (with his left foot); each side scrambled one in at the Celtic end, close-in efforts from Roger Hynd and Jimmy Johnstone. The result, a fair 2–2 draw, was enough for Celtic and they had retained the championship. The managers of Inter Milan and Bayern Munich watched impassively from the stand as they contemplated the tactics to be used against the Old Firm in the forthcoming European finals. To add to the occasion, Sean Connery, in the days when he claimed to be a Celtic fan, seemed delighted with the outcome as did the other rain-soaked Celtic supporters in the 78,000-strong crowd.

One more game remained in the league, a now meaningless fixture against Kilmarnock on 15 May. Celtic wore their all-green strip and fielded John Cushley at centre-half while choosing Billy McNeill as inside-right. Regardless of the eccentric selection, perhaps designed to confuse Herrera's spies from Milan, they won by 2–0, a goal in each half from Lennox and Wallace deciding matters.

Doubtless, the minds of the players and the supporters kept turning to another date with destiny in Lisbon on 25 May 1967.

Celtic had qualified for Lisbon by beating Dukla Prague (the Czech Army team) by 3–1 in Glasgow, and by holding on for a nervous, uncharacteristic 0–0 draw in Czechoslovakia. In the first leg at Celtic Park on 12 April, Wallace had scored twice in the second half to give Celtic a two-goal lead as a cushion for the visit behind the Iron Curtain. Once more a goal straight from the training-ground eased Celtic through: a Czech defender deliberately handled a few yards outside the penalty area and three Celtic players conferred (in the manner of the witches in *Macbeth*) about the options available to them. Auld was the pivotal figure, with Gemmell and Wallace in attendance.

At last, a decision was reached and Auld prepared to take the kick . . . but, unhappy with the placing of the ball, he stooped as if to move it . . . instead, he quickly rolled the ball a few feet to the right and Wallace's shot went round the wall which had relaxed momentarily and flew into the net past a surprised goalkeeper.

In Prague, the team chose to play defensively – in an almost unrecognisable Celtic manner. This time there would be no defeat caused by tactical stupidity. If Dukla won this match they would have to overcome a resolute Celtic defence, suitably reinforced by midfielders and even forwards. Only Steve Chalmers was left up front but, with his speed, Dukla were forced to hold back two of their men to guard him; already, in the vital zones of the pitch, Celtic had a one-man advantage. However, it was a miserable, tense match and Stein was afterwards always reluctant to discuss it in any great detail; his chairman was more forthcoming and claimed to be bitterly disappointed by Celtic's attitude.

Stein saw the match as Celtic's last hurdle in getting to the final of the European Cup and planned accordingly. Some of his squad remembered too well the experience of 'Kelly's Kids' back in 1964 when Celtic went to Hungary holding a 3–0 lead from the first leg of the semi-final of the European Cup-Winners' Cup – and played with such naïveté that they lost 4–0. Apparently, Bob Kelly attempted to justify the team's 'tactics' by claiming later that 'Celtic had a duty to entertain the public in Budapest'. In such an important match, Stein simply saw no point in 'entertaining' a meagre crowd of 22,000 – comprised mostly of soldiers in uniform – in a moribund stadium behind the Iron Curtain on a cold afternoon and thus risk losing a place on the world stage.

More and more, in the build-up to the European Cup final in Lisbon, attention was being paid to Jock Stein, and he was a man growing into his job. It is interesting to see the difference between Jock Stein, the young manager, and Jock Stein, the mature manager. The younger Stein, more particularly in his Dunfermline days, is obviously intelligent and alert but somewhat diffident with words in his interviews; the 1967 Stein has added considerable *gravitas* to his image and in interviews or press conferences is totally in command. He is the one in control, unruffled and calm but hugely attentive. The impression is given clearly that he will not blurt out anything inadvertently – what will be revealed is what was intended to be revealed. The words too are geared for the reporters: concise, exact and always quotable – in modern-day media terms, he was 'a master of the sound bite'.

His players had come to know him as a sound coach and a motivator. Some of them date their trust in him as a coach from the second-leg match against Zurich on 5 October 1966. The Swiss side had opted for a packed defence in Glasgow and Celtic had stuttered at times before winning a bruising encounter by 2–0; the players fully expected a different approach in Zurich, and were astonished when Stein informed them that he thought their opponents would not go all-out in attack. They disagreed and told him so – but the manager felt convinced he was right: Celtic, playing sensibly, could play their normal game and there would be no surprises from the Swiss. He was totally right and the players were impressed as Celtic went on to record a 3–0 victory, with Tommy Gemmell spending the last 30 minutes vainly trying to complete a hat-trick.

In the domestic game, where everything was familiar, the manager and his players could agree quickly on the tactics to be used, but Europe in 1967 was different. For one thing, TV coverage had not reached saturation level and, accordingly, the opponents were unknown for the most part. Stein, usually on the basis of one scouting trip, had impressed the players with the accuracy of his predictions. The squad were not given too many details about the opposition, but they knew roughly what to expect and where the danger would come from.

Stein, of course, was more familiar with the European scene than his Celtic players as he had led Dunfermline Athletic to unexpected glory in that theatre; Celtic, apart from one exciting campaign in 1963-64 in the Cup-Winners' Cup, had done little prior to Stein's arrival. First-hand experience was vital, but Jock Stein, an excellent listener, was steeped in the stories of European intrigue and deceptions. He had heard from other managers of the methods used to disarm British sides. In the earlier years of European competition, when foreign travel was relatively unusual, the continental clubs would often lay on tours of their cities and countryside, often on the morning of the match. These trips would stretch, lasting a couple of hours more than originally planned, and the British players would find their normal preparation for an important match seriously disrupted. Stein's professional response was to turn down all such outings. One Celtic player, perhaps not understanding his manager's thinking, summed it up: 'Jock Stein didn't like sight-seeing, so we didn't either.'

Scottish footballers were curious about their mysterious European counterparts, and Jock Stein often took considerable pains to counter their anxieties about the unknown. During the 1965–66 European Cup-Winners' Cup, Celtic faced Dynamo Kiev at Parkhead on 12 January and it was customary for the home club to give the visitors the use of the facilities at the ground on the day before the match in order that they would be familiar with the state of the playing surface and the floodlighting. Most of the Celtic squad, along with Stein and his helpers, watched the Soviet side run through a training session and were intrigued – and perhaps alarmed – to observe that the whole exercise was carried out in complete silence, apart from an occasional whistle or command from the trainer. Stein allayed any disquiet this Pavlovian session may have caused by his remarks later: 'They're good technical players, well trained and disciplined . . . they have a system and they know it well enough . . . but the best systems, especially drilled ones, can be beaten with players of flair and imagination – and we have those players.'

The Celtic players knew their boss as a formidable figure, and were delighted when he refused to be conned by any subtle European ploys. At Nantes, for example, Celtic had not been allowed full access to the pitch at the Malakoff Stadium on the grounds that it had been used recently for a rugby match and might cut up too much prior to the European match with Celtic. Stein accepted this as reasonable, but was not fooled; two weeks later in Glasgow, he informed the visitors that the playing surface at Celtic Park was 'delicate' and offered them the facilities at Barrowfield, Celtic's training-ground, in exchange.

In the tense minutes before the kick-off at Lisbon they were given a psychological boost when Stein twice thwarted gambits by Inter's manager, Helenio Herrera. There had been rumours before the final that Suarez, Inter's general in midfield, would not be playing because of injury; Stein was reluctant to believe this but had prepared for every eventuality. Right up to the kick-off, Inter's manager delayed giving the match officials the line-up of his team; in response, Stein told the referee that Celtic would refuse to play unless they were given access to that list. Celtic's manager was perfectly within his rights; as the regulations stated, he had provided the referee with the Glasgow club's list of players (and substitute goalkeeper) 30 minutes before the scheduled kick-off. Now Stein wanted his Inter counterpart to comply with the same regulations, and he was insistent about it.

On the sidelines, after the two teams had entered the arena, there was another *contretemps* and once more it ended in a victory for Celtic. Prior to the match, Celtic had been informed about which bench would be theirs, but the backroom staff spotted immediately that some advance members of Inter had claimed it. Stein, never a man to yield any advantage to opponents, ordered his staff to regain possession of the bench – a task accomplished with a suitable display of power by such formidable men as John Cushley, Neil Mochan and Sean Fallon. It may have been unimportant but the Celtic players on the pitch saw this development, and were boosted by the sight of the Italian trainers (and manager) trudging down to the far end of the field towards their bench.

The match at the Estadio Nacional in Lisbon on the evening of 25 May 1967 was destined to be greatest day in the club's history. Round the pitch, a crowd of 54,000 had gathered to witness a clash of two differing approaches to football: Inter favoured a defensive structure with a devastating ability to strike on the break, while Celtic had already earned a European reputation for swift, attacking play. Inter, as befitted their pedigree and record in Europe, were favourites to win, while Celtic had to be the underdogs. Thousands (estimated at between 8,000 and 10,000) of Celtic supporters had made the long journey to Portugal by a variety of means, and in the days prior to the European Cup final had intrigued the population of the capital city by their enthusiasm, and so there were few 'neutrals' at that final. Celtic's reputation – in contrast to Inter's – ensured that most Portuguese present would be cheering for Celtic.

Right from the opening kick-off, Celtic attacked in waves of combined play, and Inter defended in depth. The opening goal came in only seven minutes – but at the wrong end of the pitch. Inter broke from deep defence, and Jim Craig tackled Cappellini awkwardly. Despite protests that it was a harsh decision by the German referee, it was a penalty-kick, and Mazzola converted it neatly by sending Simpson the wrong way. That was a disastrous start for the Scots, who had dominated the opening minutes, and Inter Milan, past masters at grinding out results, settled in to defend. In retrospect, it could have been a flaw in their tactics, as Billy McNeill points out: 'Apart from Ronnie [Simpson] and John [Clark], we had players who could score from any position on the field. It was an open invitation for us to attack ...'

And attack Celtic did. Jimmy Johnstone was plied with the ball for the first 20 minutes of the contest quite deliberately to unsettle the Italian defenders; he twisted and turned past opponents and succeeded in spreading some unease in their ranks. Facchetti, an outstanding attacking full-back when released from defensive duties, was forced to remain in his own half for the entire match. Stein had asked that Jinky be given the ball for that period of time, but afterwards the match took on a more characteristic look.

The danger to the Italian goal was coming from every quarter, and Celtic were denied twice by the woodwork when shots from Auld and Gemmell crashed against the bar. Inter's goalkeeper Sarti made several outstanding saves – and some Celtic players recalled that Stein had suggested he was a vulnerable link in Inter's defence. It was not just frantic attack, as Bobby Charlton later commented upon seeing a film of the match: 'I knew you won, and deserved to win – but I never realised the quality of the football you played in Lisbon.'

At half-time Jock Stein was monumentally calm: the players were disappointed at the first-half performance, but Stein disguised any anxiety he may have been harbouring. He felt that only one thing needed to be stressed: too many balls were being crossed into Inter's goalmouth – a dash to the bye-line and a low cutback would do more damage.

Inter's goal fell in 60 minutes, and both Celtic full-backs were involved. Jim Craig, toying with the ball on the edge of Inter's penalty area, sensed the arrival of Tommy Gemmell; Craig rolled the ball back towards the left-back and Gemmell delivered the shot of his life – a bullet from 20 yards that exploded in the net behind the heroic Sarti. The Celtic supporters in Lisbon – and the Portuguese – danced with joy; across Scotland, in homes and pubs, the celebrations began although there were 30 minutes left.

The winning goal came with only five of those minutes left, and it was such a simple goal. Tommy Gemmell had been closed down on the left wing but slipped the ball back to Bobby Murdoch who shaped up for a shot at goal from the left-half position. It was a hard shot, fierce and low, but looked as if it would slide past the far post. Stevie Chalmers was lurking with intent in the six-yard box, and he reacted quickly by diverting the ball past Sarti. A simple goal, but not a lucky one; during the past season Stein had spent hours with his forwards encouraging them to get a touch on such a cross/shot. Those hours of hard work were rewarded in full at Lisbon.

The European Cup victory was a remarkable accomplishment – and a popular one. Across the continent, football writers praised the manner of the victory, one achieved with style and flair, one which seemed to have liberated football from the chains of defensive tactics. Millions of TV viewers had watched the spectacle and had been enthralled at the Celtic style.

It was a wonderful time to be Scottish and a Celtic supporter.

Notes

1. Jimmy Johnstone also returned early to Scotland to get married. His flight experienced such severe turbulence that the player dates his fear of flying from this time.

Chapter 3

Triumph and Disaster

When the Celtic squad reported for training on the morning of 13 February 1968, it seemed a normal day. They chatted, kidded each other, told jokes and changed for the training-ground. With Celtic falling behind in the championship race they had an idea that the session might be gruelling but, as professionals, they were prepared to work harder in order to catch up.

To everybody's surprise Jock Stein announced that he had called a full meeting of the first-team squad. This was new, because Stein rarely called meetings, preferring to speak to players individually or in small groups on the field. It turned out to be a Council of War, exactly the response the situation called for. Quietly and unemotionally, the manager outlined the situation as he saw it. Celtic now trailed Rangers by two points, and had to rely on the Ibrox side dropping points to other teams. Celtic had fulfilled their two fixtures with Rangers and could not alter the outcome in a face-to-face clash.

Stein pointed out the strain imposed on a team challenging for the championship and his attentive players needed little reminding of it. What could Celtic do to add to the pressure on Rangers? The answer was simple. They had to continue to play their own fixtures one at a time; they had to win those matches; as goal average might well be a factor, he looked for more goals, and more concentration. His conclusion was that Rangers could crack before the end of the season but only if Celtic kept the pressure.

It was scarcely a free-flowing dialogue, nor a therapy session. The normal gulf separating a manager from any group of players was too wide for that. But it was something radically different. That Celtic squad contained its share of strong-willed characters, but they respected their manager – and some feared him. Most sat in silence, weighing Stein's words. Many nodded in agreement because they accepted the fact that Celtic had shaded off. Those who were reluctant to accept fully the criticism he levelled occasionally shook their heads, and gave hints of their unhappiness.

Stein may have been the first tracksuit manager in Scottish football and may have enjoyed the training sessions, but he was a manager firmly in charge of his club. He was capable of responding angrily and savagely to any form of dissent and of overpowering opposition by the sheer power of his dominant personality. According to one player present in the crowded room, Jock Stein reacted differently this time, as if to recognise the gravity of the present situation. He picked up on the mood of discontent immediately, and made conciliatory sounds. Would the players prefer a different approach to training, or to train at a different time of day? Would they prefer that the substitute be used more often? What were their practical concerns?

The meeting reminded the players that the manager was aware of some of their emotional needs – and that he knew about the unique stresses that they, as winners of the European Cup and coming from a football-mad and divided city such as Glasgow, had been subjected to. He had reminded them too that football greatness has to be earned weekly on the field against lesser opponents who wanted to share the glory by beating Celtic at least once. Some players ventured to complain, tentatively at first: about the antiquated training gear, about the fines levied by the chairman after the South American fiasco etc, and Stein – hard man as he could be at times – listened to them with every appearance of sympathy.

It would be pleasant to record that the team were so inspired that the next match produced a breathtaking display of skill and a cricket score in Celtic's favour. Not so: Stirling Albion, frequent whipping-boys away from home, dug in at Celtic Park the next night in a poor match and confined the home side to a 2–0 win.

That meeting did, however, go some way to lancing the boil of discontent that had been affecting Celtic since that wonderful day in Lisbon eight months previously. The seeds had been sown, and it was up to the players to produce on the field in the remaining 16 league games.

What had happened at Celtic Park to have forced such a soul-searching meeting?

Simply, it was the feeling – insubstantial, but real – that nothing could ever again match the euphoria of 25 May 1967 in Lisbon. After those 90 minutes in the sun all football would be an anticlimax. One eminent Celtic historian has expressed the opinion privately that he would have been quite happy for football as a sport to have closed down on 26 May, that no other match ever be played anywhere, so that Celtic's triumph would remain in the memory as football's finest hour. At the first training session after the summer break Jock Stein told his squad: 'For some of you, football will never be the same again.'[1]

The players, basking in the glory of the European Cup triumph, would find it hard to regain enthusiasm for ordinary fare. Yet the League Cup proved an exciting and successful start to 1967–68. Celtic survived a difficult section with home and away matches against Rangers, Aberdeen and Dundee United, advanced comfortably through to the final in which they played Dundee at Hampden on 28 October, and participated in a pleasant, high-scoring encounter to run out winners by 5–3, and thus retain the trophy.

There were hints of tension early on, though. In the League Cup tie at Parkhead against Rangers on 30 August, Celtic were still a goal down to their great rivals with only 12 minutes left, and had conceded a penalty. Only after Johansen had blasted his shot against the crossbar did Celtic equalise – and go on to win an epic clash by 3–1. It had been a narrow escape.

There was no such escape in the European Cup when Celtic were eliminated by Dynamo Kiev at the first hurdle, surprisingly going down by 2–1 at Parkhead and redeeming themselves only partially with a 1–1 draw in the Ukraine.

The tension revealed itself in field discipline. Previously, Celtic had been an exemplary side, combative but sporting. Frustration now produced some odd outbursts. In an early league game (on 23 September) against St Johnstone at Parkhead – and significantly after a defeat at Ibrox the previous Saturday – Celtic were struggling. Jimmy Johnstone had rounded Kenny Aird when the St Johnstone player pulled the feet from under him. A year earlier Johnstone might well have picked himself up, and given his opponent a dirty look; this time the little winger jumped to his feet and smacked Aird full in the face with the referee standing only yards away. Parkhead lapsed into a shocked silence as Johnstone made his way to the pavilion, and came to life only after Alex McDonald (later a Rangers player, and manager of Hearts and Airdrie) scored for St Johnstone. Thankfully, Murdoch equalised and salvaged a point.

Bobby Murdoch himself was ordered off in the Ukraine on 4 October when he questioned a refereeing decision by slamming the ball into the ground. The *Sunday Observer* had little trouble in reaching a diagnosis: 'In the old days they used to talk about "all work and no play" and in more recent times "overwork" and, whether you choose to use these more homely phrases or the high-falutin "psychosomatic strain", the effect is the same . . . Irritability has ruined the wonderful discipline that had taken the Scottish champions through Europe two seasons running without being involved in any unsavoury incident . . . They have not suddenly decided that they should be ill-mannered on the field and argumentative with referees . . . They are individual human beings, and everybody knows how any normal human being reacts to working under strain over a long period.'

Starting on 30 September the side returned to some semblance of form with a 4–0 rout of Stirling Albion at Annfield – a most welcome result in view of recent results there, and one made doubly so with the news that Rangers had only drawn with Hearts at Ibrox. Following the disappointment in Kiev, Celtic came back to face Hibernian at Parkhead on 7 October before a crowd in excess of 40,000. The fans were at their most encouraging and the team responded to the roars of approval with one of the best displays of the early season. Hibs were no match for them, and they had absolutely no answer to the power of Bobby Murdoch who netted twice in a 4–0 win. Clearly, Murdoch felt the need to atone for his lapse in Kiev. A week later Bobby Lennox led the way at Firhill, scoring four goals in a 5–1 victory over Partick Thistle. It seemed that Celtic had put their bad results behind Celtic and that the way ahead was clear. But it was not so . . .

Immediately after the League Cup triumph over Dundee on 28 October the Celtic party flew out to South America to face Racing Club of the Argentine in the second leg of the so-called World Club Championship.

If Lisbon had been a triumph, South America turned out to be a disaster. Racing Club had come to Glasgow determined to avoid defeat at all costs. At Hampden on 18 October before a crowd of 90,000, Celtic scraped through by 1–0 after Billy McNeill had survived a buffeting in the penalty area to head home a corner-kick. McNeill had a remarkable talent of reaching the ball in the air despite the efforts made to impede him. The spectators – and perhaps the Celtic players – had been shocked at the brutal tactics and cynical disregard of the referee's authority displayed by the South Americans, one journalist expressing the fears of the whole Celtic party when he wondered aloud: 'If that's how they play in Glasgow, what will they be like at home in front of their own supporters?'

Celtic were soon to find out.

Even before the kick-off in Buenos Aires the Scots had been subjected to violence. As he warmed up in Celtic's goalmouth, while 120,000 bayed their hatred of the visitors, Ronnie Simpson was struck on the back of the head with a missile. Even after medical treatment he was unable to take his place in the starting line-up, and John Fallon was summoned quickly to replace him. Where the missile (Simpson believes that it was a small, metal dart-like object) had come from remains a mystery, as the paying spectators were penned in behind wire fences. It seemed more likely that the assailant was actually on the pitch, masquerading as one of the stewards, security men, photographers, reporters or officials allowed free access to the playing surface before the match – and indeed at times during it! Not surprisingly, Celtic went down to a 2–1 defeat.

The question was not where the third and deciding match should be played, but whether it should take place at all. The Celtic party was divided on the issue. Some players wanted another chance to settle the outcome against opponents whose brutality had shocked them but whose talent and skill were unquestioned; some, nursing bruises, welcomed a chance to settle old scores, while others did not want to be involved with such a cynical outfit at all. Bob Kelly advocated that the Celtic party simply withdraw from the event and fly home; Jock Stein still felt that, playing in neutral Uruguay, the Argentinians would concentrate on football as would Celtic. In the end, it was decided to proceed with the match.

The game, played in Montevideo, turned out to be a fiasco, a nightmare disguised as a football match. Racing Club won 1–0 – but the result was irrelevant. Six players, four from Celtic and two from Racing, were ordered off for a variety of offences: Jimmy Johnstone, the target for systematic abuse for all three matches, was sent off for retaliation after being savagely fouled yet again; Bobby Lennox remains mystified as to why he was ordered from the pitch, and suggests plausibly that it was a case of mistaken identity; John Hughes was banished for kicking at the goalkeeper, a hysterical reaction to what had gone on before; Bertie Auld was the last to be dismissed for violent play, but simply refused to leave the pitch – and was permitted to stay by a referee who had understandably lost control of an impossible situation.

Regardless, Celtic returned from South America with their reputation in tatters and with morale damaged. Jock Stein, often the most sociable of men, brooded alone on the long journey home. None of the accompanying journalists felt inclined to ask questions, or dared disturb him. Once the party arrived back in Glasgow, they found the situation made worse by the BBC's actions in filming selected incidents in the last clash. This editing and repeated showing by the corporation in both England and Scotland could only be described as vindictive as the film ignored what in the first two matches had led up to the outbreak of violence in the third.

It was a time of crisis at Parkhead and Stein, himself badly affected by the events of the trip, had to rally his men again for the 'bread-and-butter' programme of the league championship. It was back to the reality of a dreich November in Scotland and an immediate visit to Broomfield to face Airdrie. Despite the collective hangover incurred by the South American experience, Celtic won all four matches in November: 2–0 at Airdrie, 3–0 against both Kilmarnock and Falkirk at Celtic Park, and another 2–0 win over Raith Rovers at Stark's Park. The 100 per cent record was satisfying only from the perspective of points won because Celtic's form was understandably unconvincing. Certainly, in comparison with the sparkle of the two previous seasons, it was depressing.

Rangers too were having their problems. During Celtic's sojourn in the Argentine and Uruguay, they had sacked their long-time manager, Scot Symon. A dour, uncommunicative man, Symon had been in charge since 1954 and must be considered the most successful manager of his period, but Stein's arrival at Parkhead had changed all that. There had been no great clamour for Symon's dismissal – in fact, Rangers were actually in first place in the league at the time – but the Ibrox hierarchy apparently found it difficult to accept that their greatest rivals were occupied in playing for the World Club Championship. To his credit, Jock Stein went out of his way to commiserate with his former opponent. The replacement had been a surprise: the promising Davie White, who had done well with Clyde and had shown potential as Symon's assistant at Ibrox, but a man who seemed very young for such responsibility at Ibrox. One journalist of a biblical bent suggested that it might well be a rematch of David and Goliath, a comparison made more valid by a later (and unofficial) report that Rangers' new manager appeared on a TV programme with Stein only on condition that 'Jock go easy on him'.

If this turn of events had seemed a coup for Celtic, the euphoria was only temporary. The combination of a new manager, a young, enthusiastic one with his own ideas, and the prospect of challenging an apparently vulnerable Celtic side, proved a potent one. Rangers continued to play well and were mounting a new offensive for the league flag. Even more ominously, they were challenging from the front: Celtic would have to do the catching-up this time.

The newspapers were full of baseless – but unsettling – rumours: of players wishing to leave Parkhead, of squabbles, and about unhappiness at the £250 fine levied at each and every player who had participated in the third match at Montevideo.[2] There was some truth in the latter reportage. Even the goalkeeper, John Fallon, who had been a blameless spectator of the violence, had to pay up. Not every player accepted the decision; one, in particular, went to the chairman to protest at the treatment, pointing out that he had not been ordered off, had not been cautioned and had not even had a foul awarded against him. Appeal was useless once Kelly had made up his mind, however. Later on, Stein would suggest to his squad that the bonus for winning the league championship for the third successive season would more than compensate for any financial loss.

On 2 December Celtic stumbled again, this time when facing Dundee United at Parkhead. Perhaps it should not have been a total surprise as United had beaten Celtic twice – home and away – the previous season. The Celtic fans renewed acquaintance with Davie Wilson, a man who had scored often against Celtic in his Ibrox days, and a performer to be respected.

Wilson enjoyed one advantage in that Celtic were struggling to field a right-back to mark him: Jim Craig had returned from South America suffering from a debilitating virus and Chris Shevlane was chosen to fill the position, but he suffered a knock during the match, and Willie Wallace moved back from his striker's role to act as a defender. Wallace was a sturdy player, and not a man to be trifled with; certainly, he and Wilson had had a couple of skirmishes before the winger put Dundee United ahead in 73 minutes. Fortunately, Celtic equalised immediately from the kick-off, but the feuding continued between Wallace and Wilson. After one incident in which Wilson was sent crashing to the ground, Wallace was ordered off, the seventh Celtic player to be sent off that season. Celtic managed to hang on for a draw, but Rangers scraped through against Airdrie and increased their lead to two points.

Hearts visited Parkhead next, and continued their welcome habit of presenting Celtic with an own-goal, this time as early as the third minute. Celtic took full advantage of this pre-Christmas generosity and went on to win by 3–1.

And then to Dens Park for a wonderful game of football against Dundee, the side which had done well against Celtic in the League Cup final only seven weeks previously. This turned out to be a similar sort of free-moving and open contest, and Celtic appeared to have recovered a lot of sparkle in attack; twice they led comfortably, by 4–1 and 5–2, but Dundee fought back courageously and the visitors were glad to hear the final whistle, leaving the pitch winners by 5–4. A crowd of 16,000, vastly entertained, stayed to applaud both sides off Dens Park in what had been a splendid advertisement for the Scottish game.

Joe McBride was recovering well and had been used as a substitute, making an appearance against Dundee United in the 1–1 draw. Just before Christmas – on 23 December – he was given a place from the start against Morton at Cappielow. To the delight of everybody (with the exception of Morton and the Greenock fans) Joe resumed his scoring ways by netting a hat-trick in a 4–0 romp. Sadly, it heralded a false dawn for McBride. A competent professional with great spirit and enthusiasm, he had lost something in sharpness, a marginal shading off in speed . . . but enough to suggest that McBride's role in the future at Celtic Park would be no more than a supporting one.

Two matches remained before the clash with Rangers at Celtic Park on 2 January 1968: a home game against Dunfermline, and a first-footing of Clyde at Shawfield. Perhaps Celtic had the Old Firm match on their minds for the two fixtures resulted in only 3–2 wins, results which suggested a lack of concentration in defence. Most significantly, at Shawfield, Ronnie Simpson was injured and had to rule himself out of the Rangers match.

His replacement would be John Fallon, who had been displaced by Simpson two years previously. Fallon had accepted his demotion with equanimity. In fact, the potential rivals had become the best of friends, sitting beside each other on the team bus and sharing a room on the European trips. At practice sessions they shared the goalkeeping chores, exchanging tips and hints with each other in the accepted freemasonry of goalkeepers. A lovely man and a true Celt, John Fallon was a valued member of the squad, and one photograph taken seconds after the whistle at Lisbon shows him exploding off the bench and leaping high in the air to express his sheer delight. In the 1967–68 season his appearances had numbered only three – but they had been varied. The first had been at Somerset Park in Ayr on 27 September in the second leg of the League Cup quarter-final; with Celtic leading by 6–2 from the Parkhead leg, Stein decided to give his fringe players an outing before a crowd of 9,000. The second and third appearances were in South America when John had been summoned to take Simpson's place. In both those matches, played under bizarre and terrifying conditions, John Fallon had performed well and courageously.

And now, once again, he had been called up at short notice for a difficult, tense affair. In 1967–68, when teams in the top flight of the

Scottish League played each other only twice in the campaign, Celtic could not afford to lose again to Rangers. In fact, the champions, trailing by two points, could take little comfort from a draw.

The match followed an all-too-predictable pattern: Celtic attacked and Rangers defended. This was the practice of both sides and, given their respective league positions, it was the right policy. The atmosphere within Celtic Park was as tense as ever, but the midwinter pitch was dead and lifeless – a grey occasion brightened by the primary colours of tribalism and made almost unbearable by frayed nerves on the terracing.

Bertie Auld gave Celtic the lead in 18 minutes when his shot following a free-kick was slightly deflected by Sandy Jardine past Sorensen. By half-time Celtic were well on top and threatening to add to their lead. Ten minutes into the second half, however, Rangers' left-winger, Willie Johnston, was allowed a shot at goal, and Fallon, singularly unemployed up to that time, failed to gather it cleanly and the ball slithered between his legs into the net. The match then resumed its predestined course with Celtic on the attack and Rangers hanging on grimly. With 12 minutes left Bobby Murdoch looked to have decided the issue with a magnificent goal. He received a through ball from Brogan and shielded it from defenders just inside the penalty area. A little feint to move outside gained him some freedom, and he swivelled on the spot to blast the ball past Sorensen from 15 yards with his left foot.

That was no more than Celtic deserved, and the celebrations began in the Jungle and around three-quarters of the ground. Gaps were beginning to appear on the Rangers terracing as many of their supporters in the 75,000 crowd started to head for the exits when Kai Johansen made a sortie down the right and, running out of ideas, tried a shot from more than 20 yards. His mishit effort trundled towards Fallon at no great pace but Celtic's goalkeeper somehow managed to dive over the ball and miss it completely.

Poor John Fallon hung his head in embarrassment, aware that his two hideous mistakes had gifted Rangers a share of the points. Even worse, he may have handed Rangers the championship. A minute or so later the whistle went and Fallon, a man who normally chatted amiably to ballboys, opposing players and anybody within hailing distance, was sprinting for the pavilion anxious to escape from the ground.

It would have been a pity for Fallon's career to have ended on such a low note – and fortunately, Fate still had a few cards to deal for him – but it was a miserable time for him. John Fallon was a good goalkeeper, considered by some to be the best instinctive Scottish keeper; his mistakes occurred when he had time to think about the consequences of his reactions.

That result brought into focus once more Jock Stein's uneasy relationship with the men entrusted with the last line of defence. On the training-ground the manager used to work personally with the goalkeepers, submitting them to strenuous workouts. Fallon, described by a colleague at Parkhead as accepting criticism like 'water off a duck's back', was nervous and dreaded those sessions.[3]

Perhaps a worse result – at least in terms of decisive outcome – came in the Scottish Cup at Parkhead on 27 January against Dunfermline Athletic. The Fifers, who had suffered much from Celtic in the past two seasons, inflicted a 2–0 defeat on the Cup-holders and thoroughly deserved their win although they were helped by two favourable refereeing decisions. Simpson had returned after his injury to replace the luckless Fallon, and Bent Martin, who had spent some time at Celtic Park, was in goal for Dunfermline.[4]

It was at this time that Jock Stein started to think seriously about new ways to motivate his squad. He had always been regarded as a master of the one change in freshen up the performance of the whole side. Frequently, he had made changes among his strikers because they needed to be mentally and physically sharper; the defenders used to smile whenever Stein made a reference to 'freshening things up front' – which meant the defence would be unchanged yet again. By 1967–68 he had a different problem. At least two of the now legendary Lisbon Lions (John Clark and Stevie Chalmers) had been showing signs of decline, and Stein had begun to contemplate replacing them.

The manager had sometimes been loyal to his players to a fault, but changes are inevitable in all teams – even the most successful. A vibrant Jim Brogan, quick in every movement and sharp in the tackle, had been challenging the imperturbable Clark for some time; during this season, the two men played an equal number of league matches (18). Chalmers faced even more competition for his place from Wallace and Lennox, while Hughes could be used as a centre-forward and hopes still remained high that McBride would make a full recovery from knee surgery.

Stein pondered the options as Celtic continued to struggle, although the side went to Firhill and won 4–1 against Thistle, and travelled to Fir Park to eke out an unconvincing 1–0 win over Motherwell.

On the following Tuesday, the meeting took place.

Shortly afterwards, Rangers handed their great rivals a tremendous psychological boost. Their season had been highly successful but they had been drawn against Celtic in the Glasgow Cup semi-final and were not keen to fulfil that fixture, probably because they feared a comprehensive defeat. At any rate, they decided to withdraw from the competition, citing 'congestion of fixtures' as the reason. Nobody in Glasgow believed that, and the decision was to backfire on the Ibrox club in almost every sense.

March turned out to be a glorious month for Celtic. Seven matches were played, and all were won; 33 goals were scored, and only two given up. Four of the fixtures were away from home: at Rugby Park, Brockville, Muirton and Tannadice, and these were locations at which Celtic had stumbled even in the recent past.

The enthusiasm had returned, all the flair and panache once more on display, as the season entered the critical phase. Outstanding in the revival was an often neglected player, Charlie Gallagher. Stein (and most Celtic supporters) had great belief in Auld's talismanic powers. However, Auld was injured against Motherwell on 10 February and had to be sidelined while he recovered from a cartilage operation. In came Charlie Gallagher as a direct replacement, fitting into the midfield role which he relished. It was another reminder of the previous régime's incompetence as Gallagher, never particularly fast, frequently had been played out of position (as a centre-forward and right-winger, for example) while the chairman indulged in his own version of *Fantasy Football*.

Like Auld, Gallagher could read a game and organise strategies to break down defences. In addition, and perhaps surprisingly for one of such a slight build, Charlie Gallagher was an excellent striker of the ball and possessed a lethal shot. Those supporters who felt uncomfortable in remembering the barracking Gallagher had received previously from the less tolerant were delighted to see him take full advantage of his recall. From the deep-lying position he spread passes all over the field and, more importantly, was the ideal link man with forwards now running freely and readily into dangerous positions. Bobby Murdoch stated that one key to Celtic's success went largely unnoticed: 'For years nobody twigged that what we were doing – and looking for – was creating space.'[5]

Bobby Lennox was another who made a return to form at this time, and his contribution was a major factor in the revival. With his distinctive rolling run and his bandy-legged walk, Lennox was a great Parkhead character. His enthusiasm was infectious and an inspiration to others at times when the heads started to droop. He was apparently tireless, and Bertie Auld summed up his restless energy: 'Bobby Lennox would chase paper on a windy day.' He was a forward of genuine pace, and there were few of those around the British game. His energy and running also deflected attention away from the fact that when given a clear-cut chance, Bobby Lennox was a clinical finisher.

At Kilmarnock on 2 March Celtic ran riot and defeated the home side by 6–0. They remained four points behind Rangers but did have a game in hand. That match marked the day that Celtic's goal average edged ahead of Rangers' by 67–18 as against 67–21. Normally, Willie Wallace would have expected top-billing after scoring four goals, but the best player on view was Jimmy Johnstone, unstoppable on the wing and wherever else he cared to wander over Rugby Park. Johnstone took particular pleasure from this performance partly because it gave him an element of personal revenge against Walter McCrae, Kilmarnock's coach.[6] Acting as Scotland's trainer, McCrae had clashed with Johnstone recently; after the Celtic winger had been dropped from the national side, McCrae had asked him to act as linesman in a practice match. Revenge was sweet and, for once, the hot-tempered Jinky relished the vengeance as 'a dish best served cold', making the sarcastic comment to McCrae at full-time: 'No' bad for a linesman, eh?'

On Wednesday, 6 March, Celtic defeated Aberdeen comfortably enough at Parkhead with a 4–1 scoreline, all the home team's goals coming in the first half; this time Bobby Lennox scored a hat-trick. On 13 March, again at Parkhead in midweek, Celtic thrashed Airdrie by 4–0; Willie Wallace was on target with three goals. Three days later they travelled to Brockville where the tight pitch had always posed problems, but there was no mistake this time as Celtic ran out winners by 3–0.

Starting on 23 March, Celtic scored 16 goals in three matches, two of them away from home. At Perth, on one of the best playing surfaces in the Scottish League, Jimmy Johnstone was in his best form again, but Bobby Lennox stole the headlines with four goals, thriving on the service from the little winger. Later in the same week, Celtic crushed Dundee United at Tannadice by 5–0, settling to a wonderful performance after Johnstone had scored the opening goal in 13 minutes – he twisted and jinked past several defenders before netting. Later on, one United defender was seen to run away from him rather than risk a tackle and inevitable humiliation before his home crowd.

This was the exciting, all-conquering Celtic of the previous season – but there remained one problem. Rangers refused to lose any ground in the league although they were exhibiting signs of tension in every other competition in which they had chosen to be involved. On the same night that Celtic were beating Airdrie in the championship, Rangers went out of the Scottish Cup, defeated by Hearts at Tynecastle; in the Inter-Cities Fairs Cup (as the UEFA Cup was known then), they crashed out to Leeds United at Elland Road amid scenes of crowd trouble.

Perhaps the *Dundee Courier* of Monday, 1 April, played a part in turning things round; Tommy Gallacher, an ex-Dundee player, and son of Celtic's famous Patsy, wrote his regular column that day in which he praised Celtic for their brilliance at Tannadice, but castigated United for their supine display. The *Courier* is an influential newspaper in Tayside, not least in football grounds, and it was a totally committed and determined Dundee United which took the field against Rangers on the Tuesday night. At the end of the day, United had held Rangers to a 0–0 draw.

Both contenders now had only five matches left and, thanks to a quirk in the fixtures, Rangers had to face Dundee United again on 6 April, but this time at Ibrox where they ran out comfortable winners by 4–1. On the same day, Celtic faced Hearts, the Scottish Cup finalists, at Tynecastle and settled down from the start to win competently by 2–0.

The battle of nerves continued as Celtic went to Pittodrie in the following midweek to take on Aberdeen. Lennox, in remarkable late-season form, netted in 60 minutes to give Celtic a deserved lead but the Glasgow men were forced into desperate defence in the closing minutes as Aberdeen fought back. That 1–0 victory leapfrogged Celtic over Rangers, and put more pressure on them; Celtic now had 57 points from 31 matches while Rangers had 56 from 30.

The tension was unbearable on 13 April although the crowd of more than 41,000 thoroughly enjoyed the football displayed by Celtic and Dundee at Parkhead. The two sides continued their tradition of attacking play, and Celtic revelled in the contest to win by 5–2 – but this was all to the background of the news filtering through from Stark's Park. Raith Rovers had lost twice to Celtic in the league (by 2–0 and 5–0), and had been humiliated in a 10–2 drubbing at Ibrox ... but now they were staging a gritty recovery in the struggle to avoid relegation. On 13 April they gave Rangers a battle royal, only to go down in the end by 2–3. The Celtic fans followed the match on their radios, and were put through the whole range of emotions; that night it was made worse for them by seeing the highlights on TV – highlights which showed highly controversial refereeing decisions which helped the Glasgow side. The breaks were favouring Rangers, it appeared . . .

The events of Wednesday, 17 April, were the pivotal ones in determining the outcome of the season. Three matches, played in three different competitions, were interconnected that night: Rangers played Morton in the league fixture at Cappielow; Celtic lined up against Clyde in the Glasgow Cup final at Hampden; and Celtic Reserves played their Raith Rovers counterparts at Parkhead.

That last fixture, played before a handful of spectators, was even less than a footnote to history, but for Celtic's goalkeeper it was the longest match of his life. His team won by 2–1, but John Fallon freely admitted afterwards that he had scarcely been paying any attention. Fallon had not played for the first side since his disastrous experiences at the New Year match with Rangers. He had gone through agonies as he waited for something to happen, some other event which would take the blame away from him. Now, just under four months later, he was playing in a meaningless game inside a deserted Celtic Park and listening to the loudspeakers giving periodic progress reports about the other matches.

At Hampden Park the atmosphere was much more natural and a decent-sized crowd turned up for the Glasgow Cup final against Clyde. The mood of the spectators was a jovial one, as they remembered that this was the trophy from which Rangers had 'withdrawn'. In fact, they had little need to remember as the jokes had been flying around Glasgow ever since Rangers made their decision. The Celtic players were also in a carefree mood at the start and, before half-time, had stormed into a seven-goal lead. In their desire to see more goals from close-up, many Celtic supporters abandoned their spots on one terracing, heading in a happy procession along the running track to take up a position on the opposite terracing. The invasion was first of all resisted by the police on duty, then discouraged, later tolerated, and finally supervised. Like Canute before them, the police realised that to stop a tide is an impossible assignment.

The second half was an anticlimax, however, as Celtic, aware that they were playing fellow-professionals, eased up and scored only one more goal. Perhaps their concentration had been affected by the astounding news from Cappielow.

The procession along the Hampden track was in full spate when the tannoy spluttered into life with the announcement that the half-time score at Greenock stood at Morton 2, Rangers 0. Great was the rejoicing on the terracing (and on the track); presumably, there were a few smiles in the Celtic dressing-room, too. One punter on the terracing quickly grasped the element of poetic justice inherent in the equation, growling happily enough: 'Serves the bastards right; they should be here getting beat 7–0!' At Celtic Park, John Fallon was resuming his place in the Celtic goal, a wide grin splitting his face.

It was not over yet, though. Rangers scored soon after the interval to groans at Hampden and Parkhead; Morton broke away to score a third goal to wild cheering at the Glasgow grounds – and presumably at Cappielow. Celtic were now eight goals up against Clyde, but the crowd had forgotten about that entirely.

John Fallon recalls his feelings that night: 'And when they said it was 3–3 at Cappielow, I didn't want to hear any more announcements. I knew that if Rangers got another goal and won after being two down, there would be no holding them – and I would be the guy who had thrown away the championship at Parkhead! I didn't know whether to stand still or walk about.'

At Hampden, almost at the same moment that the Glasgow Cup was being presented to Celtic, it was confirmed that the final result at Greenock was 3–3: Rangers had dropped a most vital point and were now level with Celtic – and they had fallen behind significantly in goal average. Celtic's two remaining matches were against Morton at Parkhead on the Saturday and then ten days later against Dunfermline Athletic at East End Park; Rangers had to go to Kilmarnock on Saturday, and then finish up with a home fixture against Aberdeen a week later.

At Celtic Park there were large queues for the Morton match, and afterwards the attendance was given as 51,000. Not for the first time, the reported crowd was much less than it looked. The appearance of Morton in their all-white strips prompted a dilemma of sorts for the Celtic supporters, as there seemed no etiquette that exactly suited the occasion. In the end, the huge crowd welcomed them with a generous round of applause in recognition for their midweek exertions. With the first hard tackle, reality reasserted itself and soon the Parkhead legions were baying for goals. Wallace scored first in 14 minutes, and Celtic – in their green jerseys and shorts – seemed very comfortable until Morton stole an equaliser on the very stroke of half-time through Mason.

The second half was agony. Certainly, Celtic piled on the pressure but the Morton defenders threw themselves in front of every shot. Their goalkeeper seemed to use up an eternity to take goal-kicks. The referee turned down what looked like stonewall penalties. A more objective assessment would suggest that Celtic were well on top, but that they were affected by nervousness; the supporters were in a state of hysteria, as they sensed the unease undermining the side. A minor consolation was that the match at Rugby Park between Kilmarnock and Rangers remained deadlocked at 1–1, but consternation broke out when Rangers went ahead. Because of the crowds at the turnstiles, the start had been delayed at Celtic Park and a disappointed sigh swept around the ground soon afterwards, intimating that Rangers had won by 2–1.

Celtic were now pressing desperately, but the minutes were slipping by. Already the referee had glanced at his watch . . . already the match had entered injury-time. Some fans had started to make for the exits in absolute misery. Celtic made one last effort to break through: Bobby Murdoch gathered the ball far out on the right and floated a cross into the penalty area more with hope than conviction; Hughes went for it gamely, but only made partial contact. The ball broke to Wallace, but for once the striker miskicked and the ball bounced across the goalmouth amid agonised groans from the supporters. But somebody in a green shirt was lurking in that area only a few yards out and, of course, it was Bobby Lennox; the ever-sharp striker lashed at the ball, did not quite connect cleanly, but the ball nevertheless crossed the Morton line. Jock Stein leaped from the dugout 'like a cork out of a champagne bottle' and Parkhead went mad with delight. The pandemonium was such that nobody heard the final whistle apparently blown only seconds later.

A week later Celtic almost won the league – and they weren't even playing. The scheduled opponents, Dunfermline, were due at Hampden Park to face Hearts in the Scottish Cup final. Celtic, largely through Jock Stein – once the Pars' manager – urged their supporters to go along to Hampden for the Cup final and many Celtic followers did so. Stein practised what he had preached by taking his players to the game, but Rangers decided to proceed with their fixture against Aberdeen at Ibrox in direct competition to what should have been a show-piece final. Quite a few neutrals criticised the Ibrox decision on the grounds that a cup final in Glasgow between two East of Scotland sides needed every available supporter.

Dunfermline went on to win that match by 3–1, while at Ibrox, Rangers went down in an insipid manner to Aberdeen by 3–2 . . . and left the pitch with the boos of their supporters ringing in their ears. For some weeks they had been under a strain, struggling and playing with little confidence; they looked like men waiting to be mugged. In the very last league match of the season, the inevitable had happened; Rangers finally lost their unbeaten record and also the championship.

Jock Stein was going down the stairs at Hampden – and perhaps thinking ahead to Celtic's one remaining fixture – when he heard the news; in his jubilation he leapt into the air, only to slip and tumble on the steps.

That last match would be held at East End Park against the Scottish Cup-winners on the following Wednesday. It turned out to be a remarkable occasion as every follower of the sides wanted to be there. In fact, the crowd of 27,816 constituted a new record for Dunfermline's ground, grotesquely overcrowded with fans perched precariously up the floodlight pylons and on the enclosure roofs. The teams, league champions and Cup-winners, came out side by side. George Farm, Dunfermline's manager, entered with the Scottish Cup to the cheers of both sets of supporters and Jock Stein indulged in a mock tug-of-war with him for possession of it.

The match was a credit to Scottish football. Dunfermline led at half-time through Gardner's goal in 27 minutes, but Bobby Lennox came good in the second half with two more strikes to settle the match in Celtic's favour. Lennox deserved a special medal for himself, as he led the team's charge for the championship by scoring in each of the last 12 matches, all of which were won.

Thus ended a fiercely fought campaign, a nervous, anxious season in which character had prevailed.

Notes

1. Stein was well aware of the burden of greatness that Lisbon had placed on him. At the banquet after the match he sat amid the euphoria looking absolutely miserable. He confided to one journalist: 'Well, I don't know what they can expect us to do next.'

2. Bob Kelly, disappointed at the loss of discipline in South America, believed that the SFA would take action against Celtic or those players sent off, imposing the fines to forestall such action. His rather extreme view prevailed in the boardroom.

3. Ronnie Simpson has an interesting theory about those gruelling sessions: 'Jock Stein liked to get involved but his bad ankle meant he couldn't run much; sometimes he took it out on his goalkeepers.'

4. Jock Stein did not fully approve of the number of foreigners playing in the Scottish game. Bent Martin, a Danish goalkeeper, was his only foreign purchase – although, perhaps significantly,

he never played in a league match for Celtic. In fact, all the players who participated in the 'nine-in-a-row' sequence were Scottish-born. During Stein's convalescence, Sean Fallon signed Joannes Edvaldsson for Celtic in 1975.

5. Jimmy Farrell pointed out to the authors that many of Celtic's forwards – including Wallace, Chalmers, Lennox and Auld – had started their senior careers as wingers, and were adept at seeking out open space.

6. Johnstone made his début against Kilmarnock in 1963 at Rugby Park – and Celtic lost by 6–0.

Chapter 4

Three Times a Winner

Celtic started off 1968–69 exactly as they had ended the previous season, producing brilliant football as if to match the weather. It may be considered almost heresy, but some sound judges consider that the Celtic side of 1968–69 was an even better combination than the Lisbon Lions of 1967. A strong case could be made in asserting that this team produced more simply unbeatable performances and more frequent displays of sparkling football than its predecessor. The Lisbon Lions played with fervour and inspiration; this side also played in that traditional Celtic manner but they had added a mature professionalism which allowed them to change the pace of the game whenever they wanted to. They were a side very much in control, a dominant side but one with flair and speed.

At times they looked invincible and perhaps that is why at the end of a season in which Celtic won the domestic treble of championship, League Cup and Scottish Cup, there remained such an odd lingering taste of disappointment.

Celtic faced Rangers, Partick Thistle and Morton in their League Cup section and won it convincingly by defeating all their rivals comprehensively home and away, Thistle and Morton acting as sparring partners and Rangers providing competitive matches but little more as the scores (2–0 and 1–0) would suggest. However, September proved to be a disappointment after Celtic opened the league programme with a 3–0 win at Shawfield.

Rangers returned to Celtic Park the following week and inflicted an astonishing 4–2 defeat on the champions – a victory which marked their first win at Parkhead since New Year's Day, 1964. Rangers took command of midfield early on, profiting from the absence of Bobby Murdoch who was out through injury. They scored first through their

Swedish striker Persson who was to roast Tommy Gemmell throughout the afternoon; that was in 15 minutes, and Willie Johnston scored another two minutes later. The shock proved too much for some Rangers supporters who injured themselves in an excess of jubilation.

Wallace, who had scored against Rangers at Ibrox and Parkhead in the League Cup, continued his heroics by scoring before half-time after Jimmy Johnstone had rounded the goalkeeper to lay on the chance. Three minutes later Lennox scored again but his goal was disallowed through a linesman's intervention.

Celtic dominated the second half, but still looked nervous in defence against the fast breakaways of Persson and Johnston. In fact, Rangers went further ahead after one such break, through Andy Penman, a recent signing from Dundee. Wallace scored again for Celtic only a minute later, and throughout the remaining 24 minutes there were escapes in both goalmouths. With Celtic pressing furiously and totally abandoning defence, Willie Johnston decided the issue in the last minute.

The regular newspapers were mixed in reporting the match, but most seemed in agreement that the scoreline was unfair. The tabloids, ever keen to boost circulation, waxed dithyrambic about Rangers' 'recovery' and predicted that 1968–69 would be their season; the ballyhoo was, in the words of an ancient Roman orator, 'not without reason, but without end'. Regardless, the Rangers support were given an illusory feeling of confidence for a short period – until their team began to drop points to such as Kilmarnock and Hearts even before the end of September.

That same month was proving unsettling for Celtic. Four days after the Rangers defeat, Celtic travelled to France to play St Etienne in the European Cup, and went down to another defeat, this time by 2–0, a result made worse by the failure to snatch an away goal. On the Saturday (21 September) a visit to East End Park – nobody's idea of a picnic in the late 1960s – ended in a 1–1 draw when Jimmy Johnstone equalised in 66 minutes to cap a spirited comeback.

Teams in contention for trophies tend to get the breaks they deserve – or are helped by doubtful decisions. Very often, defending champions (especially in boxing) tend to get the benefit of the doubt. On 28 September a crowd of 38,000 saw Celtic and Aberdeen locked in a fine contest with the score at 1–1 in the closing stages. Lennox and Bobby Clark, Aberdeen's keeper, went for the ball together; the ball broke to Lennox who prodded it home. Despite the valid protests of the goalkeeper, the goal was allowed to stand and Celtic had been given the break denied them in the Old Firm match two weeks earlier. This Celtic side was too experienced and too professional not to take advantage of such a decision and ran out winners by 2– 1, Aberdeen giving up the ghost after the decision had gone against them.

Yet another exceptional midfield player had broken through for Celtic in the person of George Connelly, a tall, well-built youngster from Fife. At times he gave the impression of being slow but his exceptional reading of the game allowed him to perform unhurriedly. One admirer, with pardonable hyperbole, claimed: 'Connelly could play as a sweeper while sitting in an armchair.' Nobody on the field made better use of the ball than George Connelly, a trait obvious even from his earliest appearances in a Celtic jersey. The changes being made by Stein appeared seamless: Murdoch and Auld had been the engine-room of the 1967 team; Gallagher had taken over from Auld a year later, and now Connelly was slotting in perfectly.

Celtic needed the introduction of such a talent. Already Bobby Murdoch was showing signs of wear and tear. Apart from a tendency to put on weight – though this was still not too apparent in 1968–69 – Murdoch had been playing with a chronic ankle injury. Similarly, Bertie Auld may have recovered physically from his cartilage operation, but he did not trust the knee fully at times; the veteran Auld was a man who operated on swagger and confidence, and as a consequence his form was suffering. Charlie Gallagher had played magnificently after the New Year in the previous season's run-in to the championship but he was not a favourite of Stein, his unwillingness to mix it physically on the pitch apparently counting against him.

October saw a great improvement as Celtic gave an excellent performance – aided by some bizarre refereeing decisions – to despatch St Etienne by 4–0 in the second leg at Parkhead.

A few days later Dundee United succumbed at Celtic Park by 2–0, but the match was memorable only for yet another controversial incident involving Jimmy Johnstone. The little winger, nicknamed 'the Flying Flea' by the French press, had been scintillating against St Etienne but was having a so-so game against Dundee United. Aware that Johnstone seldom played two outstanding games back to back, Jock Stein decided to substitute him with George Connelly. It was a routine decision, a chance to let one of the promising players get on the field for 30 minutes or so, an opportunity to give one of the stars a rest – but Johnstone was furious as he left the field. Before disappearing up the tunnel, he turned to give his manager a mouthful of abuse. Stein jumped out of the dugout, limped along the track, and charged up the tunnel after the player. What transpired remained largely private – and one had to sympathise with Johnstone, faced as he was with an intimidating Stein in a justifiably angry mood. The upshot was that the player had to serve a club suspension of seven days, and was omitted from the squad to face Clyde at Hampden in the League Cup semi-final and Hearts at Tynecastle in the championship.

This was one example of Stein's approach in disciplining Johnstone; according to the normal practice, the player had to be punished but there was no point in punishing the whole team for one person's misdemeanour, nor was it wise to prolong the punishment. Later in his career, Stein mentioned in an interview that he considered his finest achievement to have been keeping Jimmy Johnstone in the game for five years longer than he had first thought possible. He was only half-joking. It was a relationship that required patience, ruthlessness and a lot of tact, although the language used might well have been forceful. The pragmatic Stein, before deciding on the length of suspension, had already calculated that Celtic without Johnstone could beat both Clyde and Hearts. If the team had had to go to Ibrox, for example, would Johnstone's punishment have been so immediate, draconian and public?

Stein was proved right when Celtic defeated Clyde in the semi-final, the goal being scored in 75 minutes by Connelly, the youngster who had replaced Johnstone against Dundee United and when Steve Chalmers' header in 76 minutes separated two closely matched sides at Tynecastle.

A week later, on 19 October, Celtic struggled against the rapidly improving St Johnstone at Parkhead after being two goals up shortly after the interval. St Johnstone scored in 69 minutes and came very close to levelling things before the end. Even the fanatics in the Jungle were relieved to hear the whistle, and were gracious enough to applaud the visitors from the pitch, recognising that Willie Ormond – one of Hibernian's 'Famous Five' and now the Saints' manager – was building a very competent side on a meagre budget.

The League Cup final against Hibs was scheduled for 26 October but a fire had destroyed part of the main grandstand at Hampden and forced a postponement until April 1969. Accordingly, the original fixture against Morton at Cappielow went ahead. Joe McBride put Celtic ahead in the first half and, after Harper equalised, Celtic went all out for the winner. Morton, however, held on grimly for a draw. Some supporters complained about the dropping of a point . . . until the news came through that Rangers had dropped two by losing 3–2 to Aberdeen at Ibrox.

Ironically, the three closest challengers to Celtic's domination of the championship did not include Rangers that Saturday; Dunfermline Athletic, Dundee United and the surprising St Mirren were grouped only one point behind the leaders. In truth, it had scarcely been a vintage year so far for Celtic in the league campaign. Still, as Stein continually pointed out, good teams can win even if they are not playing at their best.

Early in November, Joe McBride was sold to Hibernian for a relatively modest fee; the Edinburgh side were anxious to land a goalscorer to replace Colin Stein, transferred recently to Rangers for £100,000. These moves had been in the pipeline for some time and Hibs, desperate to stop the taunts of asset-stripping over the proposed Stein transfer, approached Celtic.

It had been an emotional time for McBride, in and out of Celtic's first team that season. On the morning of the Parkhead clash with St Etienne – which Celtic entered two goals down – the entire squad were walking along the beach at Seamill; Stein dropped back to walk alongside McBride. He got to the point immediately and asked McBride if he was ready to play that night; McBride's answer was characteristic: 'I'm bursting to play, Boss.' Stein pondered a bit more: McBride was a goalscorer . . . he had scored against Nantes in the away leg in the 1966–67 European Cup, and had been nicknamed 'Marlon Brando' by French journalists – a man important enough to be given a nickname was a man they feared.

Joe McBride played well that night; his goal in 87 minutes, Celtic's fourth, sealed the victory by removing the threat posed by an away goal. Joe must have thought the glory days had returned, but less than a week later he was called into the manager's office and told of Hibernian's interest. The player was stunned, and crestfallen that Celtic were prepared to let him go, asking Stein if he did not believe he had made a full recovery from his knee surgery. The manager assured him that he had, but pointed out the advantages: fit as he was, McBride could no longer be guaranteed a starting place at Celtic Park; Celtic would not make it difficult financially for Hibs and so he could negotiate good terms with the Edinburgh side who were desperate to sign him; at Easter Road, Joe, a popular personality, might well become a cult figure. By the end of the meeting, Joe McBride accepted the fact that his career as a Celt was over, and both men were close to tears.

After a competent win by 3–1 over Dundee at Parkhead on 2 November, Celtic made a rare sortie to Arbroath for a fixture against the Red Lichties, who had not played in the First Division for almost a decade. It was an enjoyable outing to Gayfield, a quaint little ground very close to the North Sea.

Local lore in Arbroath states that, when an east wind is blowing from the North Sea, the wingers can be showered with a salty spray and sometimes even struck by a Smokie, presumably also taken with a pinch of salt. However, the wind was surely blowing straight down the pitch on 9 November 1968, changing direction totally at half-time, because it turned out to be the most one-sided of matches. Steve Chalmers led the rout with a hat-trick as Celtic ran out winners by 5–0 – the ideal warm-up for an important European match against the highly respected Red Star of Belgrade on the following Wednesday.

Red Star were defeated by 5–1 at Parkhead and Celtic suffered a slight reaction on the Saturday, beating Raith Rovers by only 2–0 at home, Bobby Murdoch netting both goals, one in each half. It was a disappointing performance, made more so by the fact that Rovers' keeper Reid was ordered off for a foul on Lennox, but perhaps understandable when one considers the midweek heroics. However, at the whistle the fans were dancing in delight as Rangers – Colin Stein and all – went down by 1–0 to St Mirren at Love Street, chanting repeatedly: 'One Stein; Jock Stein!'

Before the next league match (against Thistle at Firhill on 23 November) Celtic had gone into the transfer market themselves by signing Tommy Callaghan from Dunfermline for £35,000. It seemed at first sight to be a strange transfer: Dunfermline supporters were not happy at losing the wholehearted Callaghan and Celtic supporters did not see the immediate need for another midfield player. Stein knew all about Callaghan from his time at Dunfermline, though, and he had monitored his progress since then: a versatile player, a midfield performer who could play equally well as a forward, a naturally left-sided player who could play on the right, a competent professional. Perhaps more important from Stein's perspective was the fact that Tommy Callaghan had grit and determination, having resumed his career after suffering a broken leg. Two days after signing on, Callaghan (with more than a superficial resemblance to Hen Broon of 10 Glebe Street) fitted in comfortably against Thistle and scored the second goal for Celtic in a convincing 4–0 win.

In midweek Celtic travelled to Belgrade and played cautiously to earn a 1–1 draw and qualify for the quarter-finals of the European Cup. Surprisingly, they had gone to Yugoslavia without Jimmy Johnstone, to the utter disbelief of the Red Star team and officials; their supporters were desperate to see in the flesh the little man who had destroyed their formidable side at Parkhead. After Johnstone's public squabble with Jock Stein on 5 October, the more sensationalist newspapers had started to fill up their sports pages on quiet days with rumours about Jimmy Johnstone's unhappiness at Celtic Park. Given the player's suspect temperament, the situation was a tense one.

Stein could be hard, even brutal at times, but he wanted Jimmy Johnstone to be a Celtic player and to live up to his potential as a world-class performer. Exasperated as he was at times with Johnstone's waywardness, the manager felt every effort he made was worth it; his eyes would light up at the thought of Jimmy Johnstone on song. On one occasion, after visiting journalists had praised an opposing defender (Terry Cooper of Leeds United) before a European tie with Celtic, Stein smiled and told them: 'Well, he's never played here before a crowd of 134,000 – and had a wee red-headed dwarf running straight at him all night.'

At times, the relationship was a father-son one, though perhaps the appropriate analogy might be that of a guidance teacher and a problem student in a Scottish secondary school. A 'guidie' must look after his charge and try to bring out the best in him. He must be a figure of stability, offering support and understanding as the youngster steers a path through the storms of adolescence. It means sometimes mollycoddling or going an extra mile for the gifted and socially maladjusted student; often it requires firmness, tempered with fairness. On rare occasions, it involves breaking the rules and acting on instinct . . .

That is what Jock Stein did with Jimmy Johnstone in November 1968. Johnstone had a fear of flying – not just normal nervousness but a genuine phobia.[1] As the tie with Red Star was approaching, Stein suggested to Johnstone that if Celtic had established a four-goal lead at home, the player might be excused the trip to Belgrade. It seemed a far-fetched idea because the champions of Yugoslavia were a powerful outfit, well trained in the defensive tactics necessary to survive in European competition. The story had a fairytale quality: Jimmy Johnstone had one of those unbelievable nights at Parkhead on 13 November, turning a bewildered defence inside-out, leaving opponents twisted like pretzels and delighting the Parkhead crowd of 67,000. Bobby Murdoch realised very quickly that his winger was 'on', and fed him all night with a stream of precision passes; after he had scored Celtic's fifth goal with an individual effort, Johnstone raced to the touchline shouting, 'I don't need to go, I don't need to go!' One spectator broke through the police cordon around the pitch to shake his hand; it was the closest anybody had got to Jinky all night.

Jock Stein was bemused, still hoping that Johnstone would fly to Belgrade with the rest of his team. The other players were divided in their responses to the affair. Stein tried to con him by telling him that the president of the Red Star club, hearing about the matter, had phoned Celtic Park to beg that Jimmy Johnstone, on his day the greatest football entertainer in the world, travel to Belgrade.

Following the return from Belgrade, Celtic (with Johnstone) made the short journey to Edinburgh to face Hibernian at Easter Road. For some reason, meetings between these sides at Easter Road in the 1960s produced memorable clashes. In the first half things were close, with both sides playing positively in attack. Gemmell scored from the penalty spot in eight minutes, and inevitably Joe McBride equalised for Hibernian in 23; at the interval a draw was a fair result. With 16 minutes left in an enthralling contest, Hibs were awarded a penalty, a soft one it seemed. Joe Davis, as he had done the previous season, converted it competently to give Hibernian the lead.

Celtic roared into attack immediately, reacting, in the words of one journalist, 'as if somebody had pressed a button'. Within a period of six minutes (from the 79th to the 84th) they had scored four times: McNeill equalised, John Hughes scored two spectacular counters, and Bobby Lennox added the fifth. It was devastating football, almost frightening in its unleashed power; even the Hibs fans leaving the ground shortly afterwards were awestruck.

A week later a similar fate struck St Mirren at Celtic Park; the Buddies held out until half-time and, when Celtic turned it on, had to give up five goals within 32 minutes in the second half. Long before the end Celtic were playing exhibition stuff and the new boy, Tommy Callaghan, was looking completely at home in a Celtic jersey.

Perhaps it was becoming too easy but the Celtic juggernaut ground to a temporary halt in December with goalless draws on hard pitches at Falkirk and Airdrie, and a 1–1 stalemate with Kilmarnock at Celtic Park. Despite those uncharacteristic results, a look at the league table as the year drew to an end would have reassured the faithful. Celtic were two points ahead of the surprising Dundee United, and five ahead of Rangers.

The Ibrox club were beginning to exhibit some indications of an inferiority complex. It must have seemed to them that, no matter what they did, the result would be the same – in second place behind Celtic. They had rung the changes at Ibrox: a new public relations officer in the person of Willie Allison; a new manager in David White; new players in Alec Smith (Dunfermline), Dave Smith (Aberdeen), Eric

Sorensen (Morton), Alex Ferguson (Dunfermline), Andy Penman (Dundee), Orjan Persson (Dundee United) and Colin Stein (Hibernian) had come but Celtic's regulars had seen off their challenges. Nothing had made any serious impression on the Parkhead side's mastery.

In the Queen's New Year Honours list, Celtic were given another tribute when the club's chairman, Bob Kelly, was knighted for 'services to football'. Most Celtic supporters were ambivalent about such honours, and wondered if the distinction had been bestowed because of the chairman's well-publicised stand against the Soviet invasion of Czechoslovakia. Others felt that, if honours were to be bestowed at Parkhead for football achievement, shouldn't Jock Stein be getting used to being called Sir John? When the chairman took his seat in the directors' box for the home match against Clyde, however, he was cheered to the echo in a manner which must have embarrassed him. No doubt he was relieved when the game started and Celtic went on to win convincingly by 5–0. Perhaps his thoughts turned back to the times when he (in particular) and the other directors were subjected to verbal abuse from the club's supporters. The honour represented how far Celtic had come since the fateful day that Bob Kelly 'admitted' that his tenure was a failure by asking Jock Stein to turn things round at Celtic Park[2]

And so to Ibrox on 2 January. Rangers were desperate for a win; Celtic less so. The match itself was quieter than the average Old Firm clash and looked to be heading for a scoreless draw. Rangers got the break in 60 minutes when Billy McNeill was adjudged to have handled the ball in the area. His Rangers counterpart, John Greig, took on a captain's responsibilities and scored from the spot-kick. For the rest of the contest, Rangers defended in depth and, as the commentators were fond of saying euphemistically, 'took no prisoners'.

At Parkhead two days later, Celtic looked determined against Dunfermline Athletic from the start; Willie Wallace scored in the first 60 seconds, adding a second in the ninth minute and the crowd of 43,500 relaxed as they watched Celtic run out easy winners by 3–1. A similar *blitzkrieg* destroyed Aberdeen at Pittodrie on 11 January; John Hughes netted after only three minutes, which was followed up with one from Wallace in seven minutes. Once again Celtic retained control of the situation to win by 3–1, an excellent result at Pittodrie in midwinter.

At Tannadice, however, Celtic ran into fierce opposition from Dundee United on 18 January. It rained throughout the match, and it was touch-and-go if the game could be completed as pools of water were gathering on the sodden pitch. Bobby Lennox gave the visitors the lead in 20 minutes, but in the second half United pressed furiously and Celtic defended grimly. After one, apparently valid, goal for United had been disallowed, Mitchell deservedly equalised. In the two previous matches Celtic's best spell was in the opening ten minutes; this time they applied the pressure in the last – and after Dundee United's equalizer. John Hughes scored a typical goal, an individual effort which put Celtic in front with only six minutes left, and young Pat McMahon, who had come on as a substitute for Johnstone, added an insurance goal very near the end.

Hughes, nicknamed 'Yogi Bear' by the supporters since his early appearances, remained an enigma. A gentle giant, he could run riot either on the left wing or through the centre but he never shook off the reputation of being inconsistent. Unusually, for such a talented player, he was an excellent 'bad-weather' performer. The mud of the Scottish winter never seemed to slow him down as much as it did defenders and, perhaps surprisingly for a man of his size, he could be graceful and dangerous on frosty, icy surfaces. Hughes was a consistent player in 1968–69, and deserved the recognition he received by being picked for Scotland and being included more often by Jock Stein in Celtic's plans.

The 3–1 score at Tannadice was unfair to United, who had contributed so much and deserved a draw. What it showed was that this Celtic side could produce a purple patch at critical times in a match – an invaluable asset to a team contending for major honours.

Hearts came to Celtic Park on 1 February and held Celtic to one goal at half-time; in the second half, they found it impossible to withstand the constant bombardment, and surrendered another four goals. The most watchful – and concerned – observers were a TV crew from Italy, highly impressed with Celtic's skill and determination. In the European Cup, the Glasgow team had been drawn against AC Milan, the first leg due to be played in the San Siro on 19 February. Many considered it a pity that this pairing had not been deferred until the final.

Celtic were enjoying a welcome respite from the league campaign – as well as enjoying a two-point lead (with three games in hand over Kilmarnock) at the top of the table. Rangers too had matches in hand, but were potentially two points behind the leaders. Bad weather and a pile-up of matches in the Scottish Cup meant that Celtic did not play another league match until Wednesday, 5 March 1969. They had not been idle, though. In the Scottish Cup, Celtic, at first sight, seemed involved in a 'make work' project by requiring replays to dispose of local rivals Partick Thistle and Clyde – and had struggled a little against St Johnstone at Parkhead.

In the Shawfield match, Ronnie Simpson dislocated his shoulder and had to be replaced by Tommy Gemmell in goal, but Celtic held out comfortably enough in a 0–0 draw. Sadly, this latest injury (he had only recently returned to Celtic's goal after being out since early November) marked virtually the end of Simpson as Celtic's first-choice keeper. His career path is strewn with astonishing milestones: a début appearance for Queen's Park at the age of 14 years and 304 days against Clyde in 1945, in the best traditions of amateurism . . . and a much later début as a full international for Scotland at the age of 36 years and 196 days against England at Wembley in 1967.

Despite the lapses to which all keepers are prone, Ronnie Simpson had been a reassuring figure in Celtic's goal. His withdrawal left the door open for the return of John Fallon, a good goalkeeper on his day but one who lacked the greatest gift that Simpson had offered Celtic – the ability to keep concentrating on the match despite long periods of inactivity, allied to an uncanny habit of making extraordinary saves even after such periods.

Celtic had now advanced to the quarter-final of the Scottish Cup as expected, and were looking forward to the delayed League Cup final against Hibernian at Hampden Park on 5 April, as well as an epic clash with AC Milan in the European Cup. The Italian champions must have thought that Celtic had brought along the Scottish weather to the San Siro because the match took place in a snowstorm before a crowd of 72,402. Celtic played well, albeit a shade cautiously, to earn a creditable 0–0 draw. It was an indication of Celtic's stature that the Italians had written off Milan's chances of surviving the trip to Parkhead, by now considered one of the most feared grounds in Europe.

Finally – after a hiatus of 33 days – another league fixture loomed on the schedule, although 'loomed' is perhaps not the most appropriate word to describe a game against Arbroath. The Angus side gave Celtic no contest at all in the Parkhead fixture, the home side running out the easiest of winners by 7–1.

A few days later, on 8 March, Celtic visited Stark's Park to face another candidate for relegation, Raith Rovers. The Kirkcaldy side were mounting their annual late offensive to stay in the First Division and played well in the first half; in fact, a shock result appeared likely when their striker, Gordon Wallace, scored in the first minute of the second. However, Celtic's Wallace equalised in 63 minutes and the visitors settled down to grind out a result. Bertie Auld, making one of his infrequent appearances that season, scored calmly with only ten minutes remaining, and Wallace added a third very near the end.

At last came the return leg against AC Milan . . . but the pain of the disappointment on that 12 March was palpable as the crowd, nearly 75,000 of them, emptied out of the ground. Unfortunately, Celtic had given away a simple goal early on, and were unable to penetrate the famed Italian defensive wall which closed down every approach to goal. So near, and yet so far . . . Celtic rallied to the frenzied cheers of the packed terracings, including a new chant of 'Attack, Attack, Attack, Attack, Attack' but the groans at the failure to take the half-chances given up by a highly organised defence were replaced by the funereal silence enveloping the streets outside the ground. It was a bitter disappointment after all the expectations of another triumph in Europe – and the frustrating sense that it could so easily have been Celtic's night but for one defensive lapse at a throw-in.

For those reasons it would be unfair to dwell on Celtic's dreadful performance against Partick Thistle on the Saturday. The crowd of 29,000 did its collective best to lift the disheartened players, but it was all too clear that everybody was suffering from a toxic reaction to the midweek disaster. Ironically, the Thistle players seemed equally out of sorts – and indeed some of them claimed afterwards to have been upset about the outcome of the European tie. John Hughes netted three minutes before the interval but his goal (a half-hit shot) failed to raise the tempo of a match that Jock Stein described as the worst of the season and probably of his entire time at Parkhead. Latterly, the crowd had fallen silent, and the blast of the final whistle brought a massive sigh of relief.

Once again, a hard – and emotionally draining – European match had produced a disappointing sequel in the next league fixture. Hugh McIlvanney in *The Observer* of 16 March described meeting Jock Stein on the morning after the defeat by AC Milan: 'It was like entering a bereaved household and the only possible reactions were sympathy and an embarrassed search for the right thing to say. Jock Stein, the head of the house, was there dispensing condolences and reassurance. Immaculately suited, his face shaved and polished to an optimistic shine, he came forward with a smile that was even broader than usual, a handshake that was even firmer.'

On 16 March, Celtic signed Harry Hood from Clyde, a player in whom the club had been interested for some seasons, even before Stein's return to Parkhead. In the two Scottish Cup ties against Celtic,

Hood had played well, constantly posing a threat to Celtic's defence. He, however, would not be eligible to play for Celtic in any Scottish Cup ties (nor in the postponed League Cup final), but the signing of such a professional player was an indication that Stein remained determined to improve his squad.

Against Hibernian in the next league match a strong element of dress-rehearsal was in the air, as both sides were due to meet in the League Cup final at Hampden in just 12 days' time. The match – like many rehearsals – produced a patchy performance and the teams seemed quite prepared to shadow-box throughout the 90 minutes. Wallace scored for Celtic early on, but Joe McBride (yet again) equalised for Hibernian in 73 minutes, and the fixture petered out in an unsatisfactory draw. Leaving the ground, the Celtic supporters felt some relief that McBride would be ineligible to play in the final, having already appeared for Celtic in the same competition earlier.

Stein sensed that his squad needed freshening up, and his new signing was introduced on 29 March against St Mirren at Love Street. Hood made a good impression and, like Tommy Callaghan earlier on, scored in his début. The supporters sensed a theatrical touch about it as Celtic were two goals up by then and obviously trying to lay on a goal for the newcomer. Still, it was reassuring to note that Harry Hood had established a fine rapport with his new colleagues.

On the following Tuesday, Hood would score a much more important goal for Celtic in one of the finest matches of the season, at Muirton Park. The ambitious St Johnstone side (who would eventually finish in a creditable sixth place in the First Division) shocked Celtic by scoring twice, through Henry Hall and John Connelly, before half-time. Stung by this impertinence, Celtic swarmed into attack in the second half, and an over-worked St Johnstone rearguard held out until the 67th minute when Wallace scored. Tommy Gemmell got the equaliser with 15 minutes left, and most people in the ground would have settled for that. However, almost at the moment when the referee was checking his watch for the second time, Harry Hood popped up in the six-yard area to net the winner. St Johnstone, despite limited resources, produced fine teams at this period – and, perhaps surprisingly, were one of the seven other clubs who played without interruption in the First Division in every season throughout the period of Celtic's 'nine-in-a-row' accomplishment. In fact, Bobby Murdoch suggested to the authors that the Perth side 'always gave Celtic a good match during those seasons'.

On 5 April 1969, a beautiful sunny day in the Easter weekend, Celtic played Hibernian in the League Cup final at Hampden before 74,000 spectators. Once more fielding the attack which won the European Cup at Lisbon, Celtic turned on all their style and flair to overrun a very respectable Edinburgh side by 6–2. In fact, Hibs' goals came very late in the contest – after Celtic had decided to call a halt to the humiliation. There was another reason for celebrations at Hampden because news was coming through that Rangers had lost at Tannadice; that marked the end of the Ibrox side's faltering challenge for the league flag.

Celtic would be champions if they garnered five points from their remaining five games. Frankly, the remaining league matches were fixtures to be completed, and points to be won in order to decide officially what everybody in Scottish football had privately ceded months before. On the Wednesday, Celtic picked up two of the required points by defeating Falkirk 5–2 at Parkhead with Harry Hood, now a regular in the league programme, scoring for the third successive game. A bonus was that Rangers only drew at Pittodrie.

Celtic did not play on the following Saturday in order to allow the Scottish squad to prepare for a World Cup qualifying match against West Germany at Hampden. There was not too much rest for Gemmell, Murdoch, Johnstone and Lennox, all of whom appeared for Scotland; Bobby Murdoch scored Scotland's goal in the 1–1 draw. The league could have been decided against Airdrie at Parkhead on 19 April, but Celtic seemed to be thinking of the Scottish Cup final a week later. Airdrie, who had held Celtic to a 0–0 draw at Broomfield in December, did the same on a dry, fast Celtic Park in a 2–2 stalemate. It took a late goal from Bobby Lennox to salvage a point in a disappointing display. Billy McNeill looked to have sealed a victory with another 'goal' in the last minute, but his effort was disallowed and the captain had to be restrained by some of his players, so incensed was he at the referee's decision.

The club were given another opportunity to settle the championship, at Rugby Park on the Monday night. They found themselves two goals down after only 30 minutes, but fought back in the second half; an own-goal by Frank Beattie in 63 minutes helped the cause, and Tommy Gemmell equalised with virtually the last kick of the match. Arithmetically, Rangers still had a chance for the championship but they crashed 3–2 to Dundee at Dens Park the following night. Like Celtic, the Ibrox club seemed distracted; they too were concentrating on the forthcoming Scottish Cup final.

Surprisingly, Rangers had been installed as betting favourites for the

Scottish Cup, because Celtic would have to enter the contest without their regular wingers Jimmy Johnstone and John Hughes. Rangers would be without their new striker Colin Stein, who had experienced disciplinary problems during his stay at Ibrox. Adding to the pre-match hype of a Scottish Cup final involving the Old Firm was the news that efforts, unofficial but persistent, were being spearheaded by Morton's chairman, the maverick John Thompson, to have Stein's suspension lifted for this occasion.

Once again Jimmy Johnstone would miss an important occasion as punishment for field indiscretions, but John Hughes was unlucky in that he had suffered a bad ankle injury during the Muirton Park victory over St Johnstone. Now a more consistent player, Hughes had been producing the best football of his career. Some evidence would suggest that he had been personally hurt at not being considered for the European final at Lisbon but, in all honesty, he had had to accept the fact that he could not be relied on every week. Since Lisbon, he had made conscious efforts to be a more steady performer.

During the league campaign the two wingers had shone for Celtic: Johnstone twisting and turning on the right, Hughes overpowering opponents on the left. They were a fearsome double-act and constituted one of the main reasons why the side of 1968–69 could be considered a threat to the Lisbon Lions. It was a sign of the team's awesome strength in depth that they took the field against Rangers without their wingers – and humiliated the Ibrox men by 4–0. And in that match John Fallon made his first appearance against Rangers since his personal purgatory at Parkhead on 2 January 1968; he looked confident and, in the early stages, when Rangers were pressing furiously for an equaliser, pulled off a marvellous save from close-in.

Celtic's first goal had come in only two minutes and from Billy McNeill who had had to receive prolonged treatment for an elbow in the face even earlier. Perhaps this lulled Rangers into a false security because nobody covered Celtic's captain when he strolled upfield for Lennox's corner-kick . . . and nobody was covering the post as McNeill's header bounced into the corner of the net. It was a characteristic Old Firm battle at times as both sides strove to intimidate the other, and several players were lucky to avoid being booked.

The issue was decided comprehensively two minutes before half-time: George Connelly, one of the youngest players on the pitch and one of the calmest, intercepted a short pass in midfield and prodded the ball forward for Bobby Lennox to race 30 yards towards Rangers' goal. The speedy forward slowed down only enough to steady himself before slanting the ball past Martin. Even worse was to befall Rangers a minute later, when John Greig decided to dribble past George Connelly following a short goal-kick; Connelly anticipated the veteran's move and neatly dispossessed him. Just as casually, he advanced on the goalkeeper, rounding him effortlessly before placing the ball in the empty net. Behind that goal, the Celtic supporters in the crowd of 132,870 celebrated noisily.

Earlier in the month, as the Celtic players headed for the dressing-room at half-time in the League Cup final leading 3–0 over Hibernian, Bobby Murdoch remarked to Billy McNeill: 'Not bad. It would be great to do this against Rangers.' His daydreaming had come true, and the Celtic dressing-room was a bedlam of celebration. Jock Stein had to raise his voice above the din – and to display his legendary temper – before order was restored; he reminded them eventually that the match was not yet over . . . but it was.

Rangers played with spirit throughout the second half but it was clear, despite their efforts, that they did not believe in miracles. With 15 minutes left, Steve Chalmers virtually emptied the Rangers end of Hampden Park with another stunning goal. Seconds earlier, the Celtic defenders and midfield had been passing the ball around their own half while their supporters roared their approval in the manner of the crowd at a Spanish bullfight. Auld saw the opportunity for damage and released Chalmers with a perfectly flighted pass. Chalmers raced on to it, totally in the clear and, using the speedy Lennox as a decoy, advanced on goal. At the last moment, when it appeared certain he would have to pass to Lennox (who was in a better position), he casually struck the ball past Martin at the near post.

For the first time in 40 years Rangers had lost a Scottish Cup final – and Celtic had avenged in full their loss to the Ibrox club in the famous final of 1928.

There was another footnote to the season. It took place at Celtic Park on 28 April, two days after the triumphant Scottish Cup win. Celtic entertained Morton in the last home match of the campaign, and it started off as a joyous occasion. Amid jubilant scenes, all the domestic trophies (the Scottish Cup, the League Cup, and the League Championship Trophy) bedecked in green and white ribbons were slowly driven round the track on the luggage-rack of a car. Within ten minutes of the start of the game, an unknown player named Bartram had scored probably the fastest hat-trick against Celtic at Parkhead. The home side never struck form and went down to a 4–2 defeat, only their third league loss of the season.

Jock Stein was absolutely furious with the performance and took his players to task in the next issue of *The Celtic View*. Always a pragmatic figure, Stein nevertheless had a sense of occasion, a touch of the theatrical impresario about him.

Celtic's horizons were still expanding, and were now taking in the whole of Europe. Jock Stein was one of the few British managers who attended the European Cup final at Madrid on 28 May. He must have watched with bittersweet feelings as AC Milan, whom Celtic had matched stride for stride over two legs in the quarter-finals, routed Ajax of Amsterdam by 4–1.

Notes

1. Jock Stein had seen the evidence of Johnstone's phobia at Madrid in 1967. After winning the European Cup, Celtic were invited to participate in the testimonial match for Alfredo di Stefano, Real Madrid's legendary striker. Johnstone's wife, Agnes, was flying into the Spanish capital on the day of the match but a severe thunderstorm broke out just prior to her arrival. Johnstone was so distraught at the thought of his wife in a plane in such weather that Stein was genuinely concerned about him. The plane landed safely, the emotional Johnstone played the game of his life, and the next day, rather than flying, Jimmy and Agnes took a taxi from Madrid to Benidorm, a distance of more than 200 miles!

2. Since Stein's arrival at Parkhead in 1965, the club has been well represented in the honours list; in addition to Sir Robert, the following have been honoured: Jock Stein, Billy McNeill, Bobby Lennox, Danny McGrain and Paul McStay.

Chapter 5

Twilight of the Gods

With an established pedigree in European competition, and the self-confidence derived from consistent domestic success, Celtic's attitude towards their home-grown opposition sometimes bordered on complacency and occasionally on arrogance. It was hardly surprising, given the run of success which started with Jock Stein's return to Celtic Park as manager, but a reputation in football is first of all won on football pitches against all-comers, and retained only in that arena. However, that elusive Holy Grail of another triumph in Europe continued to affect the regular weekly grind.

In the previous season (1968–69) Celtic had won another treble. Little wonder, then, that everybody at Celtic Park – players, manager and supporters – was brimming with confidence and optimism at the start of 1969–70.

Rangers provided the first jolt of reality in the League Cup section by winning the match between the two sides at Ibrox on 13 August, and a figure from the past returned to haunt Celtic. In what was later recognised as a desperate attempt to turn back the clock, Rangers had restored Jim Baxter from his exile in England. Celtic, playing a continental, close-passing game against their old rivals, went in front early on through Harry Hood but Baxter, their tormentor-in-chief during the barren spell in the early 1960s, came on strong in the second half. He was no longer the 'Slim Jim' of the past but he was still clearly capable of inspiring Rangers at Ibrox.

Airdrie and Raith Rovers provided little more than practice matches before the next Old Firm clash and Celtic won that battle 1–0, after Gerhardt Neef, Rangers' German goalkeeper, mishandled a free-kick from Murdoch. Tommy Gemmell, up with his forwards, dived low to head the ball into the net. John Hughes should have been ordered off prior to the goal for felling Willie Johnston in an off-the-ball incident after the linesman had drawn the matter to the attention of the referee, but Mr Callaghan (Glasgow) limited his actions to speaking sternly to the player. There was no question that Hughes, booked in the first half, should have been dismissed. Two points were of significance here: with Jock Stein in charge, Celtic were usually treated fairly by referees – and sometimes enjoyed the benefit of the doubt – and, when Celtic were given a break such as in this Old Firm battle, they tended to capitalise on it.

However, Rangers chose to lodge an official complaint into the refereeing that night and, as a consequence, the highly respected official, who had handled the 1969 Scottish Cup final between the Old Firm, was himself suspended by the SFA for two months. The extraordinary complaint by Rangers indicated how much they were chafing under Celtic's supremacy.

The opening league fixtures on 30 August threw up two interesting clashes: Celtic v St Johnstone and Dundee United v Rangers. Both matches finished up as draws, goalless at Tannadice but four goals were shared at Parkhead. The Perth side impressed everybody in the huge crowd of 60,000 in an enthralling contest played on a very hot day. Twice the unfashionable visitors led by a goal and twice Celtic fought back, through goals by Chalmers and Hood. The attendance was a remarkable one, and remains the largest crowd ever to see St Johnstone in a league fixture.

A visit to Kilmarnock produced a 4–2 win, a result more comfortable than the score would suggest but things started to go wrong – badly wrong – on 6 September at East End Park. Celtic looked thoroughly uneasy and, after Gardner had given Dunfermline the lead in ten minutes, Willie Wallace clashed with a Pars defender and both were immediately ordered off (after only 12 minutes' play). Jim Craig put the ball into his own net in 20 minutes, and the Fifers could have increased their lead before half-time. Celtic tried to fight back after the interval, but badly missed the influence of Wallace against a rugged defence. At the end, despite a Gemmell goal, Dunfermline deserved their win.

On 13 September, Celtic lost 2–1 to Hibernian at Parkhead after Jimmy Johnstone had given the home side the lead at half-time; Hibs kept plugging away, and Pat Stanton cracked home the winning goal in 82 minutes. It was a shock defeat, and one which could be put down to lack of concentration. This league fixture was sandwiched between more glamorous matches: against Aberdeen in the League Cup quarter-final (0–0 at Pittodrie before 32,000) and a European Cup tie against Basle (0–0 in Switzerland). Those latter results indicate a greater emphasis on tactics; Celtic were fully prepared to get a satisfactory result in the away legs, confident of completing the task at Celtic Park in the return.

A poor start to the league campaign – a win, a draw and two defeats with the surrender of two goals in each of those four matches – and the match at Ibrox against Rangers was next on the schedule. Another defeat – the third loss in a row – would throw the whole season into jeopardy.

One major anxiety was a recurring injury to Bobby Murdoch and his attendant weight problems. Murdoch was at the heart of Celtic's midfield, an exceptional player who could attack with power and flair but, whenever he was instructed by Stein to move back, any key opponent he had been delegated to mark would disappear from the contest. In the six League Cup sectional matches Murdoch had been substituted twice and rested once; he had missed the opening league match against St Johnstone and, by his own standards, had been labouring against Dunfermline Athletic and Hibernian.

Jock Stein, loath to single out an individual player, knew the value of his midfield dynamo and shared the opinion of the scout from Racing Club. The Argentinian on his visit to Glasgow in 1967 had been cajoled over a few drinks by Scottish journalists to judge the calibre of the Scottish champions; he thought for a moment, and then pronounced: 'Murdoch . . . he is Celtic.' He had noted that Bobby Murdoch could pass the ball superbly and with variety: threading the ball directly to the feet of Jimmy Johnstone, as he preferred, or sweeping the ball into the empty space in front of Bobby Lennox, as he wished.

The manager felt that a stay at a 'health farm' near Tring in Buckinghamshire would help Murdoch; he would get a chance to rest his ankle, and would benefit from a strict diet – or at least learn something about healthy eating.

So, Celtic went into the Ibrox clash without Murdoch – and he would also miss the European matches with Basle and the League Cup ties with Aberdeen. However, once more Celtic – even without their star – were able to raise their game for a critical occasion. The Ibrox match was played in a downpour, and the calibre of football was high as both teams concentrated on the game. One touch of magic from Harry Hood swung the match in Celtic's favour a few minutes after the restart. He gathered a long ball from McNeill on the right, beat

McKinnon comprehensively and cut inside the penalty area; before Greig could close him down, and before Neef had time to react, Hood hammered home a wonderful goal.

For several minutes after the sudden strike, the entire Celtic end of the stadium was engaged in a new chant celebrating the goalscorer. The Hare Krishna religious movement was one of many cults spawned in the 1960s as disillusioned young people rejected orthodox Western religions and increasingly turned to the East for enlightenment. The devotees, with shaved heads and saffron robes, could be seen in Edinburgh's Princes Street or Sauchiehall Street in Glasgow smiling lovingly at passers-by and intoning their monotonous chant about Hare Krishna — for all the world like a Buddhist version of the Salvation Army. However, the words were not hard to learn and nor was the tune, and Ibrox on 20 September resounded with the praises of 'Harry ... Harry ... Harry ... Harry ... Hood ...'

This was a much better performance from Celtic — the surge of adrenaline that a real challenge to their dominance saw to that — but they made things hard for themselves in 67 minutes. Jim Craig and Willie Johnston tussled for the ball at a throw-in, and the Celtic player was rightly ordered off for aiming a kick at Rangers' winger; Johnston, the player with perhaps the worst disciplinary record in Scottish football, was totally innocent.

The sending-off put the pressure on David Hay, who had been playing in the midfield in place of Murdoch — and doing well. He quietly slotted into the right-back role and looked entirely at ease. The frail-looking Hay always seemed to have time to complete his clearances, he appeared in perfect position whenever danger threatened, and his tackling was tigerish, but just on the right side of legality. Rangers huffed and puffed to get back into the match, but Celtic kept firm control of the situation, and the roars at the whistle heralded Celtic's first league victory at Ibrox since 21 September 1957.

The pattern of the season so far indicated that Celtic were prepared to coast in ordinary matches and make a more serious effort in what they considered the important engagements. Ironically, Rangers had not been able to take too much advantage of the situation, having lost to Ayr United. But, with Jim Baxter on board, anything was possible. After eliminating Aberdeen from the League Cup in midweek despite trailing by a goal at half-time, Celtic gave another mundane performance to beat Clyde by 2–1 at Parkhead on the Saturday, Lennox scoring both goals. The practice of living dangerously was continuing.

At last, after a European night at Parkhead (in which Celtic saw off

Basle by 2–0), the team produced its best form in a 'bread-and-butter' match. Poor Raith Rovers were the victims on 4 October, going down by 7–1. Almost everybody seemed eager to score that day, the goals being shared by Johnstone and Lennox (two each), Callaghan, Hughes and Wallace. Ronnie Simpson made an appearance in goal after a long absence, and Celtic showed a welcome return to form in a game made memorable by the début of Kenny Dalglish in a full match (he had made an appearance as a substitute against Hamilton Academical in a League Cup engagement the previous season). Young Dalglish made an immediate impression on the denizens of the Jungle, who noted his enthusiasm, saw that he could win the ball in midfield, and admired his accurate passing.

Stein was not willing to risk Dalglish in the next fixture – against a stuffy Airdrie side at tight, little Broomfield – especially as Celtic would be operating without the steadiness of Billy McNeill at centre-half. This was a game which the visitors should win, but one which was always going to be a physical struggle – and so it proved as Celtic went on to a competent 2–0 victory. Once again, Stein showed a touch of the theatrical by appointing Ronnie Simpson as Celtic's captain for the match on this, his 39th birthday. Before the kick-off, the supporters sang a rousing version of 'Happy Birthday' to honour the popular goalkeeper.

Simpson's comeback lasted only three games, as he injured his shoulder once again in the League Cup semi-final replay against Ayr United on 13 October. And, in the best tradition of fiction, the injury came when he was making a fine save which preserved Celtic's narrow 2–1 lead with 12 minutes left to play.

The problems of the goalkeeping situation multiplied in Stein's mind: Simpson's career might well have come to an end, and John Fallon remained suspect in the manager's opinion, unable to command the whole penalty area as had Simpson. The following day, on the advice of Sean Fallon, he signed up Evan Williams of Wolverhampton as cover for his regulars. Williams was a relatively unknown proposition in Scotland although he had played for the now-defunct Third Lanark before moving to England; when Celtic started to show an interest, he was on loan to Aston Villa.

Meanwhile, Celtic were enjoying a hiatus in the league programme because several players (Billy McNeill, Jimmy Johnstone and Tommy Gemmell) would be playing for Scotland against West Germany on 22 October at Hamburg. This World Cup qualifying match, lost unluckily by 3–2 to a resilient German side, had one significant outcome for

Celtic. Tommy Gemmell was ordered off after he had pursued Haller and kicked him on the backside. Even worse, from Celtic's perspective, the incident was a virtual replica of what had happened in South America – again shown on TV, but missed by an overworked referee on that occasion. Apparently, Gemmell had not learned from past mistakes.

Jock Stein may have been incensed at the indiscipline, but he did not mention it to the player as they travelled back together from Hamburg nor did he refer to it in the days immediately afterwards. Still, Stein knew very well that Sir Robert Kelly would be expecting a response from the club. The moral dilemma was that Celtic were due to appear in the League Cup final on the Saturday but against St Johnstone, a side totally inexperienced at that level.

The match in Hamburg had been an emotionally draining encounter and Stein's decisions were interesting to say the least: Billy McNeill kept his place in Celtic's side and, of course, was captain; Jimmy Johnstone was 'rested' but remained as a substitute as an insurance policy; and Tommy Gemmell was dropped entirely.

The manner of Gemmell's demotion reflected no credit on Stein. The unsuspecting player, after chatting with friends outside, entered the dressing-room his usual extroverted self, a wide grin on his face and clapping his hands to 'gee up' his team-mates. Out of the corner of his eye, he noticed David Hay preparing for the match, but was astonished – and publicly embarrassed – to be handed a ticket for the grandstand and ushered from the room.

Tommy Gemmell was a character, a totally irrepressible man. Bob Crampsey was struck by one photograph in the late 1960s which showed the Rangers and Celtic teams emerging from the tunnel prior to an important Old Firm clash; he points out the various degrees of tension obvious in the body-language and facial expressions of the players – except for one: Tommy Gemmell looks entirely at ease, and is smiling broadly. Gemmell did not have the slightest doubt about his worth; even if he had been given the run-around for 90 minutes by a skilled winger, Gemmell (not always the greatest defender) could leave the pitch at the end still convinced he was the best left-back in the world.

But he was hurt by this blow to his ego, a calculated snub, and he was not the type to take it lying down. He was one of the few players unafraid of Jock Stein at the height of his powers, mental and physical. He made his feelings known to the manager a few days later, and demanded a transfer, pointing out, quite rightly, that if Rangers had been the opponents in that League Cup final, he would never have been dropped. The matter dragged on for a period until it was resolved after a manner, but the relationship between the two men, player and manager, had been damaged.

That League Cup final was won 1–0 by Celtic, who scored as early as the second minute through Bertie Auld – once more on target in an important match. St Johnstone refused to buckle under this blow and the Perth side took the game to Celtic in a spirited display. The Cup-holders were hugely indebted to John Fallon, responding ideally to the new threat to his tenure as Celtic's keeper, for a couple of splendid saves. At the whistle, the Celtic supporters in the crowd of 73,067 reserved a vigorous round of applause for the plucky efforts of St Johnstone in an entertaining game.

Bobby Murdoch had returned from the health farm in improved condition, and played in the League Cup final. He was also picked for the team to face Aberdeen at Pittodrie in the following midweek, but Gemmell remained out of the picture. Murdoch scored an early goal but poor John Fallon may have sealed his fate with another bizarre mistake which allowed Aberdeen to equalise, the score being officially recorded as 'Fallon – own-goal', the ultimate humiliation for a goalkeeper. Celtic trailed this determined Aberdeen team until Jimmy Johnstone levelled the score with 12 minutes left to play. A draw would have been a highly acceptable result but Jim Brogan, on as a defensive substitute for Harry Hood, appeared from nowhere inside the penalty area to snatch the winning goal five minutes later. Nobody could deny that Celtic were the most capable side in Scotland at getting the maximum return for a performance indifferent by their own standards.

In the European Cup, Celtic were due to face the famous Portuguese side Benfica, who featured the incomparable Eusebio (nicknamed the Black Panther) among its galaxy of stars. It was going to be difficult for Celtic's players to concentrate on the regular fixture list and it was imperative for Jock Stein to resolve the ongoing situation with Tommy Gemmell.

Ayr United, having given Celtic palpitations in the League Cup semi-final, gave them similar troubles in the league fixture at Somerset Park. Their centre-forward Ingram continued to torment Billy McNeill and scored two goals to keep United level with 15 minutes left. Bobby Murdoch did not appear to have lost too much weight, but he was faster and had renewed his enthusiasm. In the second half he was moving forward more and more often on a heavy pitch to help his struggling strikers. He put Celtic ahead in 75 minutes, and added another goal in injury-time to seal a well-earned victory.

It was a temporary relief amid all the hype about the forthcoming visit of Benfica, and Celtic paid the full penalty for lapses in concentration in their next home match, against Hearts on 8 November. Stein restored Gemmell to his left-back position as a warm-up for the Benfica clash and played both Kenny Dalglish and the equally youthful Lou Macari among the forwards. Celtic minds were elsewhere, however, and Hearts took every advantage of the unexpected bonus to score twice before half-time. Throughout the second half, although Celtic pressed continuously, Hearts remained in control of the match.

On 15 November, Celtic were greeted enthusiastically by their own supporters at Fir Park – and the Motherwell fans also accorded the visitors a generous welcome. In midweek, Celtic had accomplished the marvellous feat of beating Benfica 3–0 at Parkhead, the fabled Portuguese side considering themselves fortunate to be let off so lightly.[1] Tommy Gemmell led the rout by hammering in a free-kick from 25 yards out in the first minute, a magnificent strike that left Benfica shattered; after the goal, Gemmell ran almost 60 yards alongside the roaring fans in the Jungle to a hero's acclaim. But, it was back to the grind of the Scottish League once more – and a feeling of anticlimax for Celtic. Dixie Deans scored for the home side in 38 minutes to equalise against a hesitant Celtic defence, but John Hughes put Celtic back in front with 15 minutes left. Motherwell pressed against a lacklustre Celtic team and were denied two valid claims for penalties and had one shot scrambled off the line with Fallon beaten.

The return match in Lisbon against Benfica, delayed for a couple of hours by a power failure in the Portuguese capital, was a dramatic affair: the home side scored two quick goals shortly before half-time, and pressed for an equaliser throughout a fraught second half. Well into injury-time one of their substitutes headed the levelling goal from a corner-kick, to send the match into extra-time. Celtic held out, and the two exhausted teams had to wait to learn which one would advance, the rules decreeing that the decision would be made on the toss of a coin. Billy McNeill was not noted for his luck in winning the toss at the start of matches but he guessed correctly this time. It had been a harrowing night for Celtic in Lisbon and for their supporters waiting back in Glasgow; the delayed start meant that it was well past midnight before Billy McNeill watched that fateful coin being tossed.

Celtic could now concentrate on solidifying their position at the top of the league and Morton were the first victims. Young Lou Macari scored in eight minutes at Cappielow, and Celtic went on to give a very solid, very professional performance to win 3–0. Greenock at the end of November would not top any list of desirable tourist resorts but Celtic were unfazed by the heavy Cappielow pitch and by the customary rain which persisted throughout.

Celtic's steadiness (and occasional brilliance) in December 1969 won the championship. Six fixtures were completed, and all were won; some challengers (Dundee United and Dunfermline) faded, while others (Hibernian and Rangers) struggled to keep up with Celtic's pace.

The match at Parkhead against St Mirren on 1 December saw the introduction of Evan Williams in goal and the newcomer played well, making two or three good stops during a spell in the first half when the Buddies were on top. Another relative newcomer made a significant contribution to Celtic's 2–0 victory by scoring both goals, on either side of half-time. Lou Macari had always impressed with his quickness and sharpness in front of goal, and his strong running in the first half delighted the spectators; in addition, he appeared to be fitting in well with his more experienced colleagues Hood, Wallace, and Auld.

On the Saturday, Celtic defeated Dundee 1–0 on a dubious penalty converted capably by Tommy Gemmell. Despite that, the match was a fine contest as Dundee usually provided entertaining and formidable opposition in the mid-1960s. They boasted a European reputation and possessed outstanding players in Steve Murray, Gordon Wallace and Jocky Scott. Gemmell displayed no anxiety or conscience about the merits of the referee's decision and blasted the ball into the net in his customary manner.

At Muirton Park on 13 December Celtic despatched St Johnstone by 4–1. On the opening day of the season the Perth side had come to Parkhead in a heatwave and held Celtic to a 2–2 draw; at Perth in December the weather conditions could not have been more different as the temperature dipped below freezing. Celtic's display, however, was heartwarming: Willie Wallace scored twice in the first half, while Tommy Gemmell and Harry Hood netted two more in the second. Four goals up after only 50 minutes, Celtic relaxed and were not perturbed when Kenny Aird pulled one back after 60 minutes.

On the following Wednesday (17 December) Celtic produced their best display of the season, despite miserable weather and the formidable opposition of Dundee United. The Taysiders may have been near the top of the league table but they were simply swept aside as Celtic raced to a 4–1 lead at the interval. Bertie Auld scored in the second minute and was in superb form throughout, winning the ball time after time in midfield to release the front runners, Hughes and Wallace, and feeding

Jimmy Johnstone a stream of tempting passes. Johnstone was not one to resist such a diet, and it was quickly evident that he was going to have 'one of those nights'. At the end of an exhilarating match, Celtic had run up a 7–2 scoreline, the last goal coming from Murdoch as early as the 74th minute. The wonder of it all was that Celtic's performance was produced on a treacherous surface for 90 minutes during which the rain and sleet (and occasional snow) did not cease for a second.

Celtic went on to beat Kilmarnock the following week, an acceptable 3–1 win at home, but the game was marred by an injury to Frank Beattie, a veteran midfielder for the Ayrshire club. It was a complete accident, an attempted tackle on Jimmy Johnstone, but it was sickeningly apparent that the result was a broken leg for the Kilmarnock player. Beattie had been a stalwart in a fine provincial side for several seasons, a much respected professional. To the credit of the crowd at Parkhead, the silence while he was treated was profound and was broken only by generous applause as he was stretchered off. Jock Stein had left his customary place in the dugout to offer some assistance and comfort; he took off his heavy coat and laid it over Beattie to protect him from the bitter cold. It could have been mistaken for a mere gesture but Stein was sincere in his admiration for such honest players as Frank Beattie.

On 27 December at Parkhead, Celtic took part in a much happier occasion – at least, it was carefree for the home side. Partick Thistle made the short trip across the city only to be thrashed by 8–1. The more sadistic among the support could take some satisfaction in watching the ex-Rangers goalkeeper Billy Ritchie attempt to hold a rampant Celtic in check but he was helpless against such an attack. Once more Bertie Auld was back to his best, but John Hughes was the man featured in the headlines with his three goals.

Meanwhile, the health of the long-time chairman, Sir Robert Kelly, was failing, and a power vacuum existed at the highest level of the club. As custodians of a 'family club', the directors were reluctant to discuss important changes under the circumstances although Celtic were now the dominant football club in Scotland, if not the most powerful financially. If ever the opportunity existed to develop as a European (and world) power in football, this was the time. However, the men who ran Celtic were dazzled by the success the club had achieved in a few short years. In their hearts they knew very well that they – as directors – had contributed very little to that success.

It was easier to put off making decisions.

Improvements were being made at Celtic Park to cater for the needs of the expanding crowds. In 1966 the Jungle, a large open-air barn, was torn down and replaced by a more modern version with paved terracing underfoot and passageways to allow easier access; in 1968 the East Terracing, by tradition the Rangers End, was covered completely and the steps concreted. These were considerable improvements, and were hailed as such in *The Celtic View*; to be honest, they made Celtic Park one of the best grounds in Scotland. By the standards of the recent past, the improvements were dramatic – but was it enough?[2]

Jock Stein continued to impress in every aspect of his role. He was a man of boundless energy and commitment to his chosen job. In the 1960s the manager's role was all-encompassing: as a coach and tactician; as a 'trainer' in the European sense; as an administrator of an organisation growing as a business; as a scout on the lookout for new prospects; and, as the most recognisable figure at Celtic Park, a man always in demand as a speaker or guest at functions up and down the country.

Those journalists, thrown into close proximity with him on European trips, often noted that he would be the last to retire at night and the first up in the morning. Scottish reporters would be phoned frequently by their English counterparts who informed them that Stein had been present at Old Trafford or Anfield or Goodison Park the night before. The Scottish journalists would be surprised as he had been at Celtic Park during the previous afternoon . . . and a hurried phone call at that moment would confirm that 'Mr Stein is unavailable right now, as he is taking the training.'

A capacity for hard work . . . or compulsion? Where is the line to be drawn? In January 1969, for example, one of Celtic's fixtures was postponed and Jock Stein took advantage of the few free hours to watch East Stirling play St Johnstone in the Scottish Cup. In an interview many years later, when asked about attending such minor football matches, he shrugged his shoulders, wrinkled his brow, and suggested: 'Why not? You just never know what you might see . . .' In this case, Celtic got an unexpectedly quick bonus because St Johnstone happened to be drawn as their opponents in the next round.

From his days as a journeyman centre-half with Albion Rovers, Llanelly Town and Celtic, Jock Stein had been recognised as a spokesman for the other players. Every club he played for appointed him captain and allowed him to dictate matters on the pitch and to discuss tactics with the manager. He was also known as a thoughtful player and, to be frank, with his limited skill he had to rely on cunning and knowledge of the game in order to survive. This meant that he understood more about the basics of the game than many of his more famous contemporary players who tended to play instinctively. Later, as a coach, he could break down the intricacies of football into its fundamentals and he had the added advantage of being able to explain things in a direct way. Bobby Lennox summed it up: 'He didnae feed us mince.' Hugh McIlvanney, in the *Sunday Observer* of 21 May 1967, put it another way: '[Stein] is one of those rare men who have common sense in such measure that it becomes an intellectual force. His thinking has an uncluttered clarity, an imaginative pragmatism. If the wagon train were surrounded by Indians, Stein would be the man to get you out.'

Stein himself traced his education as a football man to events when he was with Celtic near the end of his career. Bob Kelly decided that the players would benefit from watching the great Hungarian side defeat England at Wembley in 1953 and from seeing the World Cup in Switzerland in 1954. He was impressed with Hungary, especially their flowing attacks, initiated from movement within their own half of the field, and he was struck with admiration for the constructive play of their wing-halves, especially Bozcic, the player who linked defence and attack.

A year later in Switzerland he felt depressed as he watched Scotland stumble to an embarrassing 7–0 defeat by Uruguay in the World Cup. What he had seen was Scotland's tactical naïveté totally exposed by a sophisticated and well-prepared side, playing in a formation and style suited to the strengths of its individual members. The Scottish players, perspiring in woollen jerseys in 80-degree temperatures, remember that the only advice from the trainer's bench was the repeated admonition: 'Get stuck in!'

One other opportunity had furthered his education as a football manager. At the time he was Dunfermline Athletic's manager, he and Willie Waddell, then Kilmarnock's boss, accepted an invitation from a newspaper to visit Italy and learn at first hand from Helenio Herrera. Ironically, Waddell (a fast, marauding winger with Rangers) returned to Ayrshire with plans to initiate the rugged defence which helped Kilmarnock win their first championship in 1965; Stein (a determined, no-frills centre-half with Celtic) came back to Dunfermline, his inventive mind already grappling with the methods required to break down such defences.

Jock Stein largely pioneered many of the practices now regarded as normal within football managership. He took the training as a 'tracksuit manager', claiming that the best way to know and understand his players was to work alongside them; his predecessor at Parkhead, Jimmy

McGrory, had rarely ventured from his office. Billy McNeill, when he first started training at Celtic Park as a teenager, admitted that he did not know for sure who Celtic's manager was.

Stein insisted that the training should be done with the ball, and he largely abandoned the mindless, repetitive lapping of the track which had characterised Scottish football prior to his becoming a manager. For example, Bill Struth, the legendary manager of Rangers during Stein's career as a player, denied his players the use of a ball during training to ensure that 'they would be more hungry for it on Saturday'. Celtic's training under Stein, geared to preparing his players mentally and physically for the next football match, was varied and interesting with an emphasis on set-pieces designed for those next opponents.

As a manager with relegation-threatened Dunfermline Athletic, Stein took the Fifers to third place in the league, to Scottish Cup glory and memorable exploits in Europe. As a manager with a moribund Hibernian, he revived their fortunes and was well on course for major success when Celtic invited him to take over. As a manager of the Glasgow club, his exploits were legendary. Success with different clubs, in different times and under different situations, shows an extraordinary degree of flexibility and understanding of the changes in the game and its personalities.

As a motivator, Jock Stein could be adaptable. He knew which players needed encouragement and praise, just as he knew which players needed to be shouted at and bullied. Generally, he adopted the right tone for the occasion – but not always. Like every great manager, Stein was authoritative and did not allow anyone to take liberties. At times he was hard, almost a bully, and he was capable of punishing players in order to show them simply that he could do so. Not all his players liked or respected him . . . but often they were afraid of him. The exact methods of controlling his Celtic players would not work today, and Stein simply would not have tried to use them. He, as he had always done throughout his football career, would have adapted without compromising his principles, and by the force of his personality he would have got his way.

Jim Craig put it clearly: 'For the first five years at Celtic Park, Jock Stein was a genius. After that, it may have been a different story . . .'

The new decade opened with a visit to Shawfield. The Bully Wee gave Celtic a fright although John Hughes scored in 35 minutes to give them the lead at half-time. Throughout the second half Clyde pounded Celtic's goal and several times came very close to an equaliser. As so often happens, the visitors broke away in the last minute and Lou

Macari netted another opportunist goal. The 2–0 scoreline was manifestly unfair to Clyde, but it did appear that Celtic were preoccupied with the forthcoming meeting against Rangers on 3 January, Jimmy Johnstone and Tommy Gemmell sitting out this match as a precaution.

The referee had to think long and hard before deciding to proceed with the Old Firm fixture. The frost had been hard and there was no such thing at Parkhead as under-soil heating in those days; the playing surface had been sprinkled liberally with tons of sand and it was passed fit after a late inspection. Probably it would have been better to postpone the match until the spring but that was the last thing Celtic wanted, given their European commitments. Besides, there was the practical consideration of having to deal with the early arrivals of the eventual 72,000 crowd who were already lining up outside the stadium.

Jock Stein opted for experience in this traditionally tense encounter. Jimmy Johnstone, so often a thorn in Rangers' side, returned to replace Macari, and Tommy Gemmell resumed his position at left-back. However, Evan Williams, who had recently taken over from John Fallon, retained his place in goal.

The pitch may have been ruled as playable, but that was a long way from saying it was conducive to good football. Not even the lightweight Jimmy Johnstone was comfortable on the surface, and John Hughes, sandshoes and all, was well marked by Rangers' defenders. Both teams played very cautiously in the first half and Jim Brogan caught the eye with some timely interventions. Brogan had now effectively replaced John Clark as sweeper, a term now coming into regular usage. The main excitement came at the set-pieces and, from one corner just before the interval, Billy McNeill moved upfield to head into the Rangers net; however, the 'goal' was disallowed, presumably for a push on an Ibrox defender by another Celtic forward. To judge by the absence of any protests the referee's decision was correct and the match finished 0–0.

Bad weather hit Scotland and Celtic had to wait two weeks for the next league match, a vital clash against Hibernian at Easter Road. In fact, Hibs had several games in hand and, if they won this fixture and those games, could have closed to within one point of the leaders. A crowd of 40,839 rolled up to Easter Road, hoping for another classic. They did not get the feast of goals as in previous matches, but witnessed a hard-fought, engrossing clash. Billy McNeill scored first in 13 minutes with a header from a corner-kick, but Arthur Duncan equalised a few minutes after the interval by taking advantage of a moment's slackness in Celtic's defence. It was noticeable that Celtic, particularly in defence, had tightened things up; their performance could be described as more Roundhead than Cavalier. A draw would have been acceptable to both sides but the Hibs defence was tiring in the closing stages; John Hughes, a powerful figure, won the match through his perseverance with only four minutes left. He fought his way through and, although his powerful shot was half-blocked, the ball kept rolling . . . rolling into the net past Marshall, stranded by the deflection.

Dunfermline Athletic visited Celtic Park on successive Saturdays in late January. The first occasion was in the Scottish Cup and the Pars must have had visions of repeating their shock victory of two years earlier when Gillespie put them in front after 60 minutes. Till that point the Parkhead crowd of nearly 50,000 had been becoming increasingly subdued but then they found their voice. Celtic fought back with some determination and Hughes equalised with ten minutes left. In the dying seconds, Harry Hood grabbed the winner, an important goal because nobody at Parkhead fancied the prospect of a replay at East End Park. The league match was much easier, Dunfermline clearly still in some shock after giving up such a late goal seven days previously. Celtic coasted to a comfortable 3–1 win against a side that looked beaten before the kick-off.

On 16 February, a Monday night, Celtic trounced Partick Thistle by 5–1 at Firhill. Once more the ground was treacherous but Celtic appeared to have chosen the more appropriate footwear. Leading by 3–0 at the interval, they started to ease up in the second half, no doubt thinking of two very important engagements ahead: the visit of Rangers in the quarter-final of the Scottish Cup on 21 February, and the European Cup tie against Fiorentina on 4 March.

That Scottish Cup battle was important in two ways: Celtic advanced with a 3–1 win and Rangers, knocked out of the Cup, were so dispirited that their challenge in the league championship collapsed. Without a doubt, the Ibrox side lost their championship hopes as well as the Cup in the last five minutes of 21 February.

The match itself was a disgrace, a clash from which players and supporters of both sides could scarcely emerge with much credit. The tone was established after only five minutes' play when Jim Craig headed a cross from the right wing past his own goalkeeper in a misguided attempt to pass back to him. Two Rangers players, celebrating the unexpected gift of a goal, rushed to the furious Craig and attempted to 'congratulate' him.

Rangers, under their new manager Willie Waddell – prised from his position as a journalist with the *Daily Express*, from where (some said) he had actively campaigned for the Ibrox job – were a formidably robust side. They dug in on a wet, muddy pitch to defend that lead by whatever means necessary. Celtic matched the ferocity of their opponents. Bobby Lennox equalised in 39 minutes, his shot eluding Neef's desperate attempts, and the battle continued relentlessly in the second half.

David Hay, normally a full-back but occasionally a midfielder, had been chosen in Bertie Auld's place; the experts assumed this was because of his defensive qualities, but Hay surprised everybody in 85 minutes by moving upfield and unleashing a tremendous shot from 25 yards which left Neef helpless. Rangers had struggled to contain Celtic throughout the 90 minutes, but had little left; Jimmy Johnstone raced through a discouraged defence in the 88th minute to seal the win – an unsavoury but essential victory.

Celtic's next port of call in the league campaign was at Kirkcaldy where Raith Rovers were waging their annual struggle against relegation. The game was played in midweek – which may have explained the somewhat sparse crowd – and Billy McNeill settled the matter promptly with a goal after only two minutes. Tommy Gemmell, another defender, added the second after 59 minutes and Celtic won by 2–0. A poor Raith Rovers side was the verdict – but the Stark's Park team would beat Rangers two weeks later as the Ibrox collapse continued out of control.

Airdrie came to Parkhead on the last day of February and many Celtic supporters brought along their radios to keep abreast of the happenings at Easter Road where Hibs and Rangers faced each other. Airdrie put up a good fight, and got back to equal terms after Johnstone and Lennox had put Celtic two goals up. Jimmy Johnstone put Celtic back in front after 79 minutes, and Jock Stein did not relax his grim-faced vigilance in the dugout until Willie Wallace settled everything with a fourth goal in 86 minutes. Meanwhile, the bush-telegraph at Celtic Park was informing the 31,000 crowd of the draw in Edinburgh – a perfect result for Celtic.

The club were playing steadily in the league, but the temptation kept arising to think about more exciting prospects, namely the Scottish Cup and the European Cup. It was the manager's responsibility and the task of the senior players to keep things focused. Every match had to be won to ensure the league championship, although the players knew that Rangers' challenge was fading.

It was a different scenario from the 'Grand Slam' of 1967. Back then, the mood had been one of exhilaration and adventure, a voyage into new and uncharted waters. In 1970 it was the same journey, as hazardous as ever but more familiar. Jim Craig, a thoughtful player, has suggested that Celtic's 'innocence' was their ally in 1967 – a sort of 'gallus, Glasgow attitude' that made them fearless then. In addition, Rangers had chased Celtic virtually to the last game of the season before surrendering, but in 1970 Celtic were forging ahead in the championship without the incentive of a strong challenge from Ibrox.

Celtic took Fiorentina, one of the most famous teams in Italy, to the cleaners at Parkhead on 4 March. The men from Florence were demolished at Celtic Park by 3–0 before an ecstatic crowd of 77,240, the largest attendance ever for a European tie at the ground. Bertie Auld, to the surprise of the visitors and the omniscient Scottish press corps, was restored to the side; Auld teased and tormented the Italian side with his trickery and cheek. The swarthy, blue-jowled Auld was one Scottish player who could match any European with his macho antics and intimidate the fiercest of opponents.

Three days later Celtic went to Tannadice and won by 2–0; both goals were scored by Billy McNeill, responding to a mediocre performance in his best captain's fashion in leading by example. Significantly, however, the 32-year-old Auld was on the bench to allow him some recovery time after his performance against Fiorentina; the midfield general could not be risked every day. Stein did have to put him on the pitch, though, as Bobby Murdoch was struggling and did not appear fully fit. The more observant could see that Celtic's engine-room in the midfield was becoming a little worn out . . .

On the following Tuesday, Celtic made further advances towards retaining the title. At Parkhead, Morton held out till conceding an own-goal in 47 minutes and surrendered three more before the 59th to go down by 4–0. The next night Rangers failed to respond, losing 2–1 at Stark's Park to Raith Rovers.

Inevitably, with the security of a substantial lead in the championship, the attention was beginning to shift to the European Cup where, after a sensible performance in Florence, Celtic advanced to the semi-finals. The excitement was growing in intensity when the draw threw together Britain's two remaining representatives, Celtic and Leeds United. The press immediately dubbed the clash as the 'Battle of Britain' and, remarkably, given their record in Europe, Celtic were not the betting favourites. It was a tribute to Leeds United, a strong, physical side with steel in their make-up but also tremendous skills in every area of the pitch. Jock Stein was ambivalent about those odds: on one hand, he felt that his side were being slighted by the bookies but, on the other, it would be easier to motivate the players – if any extra incentive were required.

Meantime, there was the matter of the league championship to be settled. On 21 March, Ayr United put up a stout resistance till half-time but three goals, one by Lennox and two by Wallace, early after the restart ended any hopes of an upset. On the same day Rangers continued their collapse by going down to Dundee at Dens Park. Thus, Celtic could officially seal the title with a win over Aberdeen at Parkhead on the following Wednesday, a match that had assumed an extra interest because the two sides were due to face each other in the Scottish Cup final in April.

In a fixture reminiscent of the one against Dundee United back in 1967 (when Celtic could have clinched the championship at home in front of their own fans), the club produced another mediocre performance. Aberdeen came to Parkhead determined not to be 'just the other team', and played competently to a cohesive game-plan. They were a fast-improving outfit under Eddie Turnbull's leadership, and set out to combat the speed of Celtic's strikers by employing a well-rehearsed offside trap. A disconsolate crowd of 33,000 trooped out of Celtic Park, having seen the champions go down by 2–1 – and Celtic's goal was a mere consolation one from Gemmell in the 88th minute.

On Saturday, 28 March, Celtic sealed the championship by drawing 0–0 with Hearts at Tynecastle. It was scarcely a vintage performance, as Tommy Gemmell contrived to have his penalty kick saved by Jim Cruickshank, and both teams looked preoccupied. Hearts were already thinking about the close season; Celtic had to be concerned with the visit to Leeds' Elland Road on 1 April.

However, Celtic had won the league for the fifth time in succession and had won it on 28 March, the earliest date so far. Three more fixtures remained but these were now reduced to the status of practice games for the cup ties ahead. Rangers finished second also for the fifth season in succession but, this time, the Ibrox side were 12 points behind Celtic.

Champions once again – and League Cup winners – and yet 1969–70 ended in a bitter feeling of disappointment as Celtic, after scaling the heights against Leeds United in a 1–0 win at Elland Road, crashed to Aberdeen in the Scottish Cup final ten days later; and, after reaching the pinnacle of their form against the English champions at Hampden Park to win 2–1 before an official attendance of 133, 961 (a record crowd for any European Cup tie), went down to Feyenoord of Rotterdam in the final at Milan on 6 May.

What went wrong?

The Scottish Cup final upset is the more easily explained: Celtic had had things too easy against most Scottish teams that season and were understandably in a confident mood – too confident. They failed to remember that Aberdeen had recently won at Celtic Park, and had won convincingly. Also, it seems, a Scottish Cup final – once the highlight of a player's career – was no longer motivation enough. The prospect of a European Cup semi-final on the following Wednesday against Leeds was always lingering in the back of the players' minds.

Another factor was that ancient Celtic bugbear of refereeing decisions. There is no doubt that R.H. Davidson of Airdrie affected the outcome of this match by three bizarre decisions made within a ten-minute spell in the first half: one awarded Aberdeen a penalty-kick for 'hands' (although, to this day, Bobby Murdoch affirms that the ball hit him on the chest); another disallowed a 'goal' by Lennox; and the third rejected Celtic claims for a penalty-kick when Lennox was tripped inside the box. All the decisions went against Celtic, and all were wrong. When Jock Stein was Celtic's manager, the side were not too often the victims of an excessive number of 'mistakes' by officials; frankly, Stein intimidated many referees by his watchful presence on the touchline and, as a consequence, the club could have little complaint about the general level of refereeing competence.

Milan? Feyenoord were a very good side, on the night far superior to Celtic, but the feeling remains that Celtic could have beaten them. Those who dared to suggest at the time that Jock Stein had underestimated the Dutch team's ability and resilience were derided; the blame was fixed squarely on the players who had not performed as they had done in two epic clashes with Leeds United, matches regarded by most people as 'the final before the final'. The players were accused of being distracted by the representations made by a commercial agent in order to cash in on another triumph in the European Cup.

The blame has to be shared. Jock Stein, after scouting Feyenoord in an end-of-season match against Ajax, came back to Glasgow utterly convinced that Celtic would win and, unfortunately, that impression was conveyed to his players. As Bobby Murdoch remarked caustically: 'If Jock Stein looked at Feyenoord, he must have left at half-time.' On the most important occasion of all the players were not able to raise their game, and they paid the price of complacency. Celtic 'lost' that final, but Feyenoord 'won' it through superior organisation and a better attitude.

Like most of his contemporaries in Europe, the manager of

Feyenoord (the Austrian Ernst Happel) and his coaches had a comprehensive dossier on the Celtic players' strengths and weaknesses, their methods and their tactics. Feyenoord studied Celtic in 1970, as Celtic had studied Inter Milan in 1967.

Notes

1. At Seamill on the morning of the match, Stein put his squad through a warm-up session. The manager had spotted renovations taking place at the hotel and borrowed several cans of paint for a training exercise. The players had to weave through a line of cans, and end up by shooting at goal. Bobby Murdoch knocked over a can amid hilarity from his team-mates and Stein promptly nicknamed him 'Sam B. Allison' – the building contractor engaged in demolishing the Gorbals. Murdoch was far from amused and growled at Stein: 'We're no' playing —— paint cans the night!' The manager judged the mood of his players perfectly, assessing that they were ready for the match – and cancelled the rest of the planned practice.

2. Bobby Murdoch remembers training at Celtic Park in the pre-season prior to 1965 and watching two men mixing cement and working their way round the terracing using a wheelbarrow. That was the extent of 'annual maintenance and renovations' at that time.

The Master

Chapter 6

A New Start

The supporters of a team generally recognised as the best in Britain passed a totally miserable summer in a mood of depression and unrelieved anxiety. The disappointment of losing in a European Cup final was bitter, so high had been the expectations.

One academic suggested that the feelings generated by that defeat were an example of Einstein's Theory of Relativity applied to football (and its punters). Celtic had been favourites for both the Scottish Cup and European Cup but had come up woefully short. To lose one cup final might be considered unfortunate; to lose two sounds like carelessness. It was only natural to look for a scapegoat and the players provided the obvious target.

Only the day after the European Cup final it emerged that the players had formed a commercial syndicate in order to cash in on the benefits of playing in the European Cup, while those supporters who had travelled to strike-torn Milan were still stranded in the chaos of the airport. The fans at home, who had stared in disbelief at their TV sets watching an uncharacteristic Celtic performance at the San Siro, shook their heads in anger or dismay at the poor timing of the announcement.

It was just all too easy to blame the players, and it was manifestly unfair. For one thing, it was not the players' decision to stay in a hotel at Varese some 30 miles outside Milan, far removed from the atmosphere and the build-up to the big match; the players did not decide to be prepared and trained in the apparently casual manner that was reported later (much later); nor did the players determine the starting line-up, nor the tactics to be employed; it was not the players who chose who was to be substituted . . .

Most people in football – fellow-managers, coaches, players, directors and the media – lived in total awe and considerable fear of Jock Stein. If they suspected at the time that his tactics were wrong, they did not have the courage to state that outright. One journalist, more sycophantic than the others, pointed out that Celtic had enjoyed four spells of ascendancy in the match, each more short-lived than the previous one; the periods came after the opening kick-off, immediately after the restart in the second half, at the beginning of extra-time, and after half-time in that 30-minute period. He attributed this to Jock Stein's influence and pep-talks – and the subsequent decline to the players' performance and attitude.

The players had legitimate grievances and perhaps these were exaggerated by shock. In the previous five seasons they had become totally convinced that their manager was infallible – at least in a football sense. This time, on the pitch at the San Siro, they found themselves in a situation for which they were largely unprepared. One opponent, dismissed as a 'poor man's Jim Baxter', had the skills associated with the Rangers player but also had determination, drive and a powerful physical presence.

When things had started to go wrong in the second half, as Feyenoord applied more and more pressure, the Celtic players looked to the dugout for guidance but only one substitution was made (in 75 minutes) when George Connelly replaced Bertie Auld, who had been toiling in an outnumbered midfield. One of the team that night has confided to the authors that he felt Connelly should have been playing from the start and, more importantly, that Jim Craig should have been brought on and David Hay moved into the midfield to replace Jim Brogan (who had played throughout despite an injury sustained early on). This player did admit that he was speaking with all the advantage of hindsight but he clearly suggested that the men on the pitch would have welcomed some tactical changes in order to alter the pattern of the match.

An ill-advised close-season tour made things worse. The club had arranged a seven-game jaunt to North America, the last thing these demoralised Celtic players wanted.

The weather was hot and oppressively humid, the pitches fast and bumpy, and the crowds disappointingly low. After the trauma in Milan nobody wanted to play football. The players' boredom soon turned to that mischief for which idle hands are apparently intended. The older members, or some of them, were frustrated at such a pointless tour; they were no longer the eager young men of the summer of 1966 when a tour of the United States represented a dream. To a man, they resented the fact that Jimmy Johnstone, either through his well-publicised fear of flying or through injury, had been excused participating in this chore.

Another long-term resentment was festering away: Jock Stein had single-handedly introduced tactical planning to the football at Celtic Park – and perhaps Scotland. The temptation was to consider the men on the pitch – the players, the stars – as mere puppets or automatons carrying out the instructions of their manager. Often a Celtic victory was attributed to Stein's tactics, and a defeat to the players' shortcomings or mistakes. Hurt by the accusation that they had been arrogant and complacent, the players resented being blamed alone for the loss in Milan.

Astonishingly, Jock Stein left the party abruptly, and headed home to Scotland with no warning to anybody in the Celtic party or information regarding his intentions. Fifteen minutes from the end of a farcical match against Bari in Toronto's Exhibition Stadium (during which the Italians staged a walkout after a second of their players had been sent off) he turned abruptly to Sean Fallon: 'I'm away home.' His assistant stared at him in some disbelief, as Stein, who had been notably short-tempered in the pre-match warm-up, continued by pointing to Bertie Auld and Tommy Gemmell, who had been involved the day before in a 'misunderstanding' at a supporters' function: 'And see that those two don't play again on this tour.'

The only director on the tour was Jimmy Farrell, and it was decided that, in Stein's absence, the more authoritative Desmond White would fly out to take overall charge. Auld and Gemmell – no longer required as players on the tour – did not appear to be responding to Fallon's words, for example missing a couple of important functions in the US. And discipline continued to deteriorate in New York, where the party was unhappy with the accommodation – a seedy hotel in a disreputable neighbourhood. One of the reporters accompanying the tour as a guest of the club felt obliged to wire back to Scotland some hints of the disciplinary problems now dogging the trip . . . and the other Scottish newspapers were instantly hinting at scandals as the leaks started to dribble from the United States.

Sean Fallon made the decision to send Bertie Auld and Tommy Gemmell home to Glasgow from New York after speaking to both of them and explaining his action. Fallon was gravely disappointed at what he considered misbehaviour that reflected badly on Celtic, and was particularly hurt that Gemmell and Auld, whom he had signed (and re-signed) for the club, had behaved so. He describes it as 'the worst night of my life, but I made the only decision I could make for the good of the club'. He continues: 'There were young players starting out in the game, and they had to be considered. Young Dalglish and Macari – they were quiet and didn't say a word, but they saw everything and they have to be shown a good example.' While the players, on reflection, felt that Fallon had been right in making his decision – and courageous in carrying it out – some of them envied the pair their escape.

Jock Stein's own responses and demeanour upon arriving at Prestwick Airport had not helped the situation, and the answers from a man normally in complete control of the media corps were unconvincing: he had to catch up on a backlog of paperwork; he had to straighten out a contract wrangle with Jimmy Johnstone; his own chronic ankle injury had flared up and required immediate attention.

Stein had always been an ambitious man and as a successful manager always had the option of moving to a larger stage. After all, he had left Hibernian to take over at Celtic after less than a season at Easter Road. The rumours started to circulate: once again, Stein's name was being linked with the manager's post at Manchester United and everybody, it seemed, had tales to tell of Stein being involved in long conversations with people from Old Trafford back in the Toronto hotel. The question of the Scotland managership surfaced once more. It was suggested that many of those who had played poorly at the San Siro were to be offloaded immediately . . .

Details were starting to emerge that Jimmy Johnstone had asked for a transfer on 21 May, having demanded a huge wage increase even though he was only two years into a six-year contract. Tommy Gemmell, after his 'involuntary' return from America, was also insisting on a transfer. Jock Stein, having spent some time in assessing his own future at Celtic Park, agreed to place both Johnstone and Gemmell on the transfer list but apparently discouraged any interested clubs from bidding seriously for them. If he was going to remain at Parkhead, those two players would be required.

Nevertheless, there were some changes at Parkhead by the time the pre-season training resumed in July. Ronnie Simpson, admitting that his shoulder injury would be a recurring one, announced his retirement, and Charlie Gallagher was given a free transfer.

Jock Stein had spent some time thinking about the changes that had to be made at Parkhead if Celtic were to continue in the top flight of European clubs. He reached the conclusion that his side needed a complete overhaul, that new blood was required: 'If we had won the cup – and how we wanted to win it – we might have mistakenly taken the attitude that the present team could have gone on for ever.' The message – and the warning – was clear.

Some students of the game consider that Jock Stein's greatest accomplishment lay in resurrecting Celtic in the aftermath of Milan and after the dreadful summer of 1970. It was said that, one by one, his star players – all household names – were called in for a heart-to-heart chat with the manager about life at Celtic Park in the immediate future. At any rate, both Tommy Gemmell and Jimmy Johnstone withdrew their transfer requests, improving team morale considerably.

Ironically, in the opening league fixture against Morton at Parkhead on 29 August 1970, Gemmell hurt his ankle while making a rash challenge on an opposing defender. He would be out of action until 4 November, but this gave Stein the opportunity to experiment with his full-backs in various combinations. It was a period of transition at Celtic Park, and Jim Craig, Tommy Gemmell, Danny McGrain, David Hay, Jimmy Quinn and, on occasion, Jim Brogan, were all competing for the two spots at full-back. Stein had to do some juggling in this department but the pairing of the two Lisbon Lion stalwarts, Craig and Gemmell, was preferred most often. Danny McGrain, a youngster, was introduced for a sustained spell early in the season and did very well in both full-back positions. David Hay was the most adaptable, playing either on the right or left, although he was becoming recognised more and more as a midfielder. Jim Brogan, another midfielder, was sometimes picked for tactical reasons at left-back, and Jimmy Quinn, the grandson of the famous centre-forward of the early 1900s, was given a chance to break through at left-back.

The principle that nobody was guaranteed a starting place any more was being established. The memory of Milan assured that, as did Jock Stein's force of character. All managers have to be ruthless at times and only 11 players could be chosen to start a game. The current squad could quite easily win all the domestic titles again – but, after Lisbon and Milan, was that enough?

Rangers, in general, struggled against Celtic and never more so than in a Glasgow Cup final on 10 August, held over from the previous season. Jock Stein made a couple of points about this game through his team selection: at one swoop, by selecting several youngsters in place of regulars, he defined the new status of the venerable Glasgow Cup; and he issued an advance warning to his squad by winning the match 3–1, outclassing Rangers in the process.

Morton were the visitors on the opening day of the league campaign, and 35,000 soaked up the sunshine and enjoyed the sight of the new flag being unfurled above the Jungle. More than 20 years after he had made a memorable début for Celtic against Rangers, Bobby Collins was still playing, for Morton; he was given a friendly reception until he tripped Jimmy Johnstone and the two fiery little lightweights squared up to each other. Lennox got Celtic's goals in a 2–0 win, and both were scored confidently and emphatically. Tom Leonard, the Glasgow poet, could have been describing them when he wrote 'Fireworks':

> up cumzthi wee man
> beats three men
> slingzowra crackir
>
> an Lennux
> aw yi wahntia seenim
> coolizza queue cumbir
>
> bump
>
> rightnthi riggin
> poastij stamp
> a rockit
>
> that wuzzit
> that wuzthi end
>
> finisht

Clyde surrendered by 5–0 at Shawfield a week later, and three of Celtic's youngsters, Lou Macari, David Hay and Vic Davidson, featured in the scoring. However, for the Old Firm clash at Parkhead on 12 September, Stein relied on his regulars. Early on, Hughes headed in a corner-kick, and Murdoch crashed home a second shortly after the start of the second half. Brogan squandered a chance from the penalty spot to make it three, but Celtic were never troubled as they confirmed their mastery over the Ibrox club with a 2–0 win.

In the next league match, at Easter Road on 19 September, Celtic's form dipped and the home side won by 2–0, both goals scored in the second half by Joe McBride who gave his ex-colleague and business partner Billy McNeill an uncomfortable afternoon. At the end of the game, almost all the Celtic players were waiting in the tunnel to congratulate the still popular Joe. Celtic could scarcely blame their midweek exertions in the European Cup for this defeat; on the Wednesday they had strolled through a 9–0 victory over a Finnish side at Parkhead.

This loss would be the last one suffered in the league for a considerable time. Dundee held out till half-time at Parkhead on 26 September but had to yield to three second-half goals. Billy McNeill missed this match, his place being taken by George Connelly, and young Paul Wilson made his competitive début on the left wing. Similarly, Dunfermline survived till the interval at East End Park but two goals, from Lou Macari and Willie Wallace (from a penalty-kick), saw off their stubborn resistance.

Lou Macari was developing into a nippy, dangerous forward, eager to score goals, especially from close range. Strangely enough, his manager did not appear to be entirely convinced of his value to Celtic. Macari would play for five seasons at Celtic Park, developing into an exceptional talent and impressing the supporters as a proven goalscorer ... but not Jock Stein, apparently. In his five years at Parkhead, Macari played a total of 51 league matches, and only in 1971–72 did he feature in more than half the schedule.

Celtic were making steady progress in the league although Jock Stein continued to make changes virtually every week. The genuine competition may have produced a more concentrated performance on the field and more consistent effort but there was an underlying anxiety among the older players about their future at Celtic Park.

The young men who had been playing for the second team (known as the 'Quality Street Kids') were being given opportunities to prove themselves. Back in 1968, Celtic had applied to the Scottish League to enter their reserve team in the Second Division. It would have been an interesting solution to a problem: the Second Division consisted of 19 clubs and one team remained idle each Saturday. Celtic indicated that, of course, there would have been no question of promotion if the team finished in first or second place – and that would have been a realistic possibility. However, the proposal was turned down, largely on the objections of Partick Thistle who anticipated themselves in direct competition for spectators every second Saturday in Glasgow.

David Hay was the first of the group to break through and become established in Celtic's side, his versatility such that he could be employed in several positions and in a variety of roles. Stein liked his attitude, his frame of mind belying his slight appearance and which would earn him the nickname the 'Quiet Assassin'. By the end of 1970 David Hay had played in a European Cup final and was a regular for Scotland, his rapid progress and development serving as a model for the others.

George Connelly had filled out physically and was so talented that it was difficult to figure out the best role for him in what appeared certain to be a glittering future. Some saw him as the logical successor to Billy McNeill in the heart of Celtic's defence, and Stein toyed with that possibility; others, noting his intelligent reading of the play, saw him as a perfect sweeper; many saw his ball control as the trademark of a creative midfield player, capable of splitting defences with his accurate passing ...

Lou Macari could scarcely be denied a place, such was his goalscoring. Danny McGrain, given an extended run at right-back at the start of the season, was obviously going to be one for the future; he was quick and brave, and Stein was impressed with his willingness to overlap. Kenny Dalglish had already made some infrequent appearances, and he was being groomed for the future. Vic Davidson, generally tipped for stardom even more so than Macari and Dalglish, was now being promoted more and more regularly ...

St Johnstone gave Celtic their customary hard game in Glasgow, going down to a 39th-minute goal from Willie Wallace but fighting right to the end before an increasingly apprehensive crowd of 37,000. Similarly, at Broomfield, Airdrie put up a struggle and scored first in 13 minutes but Celtic equalised almost immediately through Harry Hood and went in front thanks to Lennox and Hood again for a convincing win at a notoriously difficult ground.

The goalscorers had a familiar ring: Willie Wallace, Bobby Lennox and Harry Hood. Much the same sort of competition was going on to be a Celtic striker as to be a Celtic full-back. The youngsters were clamouring for a place while established players such as Jimmy Johnstone and John Hughes remained very much in Stein's plans.

The veteran Steve Chalmers, although available, could no longer be considered a regular. He had played in the previous season's League Cup final against St Johnstone but in that most sporting of matches he had sustained a broken leg in an accidental collision. Chalmers, like Ronnie Simpson, had been an unexpected bonus for Stein and his career was highly unusual in one respect; no other 'ordinary player' ever improved so much so late in his career. Under Stein, Stevie Chalmers displayed hitherto hidden talents and deserves the place in Celtic folklore that his goal in Lisbon had earned him. Chalmers was a runner, a chaser of the ball, an unselfish player whose efforts created openings for others as he drew defenders out of position with his constant movement.

Celtic, meanwhile, had advanced to their annual appearance in the League Cup final – this time against a Rangers team decidedly off form. Celtic's progress had not been as smooth as in previous years: Dundee had held them to a 2–2 draw at Dens Park before falling by 5–1 at Parkhead in the quarter-finals; the semi-final tie against Dumbarton from the Second Division produced some anxious moments. The outsiders played gallantly to hold on for a 0–0 draw at Hampden on 7 October, their goalkeeper saving Wallace's penalty-kick (and the rebound) in extra-time. Astonishingly, the part-timers played even better in the replay to hold Celtic to 2–2, and going down only by 4–3 after extra-time. One of Celtic's former players, Charlie Gallagher, dictated things for Dumbarton, scoring from a penalty-kick in 65 minutes and, in general, showing all the class that had marked him as a Celt.

Fixtures that appeared routine were becoming fraught as Celtic had been living dangerously in the League Cup against humble opponents. In the semi-final Charlie Gallagher found that he was being marked by David Hay and, during a lull in the early play, the Celtic midfielder spoke to him: 'Charlie, let's play football; you let me play and I'll let you play, okay?' Gallagher, only too well aware of Hay's reputation as a ferocious tackler, agreed readily. During the second half, when Dumbarton were threatening to take the lead he (and several other players) heard Jock Stein's rasping orders from the dugout: 'Break that wee bastard's legs!' While accepting the fact that the instruction was no more than intimidation at its most obvious, Gallagher was disappointed in the attitude shown by Celtic's manager – and it is a disturbing anecdote for a Celtic historian, given Gallagher's contribution to Celtic in the 1960s and his deserved reputation for gentlemanly play.

Celtic's adventures continued in Europe against lowly opposition. At least in the second round of the European Cup the football was no matter for concern. A tie against Waterford in Dublin looked little more than a carefree jaunt, and Celtic led by four goals at the interval before a crowd of 50,000. But the referee had to keep the teams in the dressing-rooms for an extra five minutes as trouble erupted on the terracing. Bottles, cans, and other assorted missiles were being thrown at the police and into other sections of the crowd. Given the one-sided nature of the match, and Celtic's long-standing connection with Ireland, the outbreak was astonishing, but trouble had been brewing for hours before and during the first half. The group of hooligans responsible for the trouble were Celtic's first experience with soccer 'casuals', organised gangs wanting to disrupt football matches for no apparent purpose other than publicity and cheap thrills. Evidence suggested that among them were *agents provocateurs* from Ulster who had infiltrated the gangs in an attempt to discredit sport in the Republic. Fortunately, the actual injuries were few in number and the game was resumed, Celtic going on to win by 7–0.

It was back to Glasgow to prepare for the League Cup final against Rangers, and Celtic entered the match as overwhelming favourites. It is one of Scottish football's hoariest clichés that nobody can predict the result of an Old Firm clash, and so it proved on 24 October. Rangers played well and forcefully, keeping Celtic under pressure in the first half; young Derek Johnstone, a mere 16-year-old from Dundee, scored with a fine header in the 40th minute. Only Bobby Murdoch looked in the proper frame of mind for Celtic, and another feckless performance in a major cup final resulted in disappointment.

At least one lingering worry resolved itself shortly afterwards. Some Celtic followers had worried about Rangers' challenge in the league race but it was a non-starter. A week before the final, Aberdeen had won 2–0 at Ibrox and, within a month, Rangers dropped another point at Dunfermline and two more at Easter Road.

Celtic faced an immediate test of their resolve on the Wednesday after the League Cup final when Hearts visited Parkhead, and went two goals up after 53 minutes. The crowd, a mere 18,000, was muted and feared the worst but once more Bobby Murdoch was an inspirational figure as he strove to turn things round. It is impossible to overrate Murdoch's contribution to Celtic when things were threatening to fall apart; the phlegmatic midfielder, despite his assorted physical problems, was always a reassuring figure either in defence or attack. He was at his best in the hardest matches, and was never a player to hide from any challenge. Jock Stein, whose value system had been formed in the coal-mines, treasured reliability and steadiness in a player; his most frequent adjective used in praising one of his players (or a worthy opponent) was 'manly'. Bobby Murdoch deserved this accolade more than most.

Back into Celtic's side for the Hearts match had come David Cattenach, a fringe player who had been unlucky in his career at Parkhead; some supporters were unwilling to forgive him for a botched passback which led to Dunfermline's second goal in a Scottish Cup defeat in 1968. Three goals for Celtic within a ten-minute spell in the second half, including two by Willie Wallace, assured a hard-fought victory over the Edinburgh side and gave more momentum to Celtic's efforts to win the league for the sixth successive time.

Celtic once more embarked on that part of the terrain which had ensured so many of their league flags. After the first two rounds in Europe, there would be a break until competition resumed in March;

after the League Cup final there would be no other distractions until the Scottish Cup in late January.

The opposition was not too demanding, but on 21 November Celtic dropped one point at Brockville where the home side 'entertained' their fans by playing seven men in or around their own penalty area for the entire contest. The other results were reassuring, however: a 5–0 win over Motherwell at Fir Park, as well as comfortable 3–0 wins over St Mirren, Kilmarnock and Cowdenbeath, the last making a rare but short-lived appearance in the First Division, only to be welcomed by two first-half goals from fellow Fifer, George Connelly.

December produced more difficult fixtures. At Tannadice Celtic trailed by 1–0 at half-time, Billy McNeill having scored an own-goal, but a United defender did much the same after the restart. This match could have gone either way, and a draw looked the most likely and fairest result until Vic Davidson scored in 58 minutes. Celtic held on grimly for the win.

The biggest match of the league programme so far – at least in terms of winning or losing the championship – came at Celtic Park on 12 December, and it was watched by a crowd of 63,000. The attendance was a remarkable one for such a cold, foggy day, but Aberdeen always have a large travelling support and were an attractive prospect for exiled Northerners living in or near Glasgow. It was also one of those pre-Christmas Saturdays, and many Aberdeen families had come to Glasgow to divide before the match – the men to Celtic Park and the womenfolk off to the shops on Argyle Street or Sauchiehall Street.

Aberdeen were now emerging as the real challengers to Celtic and came to Glasgow trailing by only one point and with morale high after scoring seven times the previous week against Cowdenbeath. It was a tense match which had its moments of good football, but Aberdeen escaped with both points, Joe Harper's goal shortly after half-time separating two well-matched sides. Bobby Clark in Aberdeen's goal, once a target for Rangers, pulled off several fine saves and the Dons' 'double centre-half' duo of McMillan and Buchan were cool in utilising the offside trap.

Jock Stein remained calm and decided on more changes for the last two fixtures of the year against Ayr United at Somerset Park and Morton at Cappielow. Into the forward line came some of the old guard such as Harry Hood, Bobby Lennox and Steve Chalmers, who marked his return with an early goal against Morton. At Cappielow, Stein made an impression on the mood of his camp with two other changes: Billy McNeill and Jimmy Johnstone, the archetypal Celtic defender and attacker, were both dropped – although the word 'rested' was used. It was not a crisis as both players appear to have been informed of the move well in advance, and Stein explained things clearly enough to the journalists: Johnstone had not been playing well, and McNeill (blamed in some quarters for Harper's goal at Parkhead on 12 December) was looking stale.

Despite the changes, Celtic won both matches, against Ayr by 2–1 and 3–0 over Morton on Boxing Day, to set up the traditional New Year clash with Rangers at Ibrox Stadium on 2 January. The Light Blues were out of contention in the league, but a victory in an Old Firm match was as important as ever for both teams and their supporters.

The match, on a hard pitch as a midwinter freezing fog descended on Glasgow, was surprisingly well played under the conditions. Both sides played constructive football, and the contest was deadlocked at 0–0 with a minute or so to play. The Celtic supporters were more disappointed at that stage, as they had learned over the radio that Aberdeen, who had won against Dundee on 1 January, were leading against St Johnstone. Celtic were pressing and Lennox's shot struck the crossbar but Jimmy Johnstone reacted quickly to head in the rebound. At the Broomloan Road end of the stadium the Celtic fans celebrated hugely, the goal seemingly heralding another victory over the old rivals. But Rangers swept into attack from the kick-off and, as Celtic's defence (still without McNeill) hesitated momentarily, Colin Stein netted an opportunist's goal to equalise. At the Copland Road end of the ground the Rangers followers roared with delight at the reprieve of such a late equaliser.

Assuming a draw, hundreds of Rangers fans – like their Celtic counterparts – had started to leave the ground minutes before the end of the match, and that number at the Rangers end swelled dramatically when Johnstone scored his goal. Less than 30 seconds later those thousands pouring away from Ibrox down Stairway 13 halted in their tracks at the tremendous roar behind them which greeted Rangers' equaliser. Several turned to climb back up those stairs to join in the celebrations, but the match had ended and they were met by a vast tidal wave of humanity exiting the stadium . . . in the confusion somebody (or several people) fell or stumbled and those leaving, unaware of this until too late, were unable to stop or halt the progress of the thousands behind them. As anybody ever caught in one of those pre-Taylor Report crowds can confirm, there was no escape for those trapped. In that bottleneck railings buckled and collapsed under the strain. Football fans, trying to stop, were unable to prevent themselves being pushed on to fellow-fans and trampling them to death or crushing them against the fence at the side of the exit. It was death for 66 people – as hideous as one could imagine.

It was the worst disaster in Scottish football and yet thousands left the ground oblivious to the gravity of what had happened at Stairway 13. Many saw the ambulances and police cars racing towards Ibrox afterwards with lights flashing and sirens blaring, but assumed wrongly that there had been an outbreak of violence after the game. Only later, as the supporters' buses were on the way home with the occupants listening to the radio did the full horror emerge. At first, the reports were vague and then the death toll began to mount until it reached 66. On the trains between Glasgow and Edinburgh that night rival fans still wearing their colours sat in misery.

Life had to go on after those terrible events but, for a while in the West of Scotland, it appeared as if there would be a possible turning point in the sectarian divide that has scarred the region for decades. Joint remembrance services were held at Church of Scotland and Roman Catholic places of worship; prayers were offered in both religious communities and at both clubs, directors, staff, players and supporters joined in the impressive solidarity of mourning. A week later at Parkhead a minute's silence was due to be held before the league match between Celtic and Hibernian – two Scottish clubs with strong founding links to Ireland and Catholicism. The fear was that one idiot, immature or drunk, might profane the moment of respect but fortunately the crowd of 28,000 rose to the occasion – as they have done so often – and Parkhead stood utterly mute and quiet in memory of 66 fellow football supporters, rivals but men who were not enemies at all.

The fixture against Hibernian was played out against that sombre and subdued background, but Celtic won the match 2–1 with a professional performance; a week later came the best display of the season, at Dens Park against an acceptable Dundee side. Celtic won by the incredible score of 8–1. Everybody played well that day, but nobody better than Bertie Auld, restored to the side for the first time that season and revelling in the occasion. Auld was at his arrogant best, orchestrating everything from the midfield, and throughout the second half the Celtic fans were chanting his name in acclamation. However, his surprise appearance was an interlude in his last season at Parkhead. Jock Stein and Bertie Auld did not always see eye to eye over a variety of matters, among them tactics, discipline and attitude. Stein was slow to forgive the player for the alleged lapses in behaviour on the

American tour. And, in the transitional season of 1970–71, when Stein was ringing the changes on a weekly basis while maintaining a challenge for the league, there was no room for Auld until 16 January.

Nostalgia can be a deceptive thing, but football grounds in the 1960s and 1970s – dilapidated and primitive as they were, unsanitary and unsafe – somehow looked better with the terracings packed with working men absorbed by the football. Dens Park was typical of that era, and looked splendid that afternoon as the winter sun started to dip behind the Provost Road end, its rays mingling with the silver light from the floodlights. It provided a fitting farewell to Bertie Auld, basking in the spotlight once more, and making one of his few appearances in this, his last season for Celtic.

Celtic and Aberdeen had moved far out in front of the others in the championship race; even before the Ibrox tragedy, Rangers had been struggling, eight points behind Celtic. The Ibrox club, from top to bottom, were concerned about the legal consequences arising from the 66 deaths at their ground. Despite being vaunted as one of the best stadiums in the country, Ibrox Park had had a deplorable safety record, starting with the first Ibrox Disaster in 1902 when overcrowding and an unsafe terracing caused 25 deaths and hundreds of injuries. After the latest tragedy, Rangers' league form understandably declined further. Aberdeen, whose sustained challenge was beginning to cause some disquiet among the Celtic supporters, lost to Hibernian that same afternoon while Celtic were conducting their master-class at Dens Park, and the two sides were now level at the top. Astonishingly, both challenger and champion lost on 6 February, when Aberdeen went down to Dunfermline Athletic and Celtic lost at Muirton Park to St Johnstone.

Celtic gave a sloppy performance, both in defence and attack, while St Johnstone took partial revenge for some 'unlucky' defeats from Celtic in recent seasons. By that time, the Perth side had moved up to third place in the table and would finish in that position, ahead of Rangers.

Jock Stein was enraged by this defeat, and by an incident involving John Hughes. The giant forward had reason to consider Muirton an unlucky ground: in 1969 he had injured his ankle badly there on 1 April and now, yet again, he was injured in a clash with Benny Rooney (ironically, the son of Celtic's trainer). The manager felt that the player was fit to continue, and ordered him to do so; Hughes carried on reluctantly, but so ineffectively, that Stein was forced to substitute Steve Chalmers for him.

Once again, relationships between Jock Stein and one of his players were nearing breaking point. After Milan he took the pragmatic approach that he would make all the important decisions, and that he would stand or fall by those decisions. That season he was more ruthless and brutal than ever before. Jock Stein was no democrat – or socialist – when it came to running a football team; players, whether established stars or youngsters, would have to toe the line or accept the consequences.

He could be a vicious taskmaster at times: goalkeepers complained about training sessions in which they were forced to the limit. Jim Craig, by then a practising dentist, remembers asking Stein if he could wear gloves to protect his hands before playing on an icy, dangerous pitch – and the manager dismissed the idea derisively, with all the contempt that a hard, former miner could muster.[1]

The power that a manager wields is through picking the team and Stein enjoyed exercising that power. His primary task was to win the championship, and the club was on course for that. Nobody could argue with success: the older players were still performing well, winning the key matches, and youngsters were continuing to break through as if on an endless conveyor belt of talent.

Celtic toiled through a cup replay with Dunfermline, and also had struggled a bit before beating the Fifers 1–0 at Parkhead in the league earlier, but they had no trouble disposing of Airdrie by 4–1, also at Celtic Park, on 20 February. Transistor radios were becoming part of the gear of football fans by then, and thousands at Celtic Park paid little attention to their favourites beating Airdrie, involved as they were in listening to Rangers play Aberdeen at Pittodrie. Mixed emotions, indeed, as great cheering heralded the news that Rangers – luckily, it appeared – had held Aberdeen to a 0–0 draw. The challengers stuttered again the following Saturday: Aberdeen dropped a point at home in an unsatisfying 1–1 draw with lowly St Mirren, but Celtic were happier with their draw, also by 1–1, at Tynecastle.

Once more, progress in the European Cup and the Scottish Cup could have hindered Celtic's defence of the league title. Aberdeen were able to concentrate fully on the pursuit of the league flag because, when Celtic were thrashing the hapless Raith Rovers by 7–1 in the Cup at Celtic Park on 6 March, Aberdeen had been going down 1–0 to Rangers at Ibrox.

Four days later Celtic went to Amsterdam to face Ajax and this time nobody was in any danger of underestimating the calibre of Dutch sides. Celtic opted for a defensive game, despite Stein's assurances that his team would attack even away from home. At half-time Celtic had soaked up all the Dutch pressure and showed some signs of asserting themselves in attack, but they fell apart in the closing stages to go down by 3–0, the last goal coming in the final minute. Jock Stein must have realised that night that his regular first team was not quite good enough for the final stages of a European competition. The brutal side of his character emerged upon the return to Glasgow when the Celtic party was swished away by coach for a rigorous training session that had a punitive mood to it; Stein was clearly putting the blame on his players for the collapse in the last 30 minutes. It was certainly no disgrace to lose to that Ajax side, which featured such stars as Cruyff, Neeskens, Krohl and Muhren.

On the same night, Aberdeen kept up the pressure on Celtic by defeating Dundee at Dens Park by 2–0. They were now one point ahead but had played one match more.

Not for the first time that season speculation was rife in the newspapers about the situation at Celtic Park. John Hughes, for example, was incensed at being dropped and had been involved in a public row with Stein on the day of the Raith Rovers cup tie. As he had done with Gemmell before a League Cup final, Jock Stein ordered him out of the dressing-room and, in fact, John Hughes went home! For the game against Cowdenbeath immediately after the return from Amsterdam, Jimmy Johnstone mysteriously asked to be omitted from the side, and Stein, aware that his player was not 'ready for the match', agreed to the request. Of course, the rumours started immediately: Johnstone had not played very well against Ajax, and was unhappy; Johnstone had objected to flying to and from Amsterdam, and wanted a transfer . . .

The fixture at Cowdenbeath allowed Celtic to make a rare visit to Central Park. Although the mining town had not yet been butchered in the Thatcher-Scargill wars of the 1980s, it was still a depressing place. A long way from Amsterdam, Central Park in places lacked even the most basic of terracing steps and is perhaps the only 'stadium' in the country also used for stock-car racing. It was hard-pressed to contain the 8,500 who turned up to watch Celtic on 13 March and the locals, who had not experienced too many such moments since the 1920s, must have had visions of a major upset when David Hay turned the ball into his own net after only four minutes' play. Celtic settled down after that, though, and went on to win comfortably enough by 5–1.

Two excellent wins in the championship on either side of an ultimately inconsequential 1–0 win over Ajax at Hampden Park indicated that Celtic's hold on the league flag was a firm one. On 20 March, despite giving up another early goal at Rugby Park, Celtic pulled ahead to win by 4–1 and, a week later, they swept aside a token resistance from Falkirk at Parkhead to win by 4–0. For the second league game in succession Harry Hood had scored twice; in fact, Hood had scored in eight of Celtic's nine matches since New Year and could be considered another underrated player who contributed a great deal to Celtic's run of consecutive championships.

Aberdeen kept moving in tandem with Celtic and got an excellent result at Tynecastle by beating Hearts 3–1 on the same day that Celtic defeated Falkirk. The Dons missed a golden opportunity on 3 April when Celtic were busy in the Scottish Cup semi-final: Celtic had all sorts of trouble against a spirited Airdrie side and, although they twice led by two goals, were glad to settle for a 3–3 draw and a replay ... but Aberdeen could only draw at Pittodrie against Motherwell. A week later it was Celtic's turn to drop a point at home. Dundee United were the more relaxed side and took the lead in 31 minutes; Celtic pressed furiously after that, but it took until the 72nd minute before Wallace equalised. The last ten minutes were tense, as Celtic went all out for the winning goal and an ominously composed United threatened every time they broke from defence. In a postponed fixture against Motherwell, Celtic produced a much better performance on the following Monday – with a much-recast side. Two goals before half-time from Jimmy Johnstone and Willie Wallace calmed the nerves, and the inevitable goal from Harry Hood in 71 minutes settled the match.

What everybody was labelling the 'Title Decider' – the league match between Celtic and Aberdeen – was staged at Pittodrie on 17 April. The North-East had rarely seen such a build-up to a football match. As early as the Thursday, TV crews were camped on Union Street with an impressive granite building as a backdrop, asking passers-by what they thought of Aberdeen's chances of thwarting Celtic. Although the Dons led by a point, Celtic were in the stronger position as, after Pittodrie, they would have three matches left and Aberdeen had only two. There was still unrest at Celtic Park behind the scenes, however, and the worst scenario involved Jock Stein's future.

For some years Manchester United had considered Stein as the best possible successor to Matt Busby. Approaches had been made, directly and indirectly, during the previous summer in the United States and the contacts were becoming more and more insistent. Only three days before the possible title decider at Pittodrie, Jock Stein met Matt Busby at a motorway service station just outside Haydock to discuss a possible transfer of power at Old Trafford. At the end of the clandestine meeting Busby was convinced that Stein had agreed to become United's manager. On the long drive back to central Scotland with his son, Stein thought more and more about the disadvantages of accepting United's offer: his wife Jean would not welcome a move to Manchester, for one; Matt Busby, a father-figure at Old Trafford, would be in the background and would still be influential; Celtic had always been good to him, starting with the time they had resurrected his faltering career by bringing him back from obscurity in Wales; the chairman Sir Robert Kelly was in poor health suffering from cancer. Later on, in an interview, Stein would say with a fair amount of sincerity: 'I like being Celtic's manager. I like the people I work for, and I like the players. And I like the supporters.'

So, despite the temptation of the English First Division, Stein decided to stay with Celtic and the players were informed of his decision at a hotel at Stonehaven as they rested before the Aberdeen match in pleasant spring weather. The story was starting to break in the Scottish newspapers and Jock Stein was astute enough to realise that further speculation could only affect the players adversely. Not one player knew anything about the meeting with Matt Busby, and everyone had assumed that their boss had driven down to England simply to see the UEFA cup tie between Liverpool and Leeds United.

Pittodrie, crammed with 35,000 spectators, was a fine sight but the match was not an exceptional one. Celtic attacked from the outset, to the surprise of Aberdeen, and scored in three minutes – the scorer, of course, Harry Hood, who sidefooted the ball into the net from close range. After that, Celtic concentrated sensibly on defence, with their rearguard of Craig, Hay, McNeill, Connelly and Brogan – every one a seasoned campaigner – parked in the last one-third of the pitch. Aberdeen refused to be totally discouraged and kept on attacking; just before the interval they were rewarded when Alex Willoughby, an ex-Ranger, equalised.

The second half was a test of nerve, a war of attrition fought out mainly in midfield although both sides could claim spells of sustained pressure and an equal share of half-chances. At the referee's whistle the relieved Celtic following left Pittodrie cheering and singing. It would, one feels, have been a much more attractive game had Celtic needed to win.

Aberdeen had lost their chance – and they knew it. On 24 April, a Saturday when Celtic were idle, they went to Brockville and went down 1–0 to Falkirk to the great disappointment of a large travelling support. A win there would have kept up the pressure on Celtic but now, given their rivals' superior goal average, three points for Celtic from their three remaining fixtures would allow the champions to retain the league flag.

At Love Street, against a St Mirren side fighting hard to avoid relegation, Celtic found themselves in a dogfight. Twice they fell behind and twice they came back to level the match – and so collect the first of the necessary three points for the championship.

Two fixtures remained, both at home, but Fate continued to conspire against Celtic winning the league championship at Parkhead. The game against Ayr United was switched to Hampden because the grandstand at Celtic Park was being renovated; the crowd of 25,000 looked sparse in Hampden's vast terracings. However, they made a lot of noise in the 18th minute when Lennox opened the scoring, and again in the 58th when Wallace sealed the victory – and the championship.

Stein now decided that a piece of live theatre was called for in the last league game against Clyde – and it should be staged at Celtic Park. He told everybody in sight that Saturday, 1 May 1971, would be a historic occasion – and it was. A crowd of 35,000 came to claim for themselves a piece of history (and nostalgia) for, trooping out of a half-demolished stand, came Celtic's team: Simpson, Craig, Gemmell, Murdoch, McNeill, Clark, Johnstone, Wallace, Chalmers, Auld and Lennox. Ronnie Simpson had already retired but he participated in the warm-up to great cheers from the punters, before going back to his seat and leaving the goalkeeping duties to Evan Williams.

Clyde approached the match in the proper spirit and came prepared to attack, but they suffered the consequences, going down to a 6–1 defeat. Apparently, several members of Clyde's team were Celtic fans and were thrilled to be on the same pitch as their heroes. The Lisbon Lions, seasoned troupers as they were, rose to the occasion and some of their football was memorable; Clyde had no answer to the rapier thrusts of Bobby Lennox who scored three times, nor to the magic of Jimmy Johnstone, nor to the wiles of Bertie Auld, making his final appearance.

More than anybody else, Jock Stein was aware that there would never be another opportunity to see that legendary side in action. Bertie Auld, for one, knew that he was being released to make his own arrangements with Hibernian; John Clark was already talking to Morton about an imminent transfer; and there would be others.

The league campaign had ended happily and the season would end on a similarly high note on 12 May at Hampden Park when Celtic completed the double by defeating Rangers in a replayed Scottish Cup final. The Ibrox side, struggling all through the season and ending a distant fourth in the championship, were hoping to salvage their year by lifting the Scottish Cup – and having it join the League Cup in their trophy-room.

In the first match, Rangers had been considered lucky to scramble a 1–1 draw when a mix-up in Celtic's defence between Williams and Connelly gifted them the equaliser with a few minutes left. Till that moment, Celtic, leading by Bobby Lennox's strike just before half-time, had looked in complete control, and the Celtic fans in the 120,092 crowd were acclaiming their side as victors till Derek Johnstone scored with a late header.

Rangers' luck deserted them in the replay as Celtic settled from the very start; time after time they stretched Rangers' defence with Tom Callaghan thrusting down the left and Jimmy Johnstone given free rein to wreak havoc on the Ibrox defence. Both men, with such vastly differing styles, took full advantage of their opponents' decision to introduce a new player into the cauldron of an Old Firm clash. Jim Denny had been pitched in because of an injury to Miller, and he found himself having to cope unexpectedly with Jimmy Johnstone operating on Celtic's left wing. In fact, none of the regular Ibrox defenders was capable, singly or collectively, of stopping Johnstone that night. Lou Macari, who had replaced Willie Wallace in the line-up, scored from close range after McNeill had cleverly dummied a corner from the left; shortly afterwards, Johnstone was pulled down in the area by a totally frustrated defender and Harry Hood calmly converted the penalty-kick.

Celtic dominated proceedings with a display of attacking football and the match was won by the most convincing of 2–1 scorelines.

It was a great way to end a most difficult season.

Notes

1. John Cushley, another university graduate, wondered if Stein was comfortable with well-educated players with interests outwith football.

Chapter 7

The Brink of Greatness

Just before the start of the 1971–72 season, Celtic followers received some bad news. Charles Patrick Tully, a legendary figure from the recent past, had died in Ireland at the tragically young age of 47. Tully came to Glasgow in 1948 from Belfast Celtic for a transfer fee of £8,250 – a modest sum by today's standards but one quality newspaper, bemoaning the trade in mere footballers, noted acidly that the amount was the same as that paid by Glasgow's Kelvingrove Art Gallery for Salvador Dali's famous painting of St John at the Cross. At least they had one thing in common: both were highly controversial.

Charlie Tully was 'a character': witty, irreverent, lovable and exasperating in equal measure, and very talented. The boy had ball control, a devastating swerve, a football intelligence so that he passed when he should pass and held the ball up whenever required. And he had cheek in abundance because nobody enjoyed practising the art of gamesmanship better than Charlie

Cheeky, irritating, lazy, petulant: but what talent, and his skills were displayed more often than not on the big occasion. It was left to one supporter, well in his cups, to provide the epitaph: 'Aye, Charlie Tully . . . an Immortal – an' noo he's deid.'

Celtic were well represented at the funeral: supporters' associations, players past and present, directors, the club's backroom staff of Jock Stein, Sean Fallon and Neilly Mochan – all of whom had played with Tully in the double-winning season of 1953–54. The three men were grim-faced and sombre as they attended the funeral on 29 July 1971 – thinking of their own mortality, perhaps – but with the reminiscing came the smiles. John Bonnar, looking at the crowds lining the Falls Road on the way to Milltown Cemetery, turned to Celtic's manager and smiled: 'Charlie would have loved this, Jock.'

As players, Stein, Fallon and Mochan did not have the skill of Tully, nor his charisma, but they all had qualities that Charlie Tully perhaps lacked in his life. As one of them has said to the authors: 'Charlie liked the late nights, and he liked his drink . . . he didn't look after himself.'

The men in Celtic's backroom during this era were steeped in Celtic's traditions: steady and reliable men with common sense and a maturity that gained them respect and affection. It is time to look a bit more closely at these men and the contribution they were making to Celtic as the club continued to rule Scottish football and search for success in Europe.

Jock Stein dominates this narrative, just as he dominated Celtic. As has been seen, Jock Stein was idolised by some, respected and feared, loved and sometimes disliked, but nobody doubted for a moment his stature in football . . . nor the contribution he had made and continued to make to Celtic. Bobby Murdoch, another man with an aversion to 'mince', summed it up perfectly: 'Jock Stein saved Celtic.'

The manager inherited Sean Fallon as his assistant, and there is some evidence to suggest that the two men did not always see eye to eye. It was generally accepted that, in football matters, Jock Stein had forgotten more than Sean Fallon had ever learned. That was unfair to Fallon. Celtic players, while speaking of him, reminisce about his sterling character and his warmth but insist that Fallon 'knew the game'. They feel that his contribution was underrated, and that he had to perform those irksome tasks that Stein at times neglected. Fallon took the training, along with Stein, Mochan and Benny Rooney, and his sessions were just as thorough and demanding as those of the others.

Those players, household names by now, hold Sean Fallon in respect and genuine affection. For one thing, behind his grim, no-nonsense exterior, the stocky Irishman was an out-and-out Celtic man. Nobody doubted for a moment his love of the club or his efforts and hard work to make it even better. On one occasion, while taking his wife and daughters out for a drive, he stopped 'just for a minute or two' in order to complete the signing of a promising player for Celtic. The minutes passed . . . and kept passing for the young family in the car, until almost two hours had elapsed. Apparently, there had been a couple of hitches but Fallon persevered until he had the signature of one Kenneth Mathieson Dalglish on a form – and the respect of the Dalglish family, like the boy himself all keen Rangers supporters.

And he may have been the man who kept Dalglish at Celtic Park as well. The last day for retaining footballers in Scotland was 30 June; anybody not offered a contract by that date is deemed a free agent.

Three or four years later, Fallon, as conscientious as ever, was checking off the names of all the Celtic players, from the stars down to the humblest apprentice, and happened to notice that Dalglish's name was missing. In fact, he had not been sent a form at all – and the date was 30 June! The most promising young player in the country was in real danger of being released by mistake. Sean went immediately to Stein's office with the news, and the manager's face turned ashen. It was a mark of supreme trust that Jock Stein decided that the best man to go round to Kenny Dalglish's home with the vital document was Sean Fallon.

One prominent Celtic player told the authors in confidence: 'Sean would be prepared to cover up for you ... but later on he would speak to you and you knew very well what would be expected of you in future. He made you want to behave in order to maintain Celtic's good name, and you knew that he would never divulge what you had done as a daft wee boy.'

Fallon was a man of honour and principle: minor infractions could be overlooked but he was not a man to shirk the hard decisions when the reputation of the club was at stake. On the ill-fated tour of North America after Milan, he was the one who decided that Bertie Auld and Tommy Gemmell should be sent home, and, before giving the pair their airline tickets and $50 each for expenses, he explained to them exactly how they had let the club down.

Neil Mochan, who had come to Celtic as a player from Middlesbrough in 1953 in time for the Coronation Cup, was the third member of the backroom staff. He was the one most associated with the fitness level of the players. At the start of the season he had to build up stamina and strength, and throughout the campaign he had to maintain that fitness despite the cumulative effect of tiredness and injuries.

As a trainer, Neil Mochan was regarded as the most effective in Scotland, the Celtic players' fitness being considered almost legendary. Statistics can be very deceptive but one should look closely at the number of goals scored by Celtic during the nine championships won in a row. Altogether Celtic scored 868 goals, 396 in the first half of matches and 467 in the second half. Some people might point out that, in general, more goals are scored in the second half of football games than in the first – and that is a valid point. However, within these statistics can be found another suggestion of Celtic's superior fitness. The time most likely for Celtic to score in the first half occurs between the 28th and the 45th minutes, during which period Celtic scored 172 goals (44 per cent of the total). A similar picture emerges in the second-half statistics: between the 73rd and 90th minute Celtic scored 204 goals (44 per cent of the second total). In the closing stages of each half, Celtic took full advantage of their superior fitness and conditioning – and these statistics refer to matches against full-time, professional opponents.

All three men loved their work and were enthusiastic. All were strong 'family men', and that sense permeated their work at Celtic Park. All had played the game for Celtic, during good times and bad. They had an understanding of the needs of players and were idealistic even in a hard professional sport.

More than one player has described to the authors the family atmosphere at Seamill Hydro. Frankly, the hotel is not a luxury one, but it had the comfortable 'feel' that Jock Stein wanted for his players in which to prepare for an important match. Charlie Gallagher remembers the whole group (16 or 17 players and the backroom staff) playing table-tennis or golf. But, most of all, he recalls everybody sitting round the fireplace at night talking about football: the past and the present, opponents and former team-mates, various grounds and the stories about past days and great matches. Jim Craig and others remember the inevitably long walks, led by Neilly Mochan, along the shore . . .

All three men had much to offer young players and they complemented each other perfectly. Stein, although a master of small-talk, could be aloof and difficult at times. Fallon, the manager's second-in-command, was gruff in appearance and had an accent to match his 'map-of-Ireland' face, but many players felt he was more approachable than Stein; he could comfort and encourage players temporarily out of favour with the manager.[1] Mochan was friendly and affable with everybody, a reassuring presence and 'a player's friend', as he was described by one of the Lisbon Lions.

On the first Saturday of the new season the Celtic supporters were hailing the advent of a new star. Kenny Dalglish had been nursed along, making only a few first-team appearances, but he could no longer be denied a regular spot in the line-up. At the end of the previous season he played in a testimonial match for Frank Beattie of Kilmarnock at Rugby Park and his six-goal performance there guaranteed him a place for the opening Drybrough match against Dumbarton; Celtic won by 5–2, and Dalglish scored four of the goals. He had done enough to keep his place for the first League Cup match of the season on 14 August against Rangers at Ibrox. Celtic won by 2–0, and Dalglish scored the second goal from the penalty spot in 70 minutes to seal the victory.

From the start of this season, Kenny Dalglish was a complete player: his reflexes were lightning-quick, and his anticipation was uncanny in one so young. He had the coolness in front of goal to finish off moves in a deadly manner and, superbly fit, he now had the strength to handle any physical challenge. The captain ordered him to take that penalty-kick in his first Old Firm match before a crowd of 72,500 – among which was his father supporting Rangers. Dalglish nodded his agreement and calmly stopped to tie up his bootlace before sending the ball firmly past Peter McCloy in Rangers' goal.

But it was his enthusiasm that shone through his every action; he had a smile, especially when he had just scored, that could light up the dreariest day. So much talent and skill, and such a positive attitude. No wonder Jock Stein, when asked about the youngster's best position, could claim: 'With a player like that, you don't talk of positions; you just toss him a jersey no matter the number.' It was a somewhat odd remark for the manager of a team which did not wear numbered jerseys.

By the time the league programme began on 4 September 1971, Celtic had advanced comfortably through the sectional play in the League Cup, helped considerably by beating Rangers twice (2–0 and 3–0). Apart from the ease of those victories, the most surprising aspect was that both ties were played at Ibrox. The main stand at Celtic Park was being redeveloped and was not yet considered safe for large crowds. Celtic's last previous fixture in the league had been Clyde, victims of the final appearance of the Lisbon Lions; this time the Shawfield club faced only five of the European Cup winners but were absolutely no match for Celtic who won by 9–1.

A week later Celtic went back to Ibrox, this time on league business. Rangers put up a tremendous struggle before going down by 3–2. It turned out to be a controversial match, fuelled by refereeing decisions that TV coverage later revealed as dubious. For once Rangers were on the wrong end of most of those decisions, and the referee (Mr Paterson of Bothwell) was criticised for his performance.

Lou Macari scored in only ten minutes with a fine header but Rangers equalised in 31 minutes from a penalty-kick, awarded when Brogan handled the ball. Rangers took the lead surprisingly when Colin Stein, over whose abilities the Ibrox support was now divided, scored right on the stroke of half-time – always a bad time to give up a goal. Celtic came out full of confidence and dictated the play until Dalglish equalised with a crisply struck shot. This goal was highly controversial as Bobby Lennox was standing on the Rangers goal-line when Dalglish shot home; Lennox made no effort to play the ball but it was hard not to accept the argument of the Rangers fans that a man standing on the goal-line has to be considered as interfering with play.

The controversy continued. Alfie Conn, already booked by the referee, made a rash tackle on Tommy Callaghan and was ordered off. Rangers were seething with indignation about that decision but their anger boiled over a minute later. The ball was lobbed into Celtic's penalty area and Colin Stein managed to hook the ball over the head of the advancing goalkeeper but Mr Paterson disallowed the 'goal', presumably on the grounds of dangerous play. Again and again that night the incident was replayed on TV, but nothing altered the fact that, if you were a Celtic follower, you applauded a correct decision by the referee and, if you supported Rangers, you felt ill-done by.

Very few would have grudged Rangers a draw on this occasion but Celtic struck dramatically in the very last minute. A high ball was sent into Rangers' area and Jimmy Johnstone, leaping higher than Celtic fans thought he ever could, headed the cross into the net for the winning goal.

The supporters were in ecstatic mood as they left the ground that afternoon; with three wins there in the last few weeks, they might well have voted Ibrox their favourite ground. Most pleasing was the continuing excellent form of the young players: Macari and Dalglish had played well and both had scored, but George Connelly had been immense in defence and had raked Rangers' flanks with superb long passes. Rangers' challenge for the title had already foundered – perhaps to the secret disappointment of many in Celtic's support who relished a close challenge from Ibrox (as long as it ultimately ended in failure).

On 18 September Morton came to Parkhead and Celtic supporters were mildly apprehensive about this match. After the heroics at Ibrox, Celtic had travelled to Denmark to play BK 1903 Copenhagen in the European Cup . . . and had lost by 2–1 to their part-time opponents. In the time-honoured Parkhead manner there were cheers of welcome for returning heroes in the person of Steve Chalmers and John Clark, now performing for Morton. For the first two or three times they touched the ball, they were applauded, but John Clark, whose goals for Celtic could have been counted on the fingers of one hand, added to his meagre total in this match. Unfortunately for him, it was an own-goal, arising out of a misunderstanding with Sorensen, his goalkeeper. That strike, cheered to the echo by the faithful, was Celtic's second and the home side ended up winners by 3–1.

Broomfield Park, the home of Airdrie, was noted for its quaint pavilion (a detached building, much like a cricket pavilion) at one corner of the ground; it was also a ground where the local side always put up a strong resistance. On 25 September Celtic made the short trip there, and routed Airdrie by 5–0, three goals by Lou Macari leading the way. It was excellent preparation for disposing of BK 1903 Copenhagen in the return leg at Parkhead the following Wednesday although the 'Danish aggregate of teachers, bankers and office-workers' put up a defiant stand until late in the second half.

At last came the first defeat of the league campaign. St Johnstone performed the feat by winning 1–0 at Celtic Park on 2 October, a first-half goal by Connolly doing the damage, but that would be the only loss in the championship until very late in the season.

The club recovered immediately from the St Johnstone reverse and went to Easter Road to eke out a fine 1–0 win before a crowd of 40,000. Once more it was Lou Macari who netted the vital goal but the outstanding player on view was Dalglish who grabbed the headlines the following Saturday by scoring all three of Celtic's goals in a 3–1 win over Dundee at Parkhead. The fresh-faced, innocent appearance of these two youngsters symbolised the emergence of a new Celtic team.

Things were changing at Celtic Park as the team prepared for a European Cup tie against Sliema Wanderers from Malta, to be followed by the League Cup final against Partick Thistle on 23 October. Just before the tie with Sliema, two of Stein's 'regulars' departed, John Hughes and Willie Wallace signing on for Crystal Palace for a combined fee of around £50,000.

John Hughes had been at Celtic Park since 1959, and probably no such long-term player has been the subject of many arguments in Celtic's history. On his day, and there were many of them, Hughes was a world-class forward, and he scored some spectacular goals. Supporters can remember vividly one long run on a heavy Cappielow pitch ending in a goal against Morton in the Scottish Cup back in 1964. He was also responsible for a brave header against Leeds United in the European Cup semi-final at Hampden in 1970. Against those memories, sadly, there were times when he did not produce or, when he got off to a poor start, seemed to lose heart. Of late there were public disagreements with Jock Stein, and he was being chosen on fewer and fewer occasions for Celtic. The sudden move to Crystal Palace and London appeared to be the best solution for everybody.

Willie Wallace had been a later arrival at Celtic Park and, as a model professional with a non-Celtic background, he had been a considerable success. In latter seasons, as if to make room for younger talent, he had been utilised sparingly but to great effect. His departure seemed to be for no other reason than that, at the age of 31, he had passed his Parkhead sell-by date.

Nothing remains static in football; these men had performed well and sometimes heroically but they might be able to prolong their careers at decent salaries with other clubs. The manager had undergone a new lease on life with the emergence and potential of his youthful stars; at times, he seemed almost impatient for some of his veterans to move on.

The result of the League Cup final – a resounding 4–1 triumph for Partick Thistle at Hampden on 23 October – called into question the manager's judgement. Realistically, the score was the sort of headline that appears once in a blue moon. Partick Thistle played the game of their lives to win their first major trophy in half a century. Celtic played poorly by their own standards. Billy McNeill was absent through injury, and the Celtic defence looked vulnerable throughout the first half. Still, Stein was furious with his side and, as was his custom, picked on the goalkeeper as the scapegoat. It was manifestly unfair to Evan Williams but it did appease the fans somewhat when Denis Connaghan was purchased from St Mirren two days later for a modest fee and took over in Celtic's goal until late January.

The manager also surprised everybody in Scottish football by buying Dixie Deans from Motherwell. One 'football man' suggested that if Bob Kelly were still alive, Jock Stein would never have been allowed to sign this controversial player. Deans had been a problem wherever he had played. He had an innate capacity to attract trouble, on and off the pitch. On several occasions he had gone AWOL in mysterious circumstances and, at the time of his signing, was serving a six-week suspension for repeated orderings-off. A *sine die* suspension – virtually a lifetime ban – seemed the most likely denouement of such a career, and Celtic supporters with long memories recalled that, on the day Willie Wallace made his début for Celtic against Motherwell, Deans had been ordered off. Those privy to such knowledge swore that Deans had turned up to sign for Motherwell wearing a Rangers scarf!

Dixie Deans was a strange figure for a modern striker. He was short and squat and always slightly overweight. But he could score goals, as he had proved against Celtic in the past. Nobody could figure out what Jock Stein, the strictest of disciplinarians, could see in such an unlikely prospect, but within six months Dixie Deans had become a household name. In fact, Jock Stein's reputation as a shrewd operator in the transfer market could be put down principally to the success-rate of his strikers: Joe McBride, Willie Wallace, Harry Hood and now Dixie Deans.[2]

The very first thing Stein impressed upon his new recruit was the need to get fit – and not merely acceptably fit, but fit by Celtic standards. While the suspension was still in effect Deans had to work out daily under the watchful eyes of the management team and, when the player was ready to take his place in a Celtic team, he was fitter than ever before in his life. It was not all a physical grind for Deans, though; a couple of days after his signing, he travelled with the team to unfashionable Malta to savour the atmosphere of the European campaign. Journalists relate the story of how the whole Celtic party were taken to the cinema by Jock Stein in order to keep them out of the sun (or possible mischief) and, to make sure that nobody escaped, the manager placed his own considerable bulk in the seat at the end of the row. During this trip – meaningless because of Celtic's five-goal lead from the first leg – discipline wavered a little and Stein ended one argument by throwing one unfortunate player across the room. Dixie Deans, scarcely a shrinking violet, was shocked, and his education as a footballer had begun.

With Billy McNeill now restored to fitness, Celtic won at Dunfermline (2–1) and at Ayr (1–0) by doing just enough to suggest that the Partick Thistle result was a mere blip. The next crucial match was against Aberdeen at Celtic Park on 6 November, a raw afternoon with more than a hint of winter in the air. Aberdeen had resumed the challenge of the previous season and were leading Celtic by a point, having drawn with St Johnstone at Muirton whereas Celtic had lost to the Perth side at Parkhead. It was a close-fought match but the home side were on top and confirmed that superiority with a goal from Harry Hood in 59 minutes. But Celtic somehow contrived to throw away the lead with a bizarre own-goal. Connaghan, the new goalkeeper, advanced from his line to deal with a cross from Joe Harper, but McNeill, amid the hubbub of a 64,000 crowd at Parkhead, did not hear him call out for the ball and the captain gently headed the ball back to his goalkeeper, assumed to be standing on the goal-line. Aberdeen, gifted an equaliser with 13 minutes left to play, held out till the end.

Celtic appeared to be in trouble a week later when Dundee United went a goal in front after 19 minutes and held that lead comfortably till half-time. Upon the resumption, Celtic looked fired-up and Billy McNeill, a dominant figure, was seen clapping his hands to encourage his team-mates. As if a switch had been flicked, Celtic dominated the second half to win by 5–1. Harry Hood netted in 49 and 50 minutes, while Macari and Dalglish added two more. Three minutes after Dalglish had been substituted, his replacement Bobby Lennox scored the fifth.

The match against Partick Thistle at Firhill was eagerly awaited by the punters, demanding some retribution for the League Cup final. They were not disappointed as Celtic, three goals up at half-time, totally dominated the contest; Dixie Deans, largely forgotten since his surprise signing, made his début and scored the last goal four minutes from the end to seal a 5–1 victory. By that time, however, the fans were drifting away into the gathering darkness, cheered with the news that Aberdeen had lost 3–2 to Hearts at Pittodrie.

Thus, Celtic took over once again at the head of the table. It was a lead they never relinquished throughout the season although Aberdeen would keep pace until the turn of the year. Before too long, the Celtic support took the extroverted Deans to their hearts for the newcomer scored in every match in December. The cheerful Deans, grinning broadly, was responding to the approval from the terracings, leaping high in the air after each goal with both fists raised in triumph. Very quickly he had formed an understanding with Kenny Dalglish, a rapport in stark contrast to the differences in the pair: Dalglish was young and fresh, while Deans presented a more worn face; Dalglish was hard-working and an excellent provider, while Deans was a poacher, watchful and waiting for an opportunity to turn up.

Having thrashed Thistle by 5–1 at Firhill, Celtic did the same to Kilmarnock at Parkhead but on the following week the visitors put up more resistance. East Fife had been promoted to the First Division and were making a rare appearance at Celtic Park. They had not been there since the days of their formidable side containing the likes of Charlie 'Legs' Fleming, George Aitken and Henry Morris two decades earlier. But they played well: Deans scored for Celtic in 20 minutes and East Fife equalised before the interval; had the Methil side not had a player ordered off, they might well have shared the points, but Deans got a second goal to give Celtic a narrow win.

Another fine 5–1 victory followed at Fir Park, a profitable hunting-ground for Celtic in those seasons and, on Christmas Day, Hearts visited Parkhead. The Edinburgh side were a curious mixture that season, having beaten both Rangers and Aberdeen, but they had exasperated their following by inconsistency. They had come to Glasgow in a Christmas spirit and gave up a goal, netted by Harry Hood, in the very first minute. Celtic seemed well on the way to a comfortable win, leading by 3–1 with only 13 minutes left. Hearts pulled a goal back at that stage after hesitancy in Celtic's defence and the last few minutes passed with a certain amount of anxiety.

On 1 January 1972 Clyde provided their customary offering of two points to Celtic's total, this time by 7–0 at Shawfield. The two sides played each other in eight of the nine championship-winning seasons, and it was the fate of the Bully Wee never to take a single point from their Parkhead neighbours. In 1971–72 the scores were 9–1 and 7–0 in Celtic's favour. It was difficult to crow about this result, or to boast about it, as the opponents were a debt-ridden outfit, most of whose players – honest journeymen – were unashamedly Celtic-daft.

And where were Rangers at the turn of the year? So far, the highlight of their season had been the League Cup final between Celtic and Thistle but, on the other hand, their recent form had been acceptable. If they could get a result at Parkhead on 3 January, they might still be able to turn the season around. The day itself was overcast and dull, but the pitch was playable. The early skirmishes bordered on the intimidating, and it was clear that one or two players on each side had a few unresolved vendettas. Dalglish and Connelly were outstanding in midfield, spreading the play from wing to wing but unable to break through a stuffy Rangers rearguard not too particular about how Celtic's increasing number of raids was to be stopped. In the 35th minute, following another free-kick conceded near the penalty area, Harry Hood flighted over a perfect cross to find Jimmy Johnstone unmarked behind the defence. Not for the first time, Celtic's smallest player headed in a goal against Rangers.

Celtic's dominance in midfield was the crucial factor as the second half wore on, but with nine minutes remaining Rangers equalised when a through ball from Mathieson found two of their forwards suspiciously on their own. Celtic's defence appealed for offside and started their pursuit only after the linesman gave no indication of raising his flag. Too late . . . as Colin Stein strode away and netted for Rangers. A draw would have suited Celtic but Rangers conceded yet another free-kick well inside their own half in the very last minute. Billy McNeill sent the ball into the crowded penalty area and found Harry Hood who managed to gain a little space for himself and caught a glimpse of Jim Brogan, Celtic's left-back, slipping into the area. Hood's lob was accurate and controlled, aimed ahead of Brogan, and the full-back glanced the ball into Rangers' net for the winning goal. For the second time that season Rangers had lost to a last-minute goal by Celtic . . .

Brogan's brilliant piece of opportunism gutted Rangers that day as the Ibrox club fully deserved a share of the points at least. However, they had played the closing stages as if expecting disaster to strike. As one of their own supporters put it, 'like an escaped convict hearing the sound of bloodhounds in the distance'. During the rest of the league campaign Rangers' form disintegrated and they would finish 16 points behind Celtic (and in those days only two points were awarded for a win).

Only one true challenger remained in contention: Aberdeen. The Dons were a formidable, well coached and disciplined, but they would virtually abandon the race when they sold their captain and central defender Martin Buchan to Manchester United early in March. The transfer was greeted with incredulity in the North-East; it was the equivalent, one Aberdeen journalist complained, of Winston Churchill selling all his Spitfires in the middle of the Battle of Britain.

Aberdeen had dropped a point to Dundee over the New Year period, but Celtic went to Cappielow with the same side that beat Rangers and gave a fitful performance against Morton to restore the status quo by drawing 1–1. Morton scored first but, after Hood's equaliser, the Celtic supporters relaxed and expected a deluge of goals. The Greenock team stuck to their task with a solid defensive professionalism, however, to pick up a point so valuable for them in the fight to avoid relegation.

Stein, by all accounts, was angry about his team's performance and gave the players a verbal rollicking; whatever he said appeared to have been effective as the results stayed good for more than two months. The league matches, the bread-and-butter games which were also the only passport into Europe's most prestigious tournament, were approached with determination.

Everybody, especially at Parkhead, was fully aware that Celtic would be establishing a new record if they won the league title again; by winning seven titles in a row, the modern Celtic would be surpassing the feat of the bygone Celtic side of Willie Maley in the Edwardian era. That team, with men like 'Sunny Jim' Young, Jimmy McMenemy and the legendary Jimmy Quinn, had won the championship from 1904–5 through 1909–10 – six times in a row. There were still a few survivors in Glasgow who had coped with two world wars, TB, the Depression and other assorted social ills and who could – prompted by the purchase of a dram – tell the youngsters about that great team.

On 15 January Celtic defeated Airdrie by 2–0 in a drab, uninteresting match at Parkhead but Rangers, as they had done so often, visited Aberdeen and shared the points. A week later Celtic faced one of the season's most perilous journeys – a trip to Perth and Muirton Park. Dalglish scored in only five minutes and Deans, revelling in his role as Celtic's main striker, added two more in the closing stages for what ultimately proved a comfortable win. It was a good night in Perth where the generally douce citizens – more than once terrorised by mindless hooliganism in the not-too-distant past – relaxed and enjoyed themselves as the huge Celtic travelling support celebrated good-naturedly.

Celtic ended any real threat from Hibernian a week later at Parkhead on 29 January although they trailed by 1–0 at half-time, David Hay having contributed an own-goal. Harry Hood, taking over Auld's mantle as the scorer of vital goals, equalised early in the second half and Dixie Deans netted the wining goal in 74 minutes. Deans' goal was an important one in itself . . . but it was also his first for Celtic against Hibernian and marked the start of a personal persecution of the Edinburgh side by the Celtic striker. Over the next few seasons the stocky, irrepressible Deans would inflict upon the Hibernian defence his own version of capital punishment.[3]

The Scottish Cup intervened, as did the Scottish winter, and on 12 February the fixture at Dens Park was postponed in mid-morning due to a frozen pitch. Several Celtic supporters' buses were already leaving from the west of Scotland (normally a bit milder than the east coast) and, because communications were not as effective as nowadays, Celtic's manager decided to take a hand in the proceedings. He drove to the outskirts of Glasgow and stood at the side of the M80 – at no little danger to himself – trying to flag down buses to tell the supporters that the match had been called off at short notice. He was not wholly successful in turning back the cavalcade of buses heading towards Dundee. Some had driven on, ignoring the burly figure by the side of the road or, as one acquaintance who travelled on such a bus insists, saying things like 'There's a daftie oot there tryin' tae stoap oor bus. Bugger looks a bit like Jock Stein, tae.'

Dunfermline, now relegation candidates, came to Celtic Park on 19 February and made a great fight of it before going down to a Lou Macari goal in 63 minutes. Unfortunately, at the end of the season, they also went down to the Second Division.

Celtic started March with a 2–0 win over Ayr United at Parkhead through two second-half goals from Deans – a fine preparation for their trip to Hungary in the European Cup. Uijpest Dozsa were considered a formidable side in the tradition of Hungarian teams and Celtic gave one of their better performances on the Continent to eke out a 2–1 win. The winning goal came from Macari near the end: Dalglish swung over a cross that found Macari with his back to goal but the striker chested the ball down, swivelled on the spot, and scored with a lightning-fast shot celebrated hugely by the tea-time TV audience back in Scotland. Jock Stein was delighted with the result and the performance which produced it; he described it as Celtic's best 'considering the youthfulness of the team'.

The next game would go far to settle the destination of the league flag as Celtic were due to visit Pittodrie on the Saturday. Aberdeen had started to slip behind in the league, especially after the shock transfer of Martin Buchan, and they had to win in order to have any chance of catching Celtic. Pittodrie was jammed that 11 March with a crowd of 33,000, who welcomed Celtic on to the pitch with great applause after the victory in Hungary. It was good to see the Aberdeen season-ticket-holders in the Centre Stand on their feet to acknowledge their Glasgow visitors.

The newspapers described the fixture as 'a great contest', but that appears an exaggeration. Celtic are seldom at their best when they decide that a draw will be sufficient. The second half was well advanced before any goal came, and it was Bobby Lennox who scored after a spell of sustained pressure from Celtic. Although 17 minutes remained to be played, several gaps appeared among the Aberdeen supporters as some of them headed home; their team refused to give up, however, and Joe Harper scored an equaliser with ten minutes left. Those ten minutes seemed to stretch for ever but Celtic held out for the draw.

Travelling back to Glasgow the Celtic legions enthused about their young side, poised, it seemed, on the very brink of greatness. Danny McGrain had been restored to the team at right-back for the European Cup-tie and had played at Pittodrie. His performances had been outstanding and he had completely closed down the dangerous left-wing partnership of Willoughby and Graham. With McGrain filling in at right-back, David Hay took over in midfield and he was now a complete footballer: tough and wiry enough to win the ball but skilful enough to distribute it to great effect. Kenny Dalglish and Lou Macari continued to fulfil all the expectations roused by their earlier appearances; they were an exciting pair of youngsters. But the greatest bonus was the emergence of George Connelly as a world-class player.

Connelly had first come to prominence at half-time in a European Cup-Winners' tie at Celtic Park back in January 1966 when he gave a demonstration of 'keepie-uppie' – a display that awed the large crowd.[4] The boy seemed so composed and unflustered as he showed off his skills with an air of unconcern. He was versatile but, in 1971–72, he was playing alongside Billy McNeill in the heart of Celtic's defence. His strength in the tackle, his intelligent reading of the play and anticipation, his ball-control and superb passing, even from dangerous positions, all earned him the accolade of the 'Scottish Beckenbauer'. He seemed the perfect all-round player: a solid, dependable defender and a highly creative midfielder.

Goalkeeping still remained a problem for Jock Stein: Evan Williams, blamed for losing the League Cup final, had been dropped, but regained his place in late January when Denis Connaghan fell back into the reserves. Gordon Marshall, signed on a free transfer from Hibernian in the previous close season, was transferred to Aberdeen in January for a modest fee. John Fallon, at Celtic Park since 1959, was transferred to Motherwell at the end of February, and on 28 March Lief Nielsen, ex-Morton keeper, would be signed on 'as cover' for the regular goalkeepers.

On 25 March, after disposing of Uijpest Dozsa in the European Cup with a hard-earned 1–1 draw at Celtic Park and eliminating Hearts from the Scottish Cup at Tynecastle in a replay, Celtic visited Falkirk to continue the quest for the seventh league flag. It was a close struggle, as so often happens on the Bairns' cramped pitch, but young Vic Davidson, regularly touted as the best prospect on Celtic's books, scrambled in the only goal in the 86th minute. For the fifth successive league match, Celtic's goals came in the second half.

However, the match at Brockville was marred for Celtic by a serious injury to Danny McGrain who collided with Doug Somner, incidentally a friend of McGrain's; the young Celtic full-back carried on for a while but was unable to continue after the interval. The immediate diagnosis was a mild concussion but, after a precautionary visit to the hospital, the injury was reassessed as a fracture of the skull. It was the first of several serious health problem for Danny McGrain.

Vic Davidson halted the trend of second-half goals by scoring almost straight from the kick-off in the next home game, against Partick Thistle on 1 April, following that up with a second on the 14th-minute mark. After Jimmy Johnstone added the third goal in 25 minutes, Celtic visibly eased up and were content to play out time to win by 3–1. A week later Vic Davidson was once more among the goalscorers at Kilmarnock in a highly competent 3–1 win.

Victor Davidson was perhaps an unlucky player, despite a decent career in the game with Celtic, Motherwell and Blackpool. At one time, Jock Stein was toying with the idea of promoting all three of his 'Quality Street' forwards (Dalglish, Davidson and Macari) into the first team at the same time. But young players develop at different rates, and Macari and Dalglish had progressed a shade more quickly, especially in terms of confidence, and Davidson was considered to be a bit slow on the turn. And to put the pressure on three youngsters to get goals against resolute, experienced defenders might have been unfair. Once promoted to the team, however, Vic Davidson scored four vital goals for Celtic on three successive Saturdays in the spring of 1972.

Events in the European theatre were unfolding in an exciting manner – so much so that the league matches were being overlooked by the newspapers. In the European Cup semi-final Celtic renewed their rivalry with Internazionale of Milan at the San Siro on 5 April and managed a praiseworthy draw (0–0) despite being put under pressure in the second half and being forced to bring on the relatively inexperienced Pat McCluskey as a substitute for Jim Brogan.

On the Saturday before the return leg at Celtic Park, the champions clinched the title at Bayview Park, the home of East Fife. It was a quiet occasion without the slightest hint of triumphalism. In fact, it marked the routine end to another Scottish League season . . . and there were still four fixtures left! Still, it was a historic occasion, played out on a ground rich in the atmosphere of a bygone age in football: redolent of a brown leather ball and brown reinforced boots, of matches contested by part-time players who might well have worked a shift down the pit that morning and whose legs might still bear traces of coal. But that was the past; on this 15 April, Celtic won comfortably by 3–0 before an unsurprised crowd of 12,086.

The one bitter disappointment of the season – apart from the total shock of that League Cup final – was the 'defeat' at Celtic Park by Inter Milan. Everybody knew that the Italians would defend in depth after the 0–0 draw in the San Siro. Everybody knew that the danger lay in their sudden breaks from defence. Everybody knew that this tie might go to extra-time, followed by penalty-kicks. And everybody was right. The home side had dictated the play, trying to stretch that famed defence with Bobby Murdoch plying his forwards. Celtic's defenders concentrated ferociously throughout and Inter never looked menacing. One substitution was made, Dixie Deans on for Kenny Dalglish, in an attempt to produce a different dimension to the attack. And suddenly it was the moment for penalty-kicks. All week Celtic had prepared for this nerve-wracking ordeal . . . and all week their most consistent scorer from the spot had been Dixie Deans.

This time, to anguished groans and shocked silence, Dixie drove the ball over the crossbar and the crowd – all 75,000 of them – knew then that Inter Milan would go through. Deans was more than upset about it, extrovert as he was, but Jock Stein reassured him and reminded the supporters that football was a team game and that he, the manager, had selected which players would take the penalty-kicks. At the next game, against Motherwell, Dixie Deans – the one-time Rangers supporter – was reminded of how forgiving a Celtic crowd can be. He was welcomed on to the pitch, and, when their side were awarded a penalty-kick in 33 minutes, they clamoured for Deans to take it but the striker declined with embarrassed grins.

A few weeks later Deans' public redemption was complete as he atoned for that missed kick by scoring three times in the final of the Scottish Cup against Hibernian – a highly entertaining and competitive match despite the 6–1 scoreline – to bring down the curtain on yet another successful season. Each of his goals was vastly different, proving his versatility as a striker. The first came in 23 minutes when he signalled for Murdoch to hoist a free-kick in his direction and he powered home a perfectly flighted ball from the midfielder, outjumping the taller Hibernian defenders to do so. Then, in 54 minutes, he latched on to a misdirected clearance on the left inside the penalty area, got away from the goalkeeper, evaded Brownlie's challenge and rounded the goalkeeper in the confined space before steadying himself to shoot into the net – the whole manoeuvre taking an eternity to complete – before celebrating with a somersault on the Hampden turf. And in 74 minutes he gathered a neat pass from Callaghan and advanced on the despairing Herriot before shooting the ball past him. It was the first hat-trick in a Scottish Cup final since Jimmy Quinn's back in 1904, and was a spectacular finale to the season as most of the 106,102 inside Hampden Park celebrated noisily in the May sunshine.

Notes

1. When he was Celtic's coach, Fallon may have been handicapped by that accent. One famous ex-Celt told the authors that at half-time at Broomfield Park in the early 1960s Fallon kept advising his goalkeeper to 'toe the ball out!'. The keeper, genuinely puzzled, reminded his coach that he always used his instep when kicking the ball. Fallon shook his head in exasperation, picked up a ball, and threw it across the dressing-room: 'No! Toe it out like that!'
2. Surprisingly, all of these strikers were relatively short men, although all were capable in the air. Towards the end of his time at Celtic Park, the manager purchased taller players such as Tom McAdam, and considered Allan Gordon of Hibernian.

3. In 13 competitive matches against Hibernian, Dixie Deans scored 18 goals, including three hat-tricks.

4. One letter-writer to the *Celtic View* indicated that Connelly had kept up the ball 654 times without allowing it to touch the ground, a remarkable feat of ball-control (and counting).

Chapter 8

Intimations of Mortality

There is a certain truth to the assertion that the Scottish League is won over the Christmas/New Year holiday. For one thing, that is when derby matches are played, and the boost to morale given by a win over local and traditional rivals can act like a surge of adrenaline. Quite often, too, an extra fixture is crammed into that period, and only the better-organised or fitter teams benefit from the schedule. Normally, with Jock Stein as manager, Celtic supporters looked forward to the turn of the year. But not this time . . .

A flu epidemic was sweeping Glasgow and Celtic were hit particularly hard. Almost every member of the squad was affected by the virus, and those who had escaped it were told to stay away from the ground. The Scottish League co-operated with the club by agreeing to postpone the fixtures with Morton and Kilmarnock, but the key match, against Rangers at Ibrox, would be going ahead on 6 January 1973.

One person who missed that match was Jock Stein . . . but he was not another victim of the flu. Feeling unwell, he had checked himself into the Victoria Infirmary, a few hundred yards from Hampden Park. There, he was admitted immediately to the Coronary Unit and, within a few hours, everybody was aware that Stein had suffered – in layman's terms – a heart attack. His condition was spoken about in hushed whispers except by those gossip-mongers who seemed to relish telling others that 'he would never recover'.

There was ample reason for concern about the health of the Big Man. He had recently passed his 50th birthday and, although he did not smoke and took only the occasional glass of wine, he was overweight. The problem was complicated by the stressful lifestyle adopted by Celtic's manager and the cumulative strain was beginning to tell, as

John Rafferty, the noted journalist, saw very clearly: 'Stein worked extraordinary hours for the club. He never did sleep well . . . in midweek when Celtic were not playing he would motor down [to Manchester, Liverpool or Leeds] after the afternoon's work was done at Celtic Park, talk a bit, watch the football, then motor back immediately afterwards and still be the first man at Celtic Park in the morning.'

Jock Stein insisted that he listen to the Rangers-Celtic match at Ibrox on his bedside radio and what he heard could not have helped his recovery. Celtic, despite including in their line-up some players who were still under the weather, had fought back to level the match at 1–1 and seemed to have done enough to merit a draw . . . but, in the last minute of play, a cross from Young was too high for the injured David Hay to reach and Alfie Conn rose unchallenged to head the winning goal.

Stein was privy to some other matters that were affecting his club. Lou Macari wanted a transfer – or vastly improved terms. Macari was a new type of player for the manager to deal with: talented, ambitious and eager for success, the young forward had a keen sense of his own worth, and was assertive in demanding his rights. A couple of seasons earlier, just before the vital league fixture at Pittodrie, he had demanded to be placed on the transfer list. His reasoning now in 1973, as in the previous transfer request, was simple and logical: he scored more goals than some of his colleagues but their salary was higher than his. This time he had another weapon in his negotiating armoury: Manchester United were more than interested in his signature, Tommy Docherty, the ex-Scotland manager, drooling over Macari's sharpness.

With a show of reluctance, the club agreed to the transfer and Lou Macari went to Old Trafford on 18 January for a record fee of £200,000. Apparently, Stein was most irritated at the move but not just because he was losing a valued player; the manager had already been talking to Liverpool about Macari and the Anfield side had submitted a counter-offer . . . but the player insisted upon going to Manchester and Stein lost some face on Merseyside.

With some of the flair and enthusiasm missing from the play in recent weeks, the supporters were growing anxious about their side's ability to retain the championship: Rangers had won at Ibrox, Hibernian had taken a point at Parkhead on 23 December in a 1–1 draw, and in two recent away games against Falkirk (3–2) and Arbroath (2–1), Celtic had struggled before grinding out victories. It was clear that all was not well in Paradise . . .

The punters in the pubs along the Gallowgate were in an

argumentative frame of mind: head-shaking about Stein's heart attack; McNeill had lost half a step, and might well be finished; Dalglish was a 'one-season wonder'; Deans was 'too fat'; Jimmy Johnstone had 'lost it'; all of the team lacked Celtic spirit and were earning far too much money. 'If that Macari steyed wi' me in a single end in Bridgeton, he'd k.10w whit the hell he was talkin' aboot' was the general tenor of the comments.

The season had started off slowly back in August with a new variant on the sectional play in the League Cup. The changes indicated clearly that the League Cup, first introduced after the Second World War, was a competition in decline. The organisers now felt that the sections should be 'seeded' with two qualifiers from each, and thus Celtic found themselves struggling to keep awake in fixtures against Stirling Albion, East Fife and Arbroath. Supporters, although deprived of football all summer, were not interested and attendances at Celtic's home games were low, alarmingly so: 15,000 to see East Fife, 17,000 for the Stirling Albion visit, and only 4,962 for Arbroath (although, in fairness, this last fixture was played at Hampden Park).

It is sad to report that in the latter stages of Celtic's virtual monopoly of the football honours in Scotland, attendances started to drop – even at Celtic Park. During the 1970–71 season, for example, Scottish football crowds were down by 143,000 paying customers, Celtic's drop alone was 47,000! It was usually possible to drive into the carpark in front of the main stand at Celtic Park on match days at half past two and still find a vacant spot. At times, the attendance dipped below the 20,000 mark – and that had been the norm a decade earlier with a team that was going nowhere. Celtic's success was making it difficult for provincial sides to attract spectators at their own grounds: with the league championship destined for Celtic Park, and the home-town team mere fodder for the champions, why bother going to the match?

Another problem lay in a widespread increase in football hooliganism – which perhaps should have been designated the 'English disease'. The virus had now spread to Scotland and caused malaise throughout the sport. There was a bizarre incident on the opening day of the new season when Celtic went to Stirling. Jock Stein charged into a large crowd of Celtic supporters at half-time to deliver a piece of his mind to those who had been extolling the virtues of the IRA throughout a dull first half. According to one bystander, Stein's language was persuasive: vehement in tone and prolonged in length. The manager was praised in the newspapers for his efforts, but it had been a risky moment.

In 1971 Celtic had started work on a massive restructuring of the main grandstand and the on-going work necessitated switching several fixtures to Hampden Park at the start of the 1972–73 season in an arrangement with Queen's Park, the owners. Thus, because the Amateurs were playing there in the afternoon, Celtic's opening league fixture, against Kilmarnock on 2 September, kicked off at seven in the evening before a disappointing attendance of 11,651. Celtic won very comfortably by 6–2 in a soulless atmosphere in a stadium which could hold a crowd of more than ten times that figure. For the next home fixture, against Rangers, the kick-off was switched to noon in an attempt to combat any likely outbreaks of hooliganism. In those days, licensed premises opened at eleven in the morning and it was more difficult (but not impossible) to get intoxicated before the start of the match.

This Old Firm clash turned out to be one of the strangest in the fixture's colourful history. The crowd of 50,416 saw the match virtually decided after only two minutes, when Dalglish scored the opening goal; after 17 minutes, Jimmy Johnstone – who was having 'one of those days' – added another. There was scarcely a sound from the Rangers end and, after Macari scored a third goal only four minutes into the second half, many Rangers supporters started to leave. Their decision was not based entirely on the scoreline (which put the game out of their reach) but also from the indications on the pitch that this Celtic team were every bit as capable as the 1957 side in running up a 7–1 score or worse. Jimmy Johnstone could not be stopped, no matter which methods were used. Dalglish was at the top of his form, intelligent as a passer and deadly as a finisher, and Connelly was majestic in Celtic's unemployed defence, livening up the proceedings with a patented display of 'keepie-uppie' in the middle of an Old Firm clash.

Rangers scored in the last minute of play, initiating some bizarre scenes. John Greig had netted, after a fine run by Smith: very few of his colleagues had any enthusiasm left even to congratulate him; the Rangers following had largely disappeared and the Celtic supporters behind the goal decided to give Rangers' captain a cheer. That sarcastic applause indicated the vast gulf in quality separating the two sides.

Despite their total domination of Rangers, Celtic were singularly unimpressive against more lowly opposition. In the European Cup in the home leg they had defeated Rosenberg of Norway by only 2–1 – and in those days Norwegian sides posed as much threat in football as their entries would in the EuroVision Song contest. At Stranraer, Celtic had edged the locals by 2–1 in the League Cup, giving a most undistinguished performance. And at Dundee in the league they went down to a 2–0 defeat on 23 September. Dundee were chafing under the maladministration of a board of directors whose policy seemed to be to sell their best players without giving them time to make a real impact on the Scottish scene. On this particular occasion the Dens Parkers scored twice within the first 13 minutes, and a jaded-looking Celtic could never get back into the game.

At last, on 30 September, Celtic were back at Parkhead for a league match and the annual unfurling of the championship flag. Against a plucky Ayr United, Dixie Deans put Celtic ahead after 15 minutes but after that the form of the home side dropped and dropped. In the end they were fortunate to escape with the points, Ayr United's Johnny Doyle (reputed to be Celtic-daft) coming close to getting a deserved equaliser. The boos of the home crowd of 25,000 reverberating around Parkhead made a strange homecoming for a team which had just won seven championships in a row. Worse was to follow in the next match or two: Airdrie, playing their traditional robust game, held them to a 1–1 draw at Celtic Park, and on the following Wednesday, Dundee beat Celtic again, this time in the first leg of the League Cup quarter-finals. That result should have sent alarm-bells resounding through Celtic Park. An ordinary team might be able to beat Celtic, taking them a bit by surprise, but to do so twice within a period of three weeks was unthinkable.

In Europe, Celtic had struggled against Rosenberg although in the end they had beaten them home and away. As he had done throughout the two previous seasons, Jock Stein continued to make changes from week to week but, although the side was winning, it was becoming clear to everybody that something was wrong.

It may well have been that a plateau had been reached in the simultaneous development of several young players; it may have been that some of the veterans could no longer 'carry' other players having an off-day. Whatever the reason, there had been a sea-change in Celtic's attitude.

However, with Stein in charge, it was dangerous to write the team off prematurely, as some critics were starting to do. At Firhill on 14 October an evenly contested first half was entering its last minute when Celtic scored through defender David Hay. The crowd of 25,699, previously apprehensive, relaxed, but only a little. In the second half Celtic, for the first time in weeks, turned up their game; Deans, Lennox (restored to the side for his enthusiasm and strong running) and Dalglish all scored to give a resounding victory. The champions were back, it seemed – a feeling provisionally confirmed with a 3–0 win over East Fife a week later.

For the second successive week Celtic had won without conceding a goal, but in each case it had taken until the last minute of the first half to score – and against moderate opposition. They had struggled desperately to outwit the offside trap set by East Fife in Glasgow and had shown little imagination in their efforts throughout a lacklustre first half. Celtic would go on to win nine successive games in the championship, starting with the 4–0 win at Firhill, but an edge had gone from their play and it showed in some of the results: a 3–2 win at Pittodrie (after going two goals up in the first 15 minutes); a 4–2 win over Hearts at Celtic Park (after being behind twice in the match); another 3–2 win at Brockville against struggling Falkirk; and a 2–1 victory at Arbroath (achieved only through Hood's goal in 86 minutes). Consistent, but not sparkling.

Of course, there were a couple of excellent performances to remind the fans of the excitement of the previous season. At Motherwell on 11 November, immediately after returning from a disastrous trip to Eastern Europe, Celtic produced an impressive and determined display to rout the home side by 5–0, and on 2 December at Boghead, they inflicted considerable damage on Dumbarton to win by 6–1. Their most professional (in the best sense of the word) performance came against Dundee United, now managed by Jim McLean and in second place in the table, when the Taysiders visited Celtic Park on 4 November. Level 1–1 at half-time, Celtic dominated the second half and swept aside the challenge of a fine side to win by 3–1 before 32,000 spectators.

The cracks were showing on other fronts, and especially in Europe. Two seasons before, Celtic had swept aside the 'challenge' of such as Kokkola (Finland) by 14–0, Waterford (Eire) by 9–2; last season, BK 1903 Copenhagen (Denmark) by 4–2, Sliema Wanderers (Malta) by 7–1; and in 1972–73 had stuttered against Rosenberg (Norway) before winning by 5–2. The decline was shown most vividly in their displays against Uijpest Dozsa: in the previous season Celtic had surprisingly won by 2–1 in Hungary, giving an excellent display in the process, following it up by fighting back at Celtic Park to gain a well-deserved draw and advance into the semi-finals. In 1972–73, the two teams were drawn together again. The first leg was at Celtic Park and the home side won by 2–1 after falling behind in 20 minutes; Celtic dominated that match territorially but found it difficult to break down the visitors' defence. For the return leg it was clear that only an excellent performance would see Celtic through. They had opted for a semi-defensive battle but their plans were in tatters after only 22 minutes with the Hungarians three goals up. They had had no answer to the swift, probing raids of the Uijpest Dozsa forwards nor had they flexibility to change tactics during the match.

The newspapers made much of the result but, perhaps out of fear of Jock Stein, they restricted themselves to discussing what was wrong with the Scottish game in general. The remedies ranged from the farcical to the serious: the fashionable long hair sported by the players slowed down their speed, for example. More reasonable suggestions included the amalgamation of smaller, struggling clubs, the establishing of a leaner, more competitive league structure, and the hardy perennial of a British League.

In hindsight, one thing that Celtic lacked in the autumn of 1972 was a real challenge from Rangers – and perhaps what the Ibrox club lacked in Europe during the early 1990s was a similar challenge from Celtic. Having things too easy at home is not the ideal preparation mentally, emotionally or physically for contests with top European sides.

The League Cup was providing its annual share of nailbiting moments as well: back on 4 October Stranraer, down 2–1 from the first leg, had actually levelled the aggregate score by netting in the sixth minute at Celtic Park before succumbing to their opponents' greater power and skill. Dundee won the first leg of the quarter-final at Dens Park by 1–0, and went down by only 3–2 after extra-time at Celtic Park, thus forcing a play-off at Hampden on 20 November when, for the first time in the series, Celtic played convincingly to win by 4–1. In the semi-final, on 27 November, again at Hampden Park, Celtic had to fight tooth and claw to scrape past Aberdeen by 3–2.

On 9 December 1972, however, Celtic fell to Hibernian by 2–1 in the League Cup final and the Edinburgh side thoroughly deserved their triumph, the first in a major competition for 20 years. But some supporters remembered that only last May, Celtic had defeated Hibs by 6–1 in the Scottish Cup final.

The mood of the soaking-wet fans leaving Hampden that evening was as chilly as the weather: melancholy and a curious, ill-defined feeling that something was amiss. It was unlike Celtic to lose three cup finals in a row, as they had done in the League Cup: Rangers (1–0 in 1970), Thistle (4–1 in 1971) and now Hibernian. The memory of such recent setbacks should have acted as a spur. It was clear that Hibernian had dominated the midfield and that, try as they might, Celtic were unable to regain the initiative in that vital area.

The problem was that they had been missing Bobby Murdoch, out with injury since 21 October when he had limped off in the first half against East Fife. Murdoch had been fighting injury for some time and was finding it increasingly difficult to recover quickly. His chronic ankle problem prevented him from training as hard as he would have wished and, for a player cursed with weight problems, this was potentially disastrous.[1] In the previous season, Stein had reportedly called him into the office and ordered him to shed the excess pounds – or else. Murdoch went back to the health farm at Tring took up the strict diet again and worked and worked and worked. The results had been there for all to see on 6 May 1972, the day of the Scottish Cup final; Dixie Deans may have scored three goals but the difference between Celtic and Hibernian was Bobby Murdoch's performance. His absence was the difference between a sparkling Celtic and a flat Celtic.

Between the League Cup final and the turn of the year, the champions were struggling: the narrow win at Arbroath (2–1) was followed by a 1–1 draw at home to Hibernian on 23 December. Then came the flu epidemic . . . and Jock Stein's heart attack . . . and Lou Macari's request for a transfer . . . and a last-minute defeat by Rangers at Ibrox on 6 January.

The recovery was not immediate, nor was it uncomplicated. The match against Dundee at Celtic Park on 13 January was a case in point. The supporters, 27,000 of them on a raw day, were nervous: with Stein convalescing, nobody at Parkhead had the ability or presence to knock the revitalised Rangers off the back pages, and the newspapers had eaten up the Ibrox club's recovery, making a three-course meal out of the win on 6 January and perhaps helping themselves to a double dessert. The mood of depression inside the ground was lifted momentarily when Stein appeared in the directors' box to watch the game and was welcomed vociferously by the Parkhead crowd.

The match itself was evenly balanced and Dundee, who had beaten Celtic in two of four starts that season, took the game to their opponents. At half-time the score was 1–1, Jimmy Johnstone for Celtic in 16 minutes and Doug Houston equalising with a well-worked goal in 29; both teams had chances in the second half before Kenny Dalglish scored in 81 minutes. It was a victory – and two points – ground out by determination and effort, and in retrospect this result meant a great deal as another defeat at that stage would certainly have dented the team's morale.

The problems continued though, despite the reappearance of Murdoch, and the visits to Somerset Park and Broomfield late in January were fraught. The weather at Ayr was menacing and snow fell throughout. Fortunately, the match was in no great danger – but Celtic were. Ayr United scored first in only ten minutes, and Celtic took until the 35th minute to equalise through Dixie Deans. The second half was tense as Celtic pressed. At last, with only 12 minutes left and with visibility becoming a problem because of the heavy snow, Kenny Dalglish put Celtic in front and added an insurance goal five minutes from the end. At Broomfield a week later the pitch would not have passed the inspection of some referees but the game was somehow permitted to start – and, having started, was allowed to finish. Deans scored first in 52 minutes, but Airdrie equalised soon after. As those with transistor radios informed their neighbours that Rangers were leading by 2–1 against Morton, McCann shot past Celtic's goalkeeper for a very late winner. Airdrie, doomed to relegation, had avoided defeat in both fixtures with the Glasgow side and had taken three out of four points from the champions.

It had been a sad début for the new goalkeeper, Alistair Hunter, signed in midweek from Kilmarnock, as he looked at fault for the goal in the 89th minute. Bobby Murdoch was disappointed too, having missed a penalty-kick.

On 7 February Celtic went to Kilmarnock to play one of the fixtures postponed from the flu epidemic. Celtic played well and were leading comfortably by 4–0 as the match entered the closing stages. In the second-last minute Celtic were awarded a penalty and Dalglish stepped up to take it. It should have been a simple conversion but this might not be any ordinary goal.

The Celtic View had entered the contentious area of football statistics and had decided – in a rather cavalier manner – that Celtic's 5,000th league goal had been scored by Frank Brogan and that at some point in 1972–73 another Celt would score the 6,000th goal. Most statisticians would agree that their methods and arithmetic were faulty but the pressure was on Kenny Dalglish and he was aware of the situation. Usually a cool customer in front of goal, Dalglish missed the unique opportunity to add to his place in Celtic's history.

A week later, Partick Thistle came to Celtic Park and their resolve may have been hardened by the sight of the press photographers waiting for the toss of the coin before departing *en masse* to behind the goal Celtic were attacking. The whole '6,000th goal' thing was meaningless and distracting as Celtic played abysmally; hollow laughter rang out when Thistle opened the scoring in front of one isolated photographer. In the second half Celtic added desperation to their attacks as Thistle refused to become footnotes to history by giving up that goal.

At last, Celtic broke through and, for what it was worth, the scorer was Bobby Murdoch with a scrappy toe-poke from close range. Murdoch would collect the china tea-set after the game and be assured of his niche in history (as if he were not already part of it), but he was far from happy at the loss of another point in the championship. In fact, the supporters had their priorities absolutely correct: the goal was greeted with celebration, generated most of all by relief, and the final whistle with a storm of boos and catcalls. Their mood was not improved with the news that Rangers, by all accounts playing as badly as Celtic, had defeated Motherwell by 2–1 at Ibrox to reduce the gap.

Then followed a truly remarkable encounter at Methil. Celtic and East Fife played to a 2–2 draw, but Celtic should have won the game by the distance from Fife to Glasgow and back again. On that 17 February most of the matches in Scotland had been called off because of frost or snow but Bayview Park has a good record of being playable against the odds. So, 11,557 spectators crammed into the ground to watch a fast and furious match. A goal by Deans – most welcome as he had looked out of sorts against Thistle – gave Celtic the lead at half-time but, throughout the second half, the word 'penalty' was on everybody's lips.

First of all, East Fife were given one and McPhee equalised, a goal followed almost immediately by Celtic's being awarded a penalty-kick. Bobby Murdoch was designated to take it but he never looked comfortable as he lumbered forward, ballooning the ball over the crossbar. However, even as the groans of the Celtic supporters were dying down, it could be seen that the referee was signalling for the kick to be retaken as an East Fife player had encroached. Murdoch wanted nothing to do with it this time and the ball was handed to Harry Hood, a man who had scored from the spot in a Scottish Cup final replay against Rangers. Hood took his time but his shot lacked pace and Ernie McGarr dived to make the save.

With East Fife leading by 2–1 later on, the drama was not over yet. Celtic were awarded yet another penalty-kick and Kenny Dalglish was designated to take it. Again Dalglish placed the ball very deliberately, and took his time before starting his run-up. The supporters sensed that he was going to miss, such was the almost visible lack of confidence shown by the players . . . and he did, to complete a miserable hat-trick of three penalties missed by three players in one match. Fortunately, as the spectators were starting for the exits, Dixie Deans grabbed a very late equaliser but the drama was not quite over. Harry Hood was sent tumbling inside the box and there were cries for a penalty – but a humane referee had seen enough and turned down the claim (as he did two others, one for each team, in the injury-time added on).

Five penalty-kicks missed in succession; Stein was not amused. Nor was he happy about the fact that Rangers, unbeaten since 2 December 1972, were slowly overhauling Celtic at the top of the table. By defeating Arbroath comprehensively at Ibrox on the Monday night, Rangers had moved three points in front (but had played two games more). Judging by the way Celtic were playing, there could be no guarantee that those points would be picked up. In fact, at that stage in the championship, Jock Stein was conceding the title to Rangers privately though in public he remained as confident as ever.

Celtic's next match was important – a Scottish Cup tie at Fir Park on 24 February. The team gave a most impressive performance, coasting to a lead of four goals by the interval, but a critical miss by Millar of Motherwell from the penalty spot had affected the outcome. When Celtic had been only one goal in front, Millar's shot was saved by Hunter diving to his right at full stretch. It was a key save by the new keeper which did much to restore confidence in Celtic's rearguard.

This confidence proved vital in the latter stages of the season. Celtic had too many experienced hands on board to throw away a championship; Rangers – or anybody else – would have to wrest it from them. The manager, too, had a vast reservoir of experience over his competitors, and Stein was not the man to risk things foolishly in the crunch games.

St Johnstone visited Parkhead on 28 February, and left Glasgow soundly trounced by 4–0 with two late goals to rub in the message. Aberdeen came to Celtic Park a few days later and put up a stronger resistance before losing to two second-half goals from Bobby Lennox; the first one came from a penalty-kick in 62 minutes and it was particularly nerve-wracking because Lennox was a player who preferred to place the ball rather than blast it. Against Morton on 6 March a relative newcomer to the side, Paul Wilson, scored Celtic's only goal in 40 minutes to win a tense match and the team were grateful to Hunter in goal for a steady display.

Wilson was half-Indian and some opponents, trying to put him off his game, taunted him about his swarthy complexion. He also suffered racial abuse from some supporters. Stein was very protective towards the player, but perhaps had shielded him too much as, by the time he reached the age of 23, he had made fewer than ten appearances for the club despite his promise. Paul Wilson was an exceptional talent, even from a young age. He was a player for St Ninian's High School in his mid-teens when Sean Fallon called to sign him up for Celtic. The club's assistant manager was just leaving the Wilsons' house when Bobby

Calder, the veteran Aberdeen scout who had 'poached' so many West Coast youngsters for the Dons, came walking up the path. As was his custom on these occasions, Calder was carrying a box of chocolates and a bouquet of flowers for the player's mother, but when Sean told him he was too late, the Aberdeen representative took the news gracefully and handed Fallon the gifts, telling him to give them to his wife.

At Tannadice on 10 March, Celtic dropped a valuable point in a 2–2 draw. More worrying was the fact that Rangers had defeated Dundee by 3–1 at Ibrox, meaning that Celtic's lead at the top rested only on the flimsy basis of a better goal-average. A healthy lead at New Year had been whittled down. The two Glasgow giants had each garnered 43 points from 27 matches and each had seven left to play. Neither was involved in Europe but both were in the quarter-finals of the Scottish Cup. The season was building towards a grand finale . . .

The chase for the league title was suspended on St Patrick's Day to make way for the Scottish Cup: Rangers disposed of Airdrie while Celtic struggled against Aberdeen at Parkhead and earned a 0–0 draw despite having Jimmy Johnstone ordered off. To be fair to Johnstone, he seemed to be the victim of a miscarriage of justice by the referee – a view apparently shared by the SFA, who declined to suspend the player despite his disciplinary record. In the following midweek Celtic had to travel to Pittodrie, a perilous ground for visitors, and managed a 1–0 win in the replay through a magnificent header by Billy McNeill in 86 minutes. However, Rangers had taken full advantage of the schedule by defeating Airdrie 6–2 in the league at Broomfield the previous night.

Tension was mounting as Celtic went to yet another dangerous ground on 24 March, Tynecastle. There they put on a highly professional display – with the emphasis on determination and grit – to win by 2–0, a goal in each half settling things. Rangers kept pace by beating Hibernian 1–0 in an agonisingly close encounter at Ibrox, virtually eliminating the Edinburgh men from the title race at this point. On 31 March both sides won again: Celtic sweeping Falkirk aside by 4–0 at a rain-soaked Parkhead and Rangers scraping through at Boghead by 2–1 against an unlucky Dumbarton. The situation could not be much tighter: Rangers had played 30 games and had 49 points while Celtic had played 29 and had 47 points. Celtic had improved their advantage in goal average, and that was a considerable comfort.

The Old Firm avoided each other in the draw for the semi-finals of the Scottish Cup; it was to be Rangers against Ayr United and Celtic against Dundee, with the ties being played at Hampden on 4 and 7 April respectively. The staggering of the semi-finals, designed to give each potential finalist an opportunity to play at Hampden, added yet another element of psychological warfare to the league campaign.

Celtic decided to play the league fixture against Motherwell on the Tuesday night, one day before Rangers' semi-final – and won 2–0 at Parkhead. On the Saturday, when Celtic were held to a 0–0 draw in a most boring semi-final, Rangers went through to Edinburgh and managed a narrow, hard-fought 1–0 win over Hearts. The replay in the Scottish Cup complicated Celtic's bid to retain the league title, and Dundee took matters into extra-time at Hampden on 11 April before eventually surrendering by 3–0.

April 14th promised to be another stressful day. There was no margin for error; a dropped point, even in a difficult away game, would spell disaster. Celtic travelled to Perth to face St Johnstone, always 'bonny fechters' at home; Rangers, meanwhile, 'entertained' Dundee United at Ibrox. Celtic rose to the occasion, as they had done at Tynecastle, and two of the older hands, Billy McNeill and Jimmy Johnstone, scored; Kenny Dalglish added a third before the Saints pulled one back. Once more, the tinny, scratchy sound of transistor radios brought bad news: Rangers, although outplayed by Dundee United, had scraped through yet again. In midweek, however, Celtic caught up on their rivals in both fixtures and points by hammering Dumbarton 5–0, Dixie Deans leading the way with three goals. That was a pleasant night: the team had played well and their substantial edge in goal average virtually meant another point advantage.

Both sides had two matches left, a difficult away fixture and an easy home match. The schedule potentially favoured Celtic as Rangers had to visit Aberdeen first while the champions' difficult match was the following week, on the last day of the season (by which time the game might be irrelevant).

A nervous Celtic struggled a bit against Arbroath but, after Harry Hood (the scorer of so many important goals) opened the account shortly after half-time, the home side pulled away to win by 4–0. Everywhere at Celtic Park among the crowd of 28,000, people were clustered around their radios – there was even one in the Celtic dugout – and willing Aberdeen on against Rangers. The match at Pittodrie was closely contested to the very end and finished up as a 2–2 draw. In recent seasons Rangers had hampered Aberdeen's bids for the championship by drawing at Pittodrie; this time Aberdeen returned the compliment.

Things had swung in Celtic's direction: a draw at Easter Road on the last day of the campaign (28 April) would be enough to retain the championship regardless of what happened at Ibrox where Rangers were playing East Fife. It would have been dangerous to play exclusively for a draw against Hibs, in third place in the league, the current League Cup winners, and a formidable side at home. Celtic would have to take the initiative.

Rain had given way to bright sunshine by mid-afternoon and those who subscribe to the belief that Celtic play their best in sunshine had ample proof to back up their theory. Dixie Deans scored in 22 minutes. Hibernian threatened briefly at the start of the second half but Celtic always appeared capable of moving up a gear. Kenny Dalglish settled the game – and the championship – with a second goal in 71 minutes before Deans rounded off a good afternoon's work with a third.

The referee signalled time up and unleashed the annual celebration. But this eighth such orgy contained more than a hint of relief. Rangers had pressed hard and credit has to be given to a team unbeaten since 2 December – and some was grudgingly admitted in the hostelries of Leith Walk and Rose Street and in the pubs of the Gallowgate later that night.

It had been a triumph for Celtic against all the odds in a most difficult season.

However satisfying the contemplation of another league flag flying at Celtic Park, there had been bitter disappointment in recent cup competitions . . . and once more the Old Firm were to meet in the Scottish Cup final on 5 May 1973.

In the frenzy of the first half Celtic played some very composed football, but several times when trying to build things from the back their defenders risked interceptions from Rangers' forwards, who had obviously been given instructions to chase every ball. Dalglish gave Celtic the lead in 24 minutes by taking a neat pass from Deans and placing the ball wide of McCloy, but Parlane equalised ten minutes later with a brave header at the near post.

The second half opened sensationally with Rangers scoring almost directly from the kick-off; Parlane's flick sent Alfie Conn roaring through and his pace took him clear of the Celtic defence to finish clinically. Both McNeill and Connelly had looked sluggish as Conn raced past them. It was now an old-fashioned cup-tie as Celtic largely abandoned their studied approach in their efforts to equalise. Only eight minutes later, they were awarded the most definite of penalties when John Greig had to handle a scoring shot from Deans on the goal-line. It was a nerve-wracking moment for George Connelly – who had a recent history of erratic behaviour – as he placed the ball very deliberately on the spot and studied Rangers' goalkeeper McCloy, the tallest in the country. Behind the goal the packed Rangers end howled and roared to distract him as he approached the ball but Connelly shot firmly low past the keeper into the net for the equaliser as half of the Hampden crowd of 122,714 went wild with delight and relief. Celtic's recent travails from the penalty spot had not been forgotten.

Cup finals are often decided by passion and commitment . . . and Rangers appeared to have slightly the more of both. Celtic's defence was still uneasy with the pace of Rangers' attacks and gave away a free-kick on the left wing in the 60th minute. Play was held up while Jim Brogan was helped from the pitch and Bobby Lennox took his place. McLean took the delayed free-kick and curled over an inviting ball, met powerfully by Johnstone. His header beat Celtic's goalkeeper but rebounded from the inside of the right-hand post, rolling along the goal-line before resting against the other post. The player quickest to react was Rangers' Tom Forsyth who managed to scramble the ball into the net.

Something had gone wrong with Celtic's communications: the player normally detailed to cover that post at corner-kicks or set-pieces was Jim Brogan. But he had been taken off seconds before the free-kick and his replacement was Bobby Lennox, a forward, who may not have been given specific instructions to guard that vicinity.

The remaining 30 minutes produced countless thrills but no more goals – although Celtic partisans saw nothing wrong with a Jimmy Johnstone effort disallowed by the referee. Celtic pressed furiously while Rangers defended grimly and tried to strike on the counter-attack. The excitement was intense, but Celtic lost the Scottish Cup and Rangers won it deservedly on the day.

Any reviewer of this season would have noted the annexation of the championship for the eighth successive time but would have to register the defeats in two cup finals. And the reviewer might well have concluded that Celtic's reign in Scotland was trembling on the brink.

Notes

1. Astonishingly, given the length of the player's career, the injury was sustained very early – in a match against Hearts when he was 18. Thus, Bobby Murdoch played virtually his whole career on a weak ankle.

Chapter 9

Nine in a Row

The last of Celtic's nine championships in this remarkable sequence came in 1973–74, but it was scarcely the most memorable campaign. It was a season without a theme and without real excitement.

In the world outside football, real life had a disconcerting habit of intruding: in Britain, skirmishing between the government and the miners was escalating; in the Middle East, the Yom Kippur war had 'settled' things between Israel and her neighbours until the next stage in that never-ending crisis; in the United States, the President – caught in the net of the Watergate scandal – put his forces on nuclear alert in order to divert attention from the unravelling of his corruption. Granted, the phrase 'close to the brink' so beloved of journalists had a touch of hyperbole about it, but 1973 was still a worrying time.

There were distractions in football from a variety of sources: players unhappy with their wages, bonuses and life at Celtic Park; too little genuine competition for Celtic from the other sides in the First Division; a preoccupation with the national team which had qualified for the 1974 World Cup to be held in West Germany . . .

At long last the Scottish football authorities had recognised the need for reform, and plans were in place to establish the Premier League, due to start in season 1975–76. It was scarcely a visionary or idealistic approach since the legislators had little option if the game was to survive. Match attendances had dropped rapidly and would continue to do so, football hooliganism was on the rise, and the fare on display for the public was largely unappealing.

Jock Stein used to maintain that the reforms made by the Scottish League were intended to break Celtic's monopoly in the championship. He was perfectly correct, but not in any sinister sense. Celtic's dominance, admirable as it was, could no longer be described as beneficial to Scottish football in general. Walter Hagen, the flamboyant American golfer, used to arrive on the eve of the tournament, look around the locker-room and ask: 'Well, boys, who's going to be second?' Jock Stein was too astute (or Scottish) to be caught in such a presumption but he knew – and everybody else knew – that few teams would be able to make and sustain a long-term challenge. Some years previously he had expressed his concern to Cyril Horne, and among his fears was the probability that the club would slide back to the level of their challengers rather than those contenders rising to Celtic's standard.

The Scottish League again messed up the administration of the League Cup. The organisers managed to have Celtic and Rangers drawn in the same section as Arbroath and Falkirk – and there were no prizes offered for guessing which two teams would qualify. Later on in the competition, Celtic and Rangers would face each other for a third time in the semi-final – and the final was scheduled for 15 December! To compound the folly, an experimental offside rule was put into effect for all matches in the bastardised competition; no player could be pulled up for offside outside the 18-yard line (extended to the touchlines for the occasion). In effect, a Scottish side was going to qualify for European football from a tournament using different Rules of the Game from everybody else – a bit like making it to a snooker final by playing billiards.

It was not surprising that Celtic's march to the ninth title in a row went largely unnoticed; it was nothing more than what was to be expected, the norm, the average, the same old thing . . . and the spectators continued to lose interest. Few punters are willing to bet on the probability of the sun not rising tomorrow no matter how enticing the odds offered.

Despite the apparent lack of interest elsewhere, Celtic played some exceptional football that winter and Kenny Dalglish fully merited his recognition as a world-class player. He was simply superb in every aspect of the game, the key man in Celtic's line-up despite his relative youth. Nobody excelled him in unselfish running off the ball into space to unsettle the opposition and provide another option for Celtic's attack. Nobody had a greater awareness of what was 'on', and his flawless distribution reflected that sense. Nobody in Scotland was a more clinical finisher. Kenny Dalglish could partner anybody, and he struck up an unlikely and effective alliance with Dixie Deans who, despite the training régime at Parkhead, was still an unathletic-looking figure.

Another important figure was David Hay who emerged as a most versatile player in the midfield. On televised games viewers could judge the state of an important match by a glance at Stein's deployment of David Hay: if the scores were level (or Celtic behind) Hay would be moving into attack and urging on his forwards; if Celtic were holding on to the lead, Hay would be further back, winning the ball and marking the most dangerous opponent.

Hay had one other contribution to make to Celtic and that was his friendship with George Connelly. The 'Scottish Beckenbauer' was a magnificent player but he was already exhibiting signs of an inability to cope with the emotional side of the game at its higher levels.

Footballers react to situations on the pitch with split-second timing, almost without thought in a manner of speaking, their bodies adjusting instinctively to a poor pass or an awkward bounce. In the dressing-room, and on the practice ground, the banter can be incessant,[1] and the Parkhead dressing-room could be a cruel place. In the modern world the lives of footballers off the field are open to scrutiny, questioned endlessly about matters outside their scope . . . and Old Firm players must become used to such a fish-bowl existence.

Unlike most players, George Connelly was introverted with no liking for the limelight and rumour had it that his marriage was in trouble. In that Celtic squad of resolute characters, of young men with their minds set on football stardom, Connelly was increasingly becoming a loner.

One newcomer had arrived at Parkhead in the close season, Steve Murray from Aberdeen, and his arrival marked the end of a legendary Celtic career. In signing Murray, Jock Stein was indicating further changes in Celtic's style with the emphasis now on a busy, hard-running midfield . . . and that meant that Bobby Murdoch, a stalwart in the previous eight championships, was now considered expendable. After playing only one League Cup match for Celtic in 1973–74, Murdoch was released in September and signed for Middlesbrough. Jack Charlton had phoned Celtic Park early in the season to ask Stein's advice on a Scottish midfielder and was astonished when Stein informed him: 'I can give you Bobby Murdoch.'

It was not quite so hard-hearted as it seems because Celtic's manager was doing Murdoch a favour; the long-time star (who had only recently signed another contract), if released, could make his own terms with the English club. Ironically, Jack Charlton was hesitant about the transaction, suspicious that Murdoch or Stein was hiding a serious injury, but he contacted Murdoch and was reassured about his fitness and training habits. Charlton was ecstatic about the success of his purchase and succinct in his praise for the ex-Celt: 'The most honest player I've known.'

Celtic began the league campaign in a low-key manner with a visit to Dunfermline; in fact, the Scottish football season had tiptoed into action with the meaningless Drybrough Cup and the sectional play in a League Cup from which competition had been removed. At East End Park, Celtic won more comfortably than the 3–2 score might suggest.

On 8 September Celtic unfurled the new league flag at their stadium and celebrated the occasion by winning 5–0 against a luckless Clyde, fated to be attendants at Celtic festivities. The game was memorable for two reasons, neither connected to the excellent attacking football displayed by the home side. Every Celtic player wore a number 8 on his shorts in recognition of the league championship feat, and a young Celt suffered a horrendous knee injury which ended his career as a top-flight player. As was his custom, Jock Stein was introducing youngsters into the side in less important fixtures and Brian McLaughlin, a promising midfielder said to be 'better than Dalglish at a corresponding age', was fielded. The promise certainly was there in his ball control and passing, and the indefinable air of maturity was present even at the tender age of 18. But, in an accidental clash, his knee was damaged and Jock Stein, who once described himself surprisingly as 'a big, soft-hearted old miner', cried tears of pity when he learned the extent of the boy's injury.

The next league match was at Ibrox. On paper, at least, both teams looked evenly matched: each had won a match from the other in the League Cup. This game, on 15 September, was a poor one, played out on a firm, dry pitch, and the only goal came in 69 minutes when Jimmy Johnstone headed a low cross from David Hay under and past Rangers' giant keeper Peter McCloy. Johnstone had lived up to his reputation as the tormentor of Rangers at Ibrox: he had previously scored from 25 yards with his left foot, tapped in another from less than a yard out with his right, leapt high to head the winning goal in 1971, and this time he stooped low with the same effect.[2] Rangers, previously contending for every ball, seemed to give up at that point, as if admitting they could do nothing against Jock Stein's Celtic.

An odd incident in Scotland's World Cup match against Czechoslovakia at Hampden Park on 26 September affected Celtic adversely. Four Celtic players (Hunter, McGrain, Connelly and Dalglish) were included in the Scottish line-up against the redoubtable European side and, for once, the nation seemed united in patriotic fervour as Scotland went on to win by 2–1 through goals by Joe Jordan and Jim Holton. The days of players like Jimmy Johnstone being booed and jeered by a sizeable minority in the Rangers end at Hampden seemed over.

However, the goal scored by Czechoslovakia was a soft one, and Alistair Hunter looked badly at fault. Despite the fact that Scotland had recovered to win the match, this latest mistake affected the keeper's confidence badly during the rest of the season as Hunter was reminded often about the goal when the TV networks played it time after time, showing off their new toy, the instant replay. In 1973–74 Jock Stein reverted to form and never really settled on a regular goalkeeper, Denis Connaghan and Hunter sharing the responsibility, and Evan Williams being restored for one important European Cup tie.

The topsy-turvy progress continued in the League Cup. In the second round Celtic won by 2–1 at Fir Park against Motherwell, but lost the second leg by 1–0 at Celtic Park. In this extremely complicated tournament, extra-time could not separate the sides; a play-off game was required and Celtic got through by 3–2 after Motherwell had fought back twice. That was on 29 October, a Monday night, and only two days before Celtic faced Aberdeen in the quarter-final. The schedule was brutal: Celtic had beaten Hearts by 3–1 at Tynecastle in the league on Saturday, defeated Motherwell 3–2 in the League Cup on the Monday, and followed that up by edging Aberdeen 3–2 on the Wednesday and completed the week by beating East Fife 4–2 in the league on the Saturday. Seven days to make one weak, indeed! The problem was partly due to efforts to complete the season early to allow lots of time for Scotland to prepare for the World Cup, but it underlined the fact that the competition was losing even more credibility.

Celtic's form at this time was scarcely convincing but they were making steady progress on all fronts: in the European Cup, they had disposed of Turku (Finland) by an aggregate of 9–1, but struggled against Vejle (Denmark). At Parkhead in the first leg, with Jimmy Johnstone acting as captain in the place of McNeill, who was out with an injury, the match ended 0–0 and, in the return, Celtic scraped through against the part-timers with a Lennox goal that most observers considered offside. In the championship a late goal by St Johnstone's Pearson in the 84th minute meant that Celtic had lost yet again at Muirton Park, this time by 2–1.

It was hard to complain while the team held on to top position in the table and had a game in hand. Stein was so concerned about the lack of goals that he repeated his enquiries about Dundee's John

Duncan and increased his early season bid from £50,000 to £60,000, but the Tayside club felt he was worth more.

Behind the scenes, difficulties with unhappy players were not being resolved. David Hay had been injured in a cup-tie almost two years previously, missing several matches as a consequence. He argued that he was entitled, when laid off through an injury sustained at work, to the same amount of money as other players. The problem almost certainly was complicated by Celtic's salary structure which consisted of a relatively low wage topped up dramatically by a bonus system. Over that period of time, Hay and Stein could not reach an agreement about the issue and the player asked for a transfer early in the new season. Surprisingly, David Hay was not snapped up by any ambitious club in England, fuelling suspicions that Jock Stein had refused to discuss approaches with interested clubs. The matter – distressing to the supporters and unsettling to the players – was dragging on far too long. In fact, in mid-November, Hay simply refused to attend training and was immediately suspended by the club.

Another player was causing concerns: Hay's friend, George Connelly, a man with emotional problems in proportion to his talents. Back in June 1973, for no apparent reason, Connelly had left the Scottish party at Glasgow Airport only an hour before they were due to depart for Switzerland. Now, in November, perhaps in sympathy with Hay, he walked out of Celtic Park . . . and a long-running drama had been set in motion.

Stein claimed that the Connelly affair had been patched up but any resolution was only short-term.[3] There would be a solution of sorts to Hay's problem over payment, however, and the midfielder performed brilliantly for Celtic on his return.

Despite the gentle approach accorded Connelly, some questions were being asked about Stein's increasingly high-handed methods in dealing with unsettled players. When he had taken over at Celtic Park back in 1965, the players were desperate for success and the manager had inspired them to fulfil their ambitions. The new wave of professionals at Parkhead had never known defeat or discouragement, and felt they had contributed just as much to Celtic's long-running success as the manager. The new breed were not as malleable as those of the old school. In fact, Jock Stein was becoming a victim of better times; the manager, brought up in harsher economic conditions, found it increasingly difficult to adjust to the wavelength of players whom he considered well paid and affluent.

A generation gap always exists between managers and workers and in football the generations are shorter. When Jock Stein arrived at Celtic Park in 1965, he was 42 years of age and probably approaching his peak as a manager; his players were young men in their early 20s. By October 1973 Jock Stein had reached 51 years of age . . . and his players, for the most part, were young men in their early 20s. He had lost the ability to surprise his charges.

It required mental gymnastics to come to grips with the changing attitudes of a new generation of players at Celtic Park. Billy McNeill, always a fierce competitor, admits candidly that he was 'hell-bent on winning, especially after the years of frustration'. The present squad were largely young professionals with skills to offer, and wanted remuneration during the relatively short career of a footballer. Nowhere had the game changed so much as in the matter of players' wages: Jock Stein had played for £14 a week in the 1950s, Billy McNeill and the Lisbon Lions played for £60 a week in the mid-1960s . . . and now competent performers such as Harry Hood could obtain £125 in the 1970s.

At Celtic Park, prior to Stein's arrival as manager, wages were traditionally low and the new manager did something to change this perception, but not too much. The manager favoured a system of handsome bonuses, but the basic wage remained low. Stein recognised the value of incentives and, in general, the football results stand as the most compelling proof of his thinking. However, such a practice was bound to provoke resentment from players deprived of the opportunity to play in important matches for whatever reason: a temporary loss of form, the effects of injury, or being omitted from the line-up 'for tactical considerations'.

It should be recalled that Stein's practices as a manager were different from his conduct as a player. Webber Lees, the wily old manager of Albion Rovers when Stein was a youngster there, described him accurately enough as 'a thrawn bugger'; Lees was frustrated at Stein's habit of holding out at the start of a season for an increase in wages – and in the 1940s the 'increase' might only be as much as £1 per week. As captain – a position to which he naturally gravitated – Stein was the spokesman for the Coatbridge players when they objected to playing against Stenhousemuir in a postponed Scottish Cup tie. The players, some of whom were part-timers, resented taking time off work without suitable recompense, but Stein's approach to the manager (and directors) less than an hour before the kick-off was curtly dismissed. Not too surprisingly, Albion Rovers (then in 'A Division') went down to a 5–1 defeat from Stenhousemuir (then in the lower reaches of 'B

Division').[4] And, of course, Jock Stein was quick enough to leave Scotland for non-league football in Wales in order to better himself financially.

As manager of Celtic, his attitude appeared to have changed; Ronnie Simpson, a man who had been around football for a long time, commented grimly: 'You would think it was his own money he was giving away.' Perhaps Stein was being an efficient 'manager' of the club's money; perhaps he was becoming older and more cautious.

On 17 November came a performance to gladden the heart of all Celtic followers. Partick Thistle, a side whom some Celtic fans wanted to punish perpetually for the indignity of that League Cup defeat, were drubbed at Celtic Park by 7–0. Dixie Deans scored six of the goals, a hat-trick in each half. Deans' six goals constituted a post-war scoring record for a competitive match. Watching from the stand was Jimmy McGrory, the holder of the all-time record with eight goals in one game against Dunfermline back in 1928. After the match Dixie Deans was presented with the ball, autographed by the players of both teams; it was said unkindly by one denizen of the Jungle that that was the only time some of the Thistle players had touched it.

Another landmark was established in the fixture against Partick Thistle, largely unnoticed in all the fuss about Dixie's feat: Bobby Lennox had also scored to bring his tally of goals up to 241 and to equal Steve Chalmers' post-war record. A week later, on 24 November, Lennox scored from the penalty spot in a 2–0 win over Dumbarton at Boghead to stand alone as the top post-war scorer. Among modern strikers, Bobby Lennox was perhaps unique as a goalscorer. He was never a 'poacher', lurking around the penalty area for scraps to fall his way. His natural speed allowed him to break away from defenders, but usually that pace gave him the time to survey the options available as he raced in on goal. Strikers tend to react instantaneously to happenings around them, but Lennox was frequently faced with the prospect of only the goalkeeper to beat . . . and with time to consider the consequences of failure. To his credit, the cool-headed Lennox was clinical in his finishing – never better illustrated than his decisive goal against Rangers in the 1969 Scottish Cup final.

The League Cup was still lumbering on and, at Pittodrie on 21 November in the second leg of the quarter-final, a stern defensive display saw off Aberdeen in a 0–0 draw, and keeper Hunter was outstanding. On Wednesday, 5 December, the semi-final match between Rangers and Celtic was played with 54,864 in attendance for the third meeting between the clubs in the same competition. The rain poured down, a chill wind blew and Celtic destroyed Rangers by 3–1. Harry Hood scored a fine hat-trick and Rangers were totally outclassed on this occasion; also outstanding in Celtic's victory was David Hay, restored to the team and apparently reconciled with his manager, the impending clash with Rangers in a semi-final having accelerated the negotiating process.

By November the protracted miners' overtime ban was beginning to affect life in Britain. The government had imposed a State of Emergency, a knee-jerk reaction to the situation. Among the provisions of such an action were that television transmissions had to end at 10.30 p.m., and floodlit football matches were prohibited in order to conserve energy. Those measures – coupled with a general unease over the petrol crisis and the certainty that things were going to get worse between the miners and the Conservative government of Ted Heath – added to the midwinter blues of the football season.

The final of the League Cup was staged at Hampden Park on 15 December with a kick-off time of 1.30 – another attempt to circumvent the effects of the State of Emergency. Those spectators who turned up – a paltry 27,974 of them – trudged through puddles outside the national stadium to stand huddled in forlorn groups on the exposed Hampden terracings as the wind howled and rain and sleet fell in sheets. They must have wondered why the vast stadium had ever been called the 'Classic Slopes'. The pitch was virtually unplayable, made treacherous by snow and ice. Both sides had made their feelings known to the match official but he deemed the surface acceptable for a major cup final.

The referee was Mr R.H. Davidson of Airdrie, a frequent adversary of Jock Stein over the years. Like Stein, Davidson was a Lanarkshire man, and equally thrawn. Stein had been fined £100 once and censured after Davidson had reported him for directing remarks to a linesman during a Scottish Cup tie between Celtic and Dunfermline. The pair had clashed again, this time openly, during and after the Scottish Cup final of 1970 when, as the members of the Aberdeen team went up the stairs to collect their medals, some Celtic players had suggested that Mr Davidson join them. Jock Stein's comments were vitriolic and public but this time Celtic's manager was fined only £10. Apparently, many officials in the SFA, attending the cup final in their capacity as the game's legislators, sympathised with Stein's feelings.[5]

However, Celtic had no real reason to complain about Mr Davidson's handling of the 1973 League Cup final after the decision had been made to play it. They gave a totally lacklustre performance and came to life only after Gordon Wallace had given Dundee the lead in 75 minutes. Tommy Gemmell, now of Dundee, was playing with much of his former swagger and flamboyance, to such an extent that the Celtic fans were reduced to borrowing the Rangers chant of 'Gemmell's a bastard' in the closing stages of a depressing day. One Dundee supporter, leaving the ground, sodden but happy, commented pithily on the weather: 'No' a day for a tree to be oot in.'

Typically, Celtic managed to raise their game immediately afterwards, as if in atonement, by defeating both Falkirk and Dunfermline by 6–0 as New Year approached. Dixie Deans, missing from the League Cup final through injury, led the way with four goals against Falkirk and two against Dunfermline Athletic. The revival continued into the early days of 1974 as Celtic went to Shawfield on New Year's Day for the ritual beating of Clyde by 2–0 and then defeated Rangers by 1–0 at Parkhead three days later.

Bobby Lennox scored the only goal in 27 minutes to complete the championship double over their rivals. Later on, both Lennox and Deans, normally efficient finishers, should have added further goals but missed clear-cut chances. Rangers virtually dropped out of the race for the championship flag after this result, and their pitiful challenge in the second half at Parkhead prompted Ian Archer to suggest in the *Glasgow Herald* – ever so gently – that Rangers' 'policy' of not signing Roman Catholics might be having an adverse effect on them at least on the playing-field. Most encouraging for Celtic was the form of Steve Murray and David Hay in the midfield. Hay had put aside any troubles over wages and bonuses, while Murray had impressed everybody with the way he had settled at Celtic Park.

After a routine win over St Johnstone by 3–0 at Parkhead on 19 January and a 6–1 rout of Clydebank in the Scottish Cup on the 27th – their first-ever Sunday fixture – Celtic suddenly lost form. On 2 February Motherwell fought back from being two goals down at Fir Park to defeat Celtic by 3–2 and, little more than a week later, Dundee came to Celtic Park and won by 2–1. The only distinction about this match was that it marked the first league game to be played by Celtic on a Sunday.

The reason for the switch to Sunday football – a move which offended many in Scotland at the time – lay in politics. The miners, still on work-to-rule, had imposed a ban on overtime and were threatening to call an all-out strike. The government, probably in a bid to turn public opinion against the miners, introduced a three-day week, ostensibly to conserve power, particularly electricity. In simple terms, this meant that some workers worked on Mondays, Tuesdays and Wednesdays and others on Thursdays, Fridays and Saturdays. Clearly, this was going to have a harmful effect on attendances; so, Sunday football was introduced as a counter-measure. In the short term, the move was successful as more than 40,000 attended the league match against Dundee.

A general election was called for 28 February to determine the question of 'Who really governs Britain?'. Another question, equally pressing for football followers in Scotland, was going to be answered on 23 February 1974 at Easter Road. This match could lay claim to the hyperbole of 'league decider'. As Celtic had been dropping points, Hibernian had been gaining ground and, from what Celtic supporters had seen of them on TV, they looked a very useful side. A team with Stanton, Black and Blackley in defence and O'Rourke, Edwards and Duncan up front were not going to be pushovers. The gap between the teams was three points in Celtic's favour, but a win for Hibernian would give the momentum to the Edinburgh side.

It was another memorable occasion at Easter Road. The crowds on the way to the stadium thronged Leith Walk and London Road, and were assailed by other zealots, political ones, handing out leaflets for the Leith Labour Party or the Scottish Nationalists. One lone Conservative drew reluctant admiration from the punters for sporting a giant blue-and-white rosette: 'See him ower therr? That is wan brave ★★★★.'

Eventually, 48,554 crowded into venerable Easter Road to witness the clash. Both teams came out prepared to attack . . . and Dixie Deans inevitably gave Celtic the lead in the very first minute of play. Deans was to score again that day, and in the last minute. In between those goals, the two teams produced a pulsating match and shared another four goals between them but, at the end, the champions had withstood another challenge to their supremacy and triumphed by 4–2. In a tremendous team performance by Celtic, McNeill was his imperious self at the centre of defence and, beside him, George Connelly was the epitome of coolness, the midfield of David Hay, Steve Murray and Kenny Dalglish worked tirelessly from the opening whistle, while Deans had imposed his psychological edge over Hibernian yet again.

Stein had revealed his pragmatism once more: George Connelly, out of favour with the club and out of sorts with himself, had asked for a transfer on 2 February . . . and the manager had 'retaliated' by restoring him to the side in time for this fixture. In fact, during that season, Celtic's most effective (if not their best) performances had been against their immediate challengers; Hibernian (1–1 and 4–2), Rangers (1–0 and 1–0) and Aberdeen (2–0 and 0–0). The loss of only two points in six matches in face-to-face confrontations suggested that Celtic's experience in winning championships – and the vital matches – was a key factor.

Just before the general election, Celtic flew to Basle on European Cup business. Their opponents were a workmanlike side, competent and robust in equal measure, but Celtic went down to a 3–2 defeat. Suggestions that they were in a relative decline – at least in a European sense – were being made and the club's reaction in *The Celtic View* indicated a certain sensitivity. The *Sunday Mail* had arranged for Jim Baxter, the ex-Ranger, to cover the match as a special correspondent and Celtic were angered by this action, especially as the report was critical of the team's display. The subsequent furore served to deflect attention from a mediocre performance in Switzerland.

By the time Celtic beat Hearts by 1–0 on the Saturday through a Dixie Deans goal, it was clear that Labour had won more seats than the Conservatives but also that Ted Heath was most reluctant to give up power. The Prime Minister spent the weekend wooing the hitherto despised Liberals of Jeremy Thorpe in an attempt to queer Labour's pitch. All his efforts fell through, however, as the Queen sent for Harold Wilson, and Labour set out to run the country with a minority government. At least the question of a miners' strike was shelved and Scotland returned to the national preoccupation with football.

Celtic struggled through March, but neither Hibernian nor Rangers could make any inroads; Celtic's 'struggles' consisted of league wins over Hearts (1–0) and Ayr United (4–0), a loss to Thistle (0–2) and a draw with Dumbarton (3–3). They then managed a 2–2 draw in the Scottish Cup at Parkhead against Motherwell, in which Celtic were a goal behind twice, followed by a 1–0 win in the replay at Fir Park. After that came an extra-time victory over Basle in the second leg of the European Cup quarter-final, all the while holding on to first place in the race for the championship.

The European tie was another memorable match as Celtic, spurred on by a massive crowd of 71,000, wiped out Basle's lead early on and went ahead after 15 minutes . . . and then gave up two goals before half-time through careless defending and questionable goalkeeping. Celtic were once more experiencing anxieties about their keepers: Williams had not impressed in the first leg in Basle and Connaghan had replaced him for the second leg, but understandably looked shaky . . .

The match finished with the teams still deadlocked at 5–5 on aggregate, and extra-time had to be played. Parkhead erupted, as only it could, eight minutes into the first period of extra-time: Hood's curling cross to the far post was knocked up into the air and Steve Murray reacted first to jump high and head the ball into the roof of the net.

Exciting, absorbing, draining – but also somehow worrying. Basle were not in the highest rank of European clubs and yet they had given Celtic the fight of their lives. In the end, Celtic advanced into the semi-final of the European Cup for the fourth time but the signs of decline were there to see.

One would have thought that progress in Europe and entry into the Scottish Cup final would also have guaranteed an easy ride in the league championship but there was severe turbulence on the journey. The last league fixture before the European Cup semi-final against Atletico Madrid was against lowly Arbroath but Celtic, apparently preoccupied with thoughts of the following Wednesday's match, struggled before winning by 1–0.

The semi-final first leg has to stand as one of the most brutal matches ever played at Parkhead. It was a display of overt violence by the Madrid side which shocked the Celtic supporters by its blatant cynicism; it was a disgrace to football. Atletico came to Glasgow with one intention in mind: to disrupt the flow of the game, to kick Celtic off the park and to do so at any cost, having packed their team with largely expendable thugs who would not have figured in the second leg regardless of what happened in Glasgow.

The Spanish side was managed by Juan Carlos Lorenzo, from the Argentine, and therein lay part of the problem. Argentina, since the 1966 World Cup match against England at Wembley, had harboured a strong dislike of the British game. In the notorious World Club Championship between Celtic and Racing Club in 1967, the Scots had felt the full fury of that backlash.

Perhaps the tactics of Atletico Madrid were designed to provoke a chaotic match in which they would have gained the upper hand. Another serious suggestion arose from the behaviour of the Rangers supporters in Barcelona after the European Cup-Winners' Cup final of 1972. Similar crowd trouble at Celtic Park could well have led to an invasion of the pitch and the forfeiture of the tie – the customary punishment for crowd trouble was the awarding of that leg to the 'innocent' side by a score of 3–0.

Regardless of the reason, the match was an absolute disgrace from beginning to end. Three of the Atletico Madrid players were ordered off, and seven were booked in the course of the tie. The spectators and journalists were convinced that several others should have joined them in the dressing-room as Jimmy Johnstone in particular was singled out for vicious treatment. To their infinite credit, the Celtic players did not rise to the bait of such provocation and only two were booked, and the supporters stayed within the bounds of responsible spectating.

However, the result was a 0–0 draw, despite the advantage in manpower throughout much of the game, and that was a major disappointment. At the end of the match, as the teams were entering the darkened tunnel, there were skirmishes between players in which the Celtic men were far from passive. The Spanish press made the most of these incidents in order to whip up a hate-campaign against Celtic for the return match in Madrid – a match which should not have been played at all, given the outrageous behaviour of the visitors at Celtic Park.

UEFA displayed a curiously ambivalent attitude and refused to expel the Spanish side from the competition. Nor did they respond to the suggestion that the second leg be played at a neutral venue to lessen the possibility of further violence on and off the field. Instead, the three players sent off were simply banned from the return leg, an automatic consequence of their misbehaviour in any case.

The controversy continued for the next two weeks but Celtic were forced to travel to Madrid to fulfil the match . . . and did so despite death threats to Jimmy Johnstone and Jock Stein over the hotel telephone. Stein tried to joke about it: at least Johnstone could run around the field while the manager had to sit in the dugout. Not surprisingly, Celtic lost by 2–0, going down to late goals.

Events like the Atletico Madrid fiasco can drain a side of energy and can cause a wavering of the concentration needed to be champions. But Jock Stein made no mistakes in the closing stages of the championship. Before they flew out to Spain, Celtic had played three league matches which did much to guarantee that the flag would be flying at Parkhead for the ninth successive time.

On 13 April, a few days after the match at Parkhead, Celtic went to Tannadice and fielded a much-changed team; Jimmy Johnstone, quick healer that he was, could not recover in time to take his customary position. Celtic were welcomed on to the pitch with the usual roar from their supporters, and with a sympathetic round of applause from the United fans. Surprisingly, after their Spanish ordeal, Celtic played superbly to lead by two goals after half an hour and held on to the lead. To the delight of the visiting fans, the news on the transistors was that Rangers had gone down at Ibrox to Dundee, and Hibernian had lost at

Arbroath. On the following Wednesday, Celtic turned on the power at Methil after East Fife had the temerity to score first, winning convincingly by 6–1. The attendance was only 6,970, however, and an indication of the lack of interest being generated in the Scottish League. And, on Saturday, 20 April, at Parkhead, Celtic disposed of Aberdeen by scoring an early goal (through Deans in five minutes) and a late one (through Lennox in 85 minutes).

The flight back from Spain was a return to reality, to a Scotland which suddenly seemed more secure and safe. It was also back to the normal practice of winning the league championship yet again although five fixtures – including the Scottish Cup final against Dundee United – had to be squeezed into the last ten days because of the perceived need to finish the season early for the Home Internationals and World Cup preparation. The first of Celtic's matches was the most important, against Falkirk at Brockville on 27 April; Celtic duly earned the draw (1–1) which gave them the flag . . . and relegated Falkirk.

The league had been clinched once more – for the ninth consecutive time on a ground other than Celtic Park – and the newspapers duly recorded the annual event. Football followers throughout Scotland were underwhelmed at the news. The remaining league matches, now of importance only to statisticians, were completed; significantly, all ended in draws.

To describe the end of such a historic season as an anticlimax is only true, but it had been a bizarre season from the start; all sorts of intrusions kept getting in the way of the football . . .

In fact, the Scottish Cup, so often the source of excitement, was of little interest in 1973–74, apart from the struggle against Motherwell in the quarter-final. Twice the visitors had led at Celtic Park on 10 March, and twice Harry Hood had equalised before a relieved 47,000. Again Motherwell put up another grim fight at Fir Park before going down to a goal by Dixie Deans in 60 minutes. The same Motherwell side had previously forced Celtic to a play-off game in the League Cup when Jimmy Johnstone's goal in the 89th minute had given his team a 3–2 win – and separated the sides after 300 minutes of football.

Once more Dundee were drawn against Celtic in the semi-final, and once more the Dens Park outfit went down to another honourable defeat at that stage. Like Celtic's supremacy in the championship, even the Scottish Cup was becoming static. The final on 4 May produced a surprise appearance by Dundee United but, sadly, their side, playing in their first-ever final, froze before the Hampden crowd of 75,959. After only 24 minutes' play Celtic were two goals up and in complete control. The third goal in a dull match came from Dixie Deans in the last minute after he swooped on to a cut-back from Dalglish.

Another domestic double for Celtic but little jubilation. The word 'another' tells us that it was becoming just too predictable.

Notes

1. To this day, when he meets some members of the Lisbon Lions, Bobby Murdoch points to his shoulder and mutters: 'I've got a humph from carrying you all those years.'

2. Campbell Ogilvie, presently Rangers' secretary and a lifetime supporter of the Ibrox club, has admitted privately: 'My heart used to sink – and I was filled with dread – whenever that wee man trotted on to the field.'

3. Stein and Sean Fallon spent hours at Celtic Park with the player; both men travelled regularly over the Kincardine Bridge to Connelly's home to encourage a change in the player's attitude.

4. A somewhat similar situation developed when Stein was Celtic's captain at the time of the Coronation Cup, held after the 1952–53 season. The players questioned the paltry amount they were due to get for appearing in the prestigious tournament and made their views known to the chairman. The matter was resolved eventually, and it appears certain that the players were given much higher rewards than the original £10 per match offered by the organisers.

5. To be fair to Mr Davidson, he had first come to prominence by disallowing a Rangers 'goal' in the 1958 Scottish Cup semi-final. The Hibs players protested *en masse* that Brand had punched the ball out of their goalkeeper's hands prior to the score, and Davidson, after consulting his linesman, changed his mind. Surprisingly, Davidson was also accused by Hearts of favouring Celtic in a Scottish Cup tie played at Tynecastle in February 1962, a match won 4–3 by Celtic. The home side claimed reasonably that one Celtic goal was scored from an offside position, but their major argument was that the official ordered Pat Crerand to retake a penalty-kick which he had missed; Crerand scored at the second attempt – in the 86th minute!

The Old Fox

Chapter 10

End of an Era

On 14 December 1974 most people on the Celtic FC bus coming back to Glasgow from Dundee were delighted: their team had just given one of their best performances of the season in trouncing Dundee by 6–0 at Dens Park. Kenny Dalglish had led the way with three goals; Jimmy Johnstone, restored to the side after injury, had scored twice and given a virtuoso performance. After some stuttering displays in recent weeks, the goals had come freely.

In fact, everything looked good for Celtic at that point, and few would have anticipated the disturbing turn of events that the New Year would bring.

Already that season, Celtic had won two trophies, managing to collect the Drybrough Cup for the first time in four attempts by beating Rangers on penalty-kicks after extra-time in the final. This trophy had come into being as a pre-season competition sponsored by a brewery in a blatant move to advertise its products. It had never been fully accepted by the public but a crowd of 57,558 turned up at Hampden Park to watch an Old Firm final – which ended in a 2–2 draw. Denis Connaghan, Celtic's goalkeeper, was the hero of the occasion, twice saving from Rangers' penalty-takers in the finale. The same player had featured in an extraordinary incident at Broomfield in the first-round match on 27 July. Celtic were playing out time when Connaghan, in attempting a throw-out, succeeded only in hurling the ball into his own net. Jock Stein stared in utter disbelief before bursting into laughter at the keeper's discomfiture – further evidence of the unreliability of goalkeepers, in the manager's opinion.

After a barren spell in the League Cup, Celtic stormed to victory in this competition in another memorable final. Once more, Hibernian were the victims, and yet again Dixie Deans was the executioner-in-chief.

Only one week before the League Cup final Celtic played Hibs in a league match at Parkhead and re-established a psychological edge by winning 5–0, producing their best form of the season up to that point. Hibernian came to Parkhead for the league fixture in a reasonably confident mood. They were only one point behind Celtic in the table and had a comparable goal average; in addition, *en route* to the forthcoming League Cup final, they had beaten Rangers. But they had no answer to Celtic's attacking play: Jimmy Johnstone tormented their left flank and Dixie Deans was his customary predatory self, scoring three times.

Hibernian may have consoled themselves with the theatrical cliché that a poor rehearsal makes for an excellent opening night; they were doomed to disappointment at Hampden Park on 26 October. The weather was perfect for football, a mellow, autumn day in vivid contrast to the misery of ill-planned December finals. Within six minutes Dalglish had continued the previous Saturday's good work when he opened up Hibernian's defence for Jimmy Johnstone to score. Celtic continued to press and Deans netted in 34 minutes after picking up a long through-ball from Pat McCluskey. Harper pulled one back for Hibs just before half-time with a fine effort that dimmed the celebrations on the King's Park terracing . . . but not for long. Paul Wilson, who seemed to reserve his best displays for cup finals that season, scored from close range three minutes after the restart. Celtic, with Jimmy Johnstone back to his impish best, were putting on the style, and Dalglish was spreading the play beautifully in partnership with Steve Murray.

Hibernian made the fatal mistake of scoring again in 61 minutes to make the score 3–2. In the dugout, Jock Stein stirred uneasily and looked pained. On the field, Billy McNeill shouted at his team-mates and gestured menacingly. Within the next quarter of an hour Celtic scored three more goals to lead by 6–2: Deans led the way with two of them (thus gaining yet another hat-trick against the Edinburgh side) and Murray finished things off with his goal in 74 minutes. Dixie Deans' third goal – Celtic's fifth – was a remarkable effort. Harry Hood's corner on the left drifted out to Johnstone on the far edge of the penalty area; the winger swung at the ball, probably attempting a full-blooded effort at goal, and the ball swerved across the goalmouth viciously; but Deans dived at it instinctively and headed the ball past a startled McArthur. Hampden Park erupted. Deans regained his feet, a grin splitting his face, as he was mobbed by his colleagues. Johnstone raised his arms and looked heavenward at such a gift from the gods of football.

The historian cannot refrain from adding a footnote or two to this match: Joe Harper, Hibernian's striker, scored near the end to complete his own hat-trick in a losing cause, and this was the last League Cup final played under the short-lived experimental offside rule.

Celtic's supporters may have felt that 'normal service had been resumed'. In fact, on the evening of 26 October 1974, every domestic piece of silverware was resting in the Parkhead boardroom: the Scottish Cup, the League Championship trophy, the League Cup and the Drybrough Cup.

However, that season (1974–75) was a strange one for Scottish football. The World Cup finals had been held in Germany in the summer of 1974 and three Celtic players (Danny McGrain, Kenny Dalglish and David Hay) played in all of Scotland's matches: against Zaire (2–0), Brazil (0–0) and Yugoslavia (1–1). Despite being undefeated, Scotland were eliminated at the initial stage, and the country's greatest football entertainer, Jimmy Johnstone, was denied the chance of gracing the world's biggest stage. Manager Willie Ormond had decided to use Johnstone as a substitute against Yugoslavia and the little Celt was warming up on the touchline in the closing minutes, but the referee did not notice him and time ran out for Johnstone and Scotland before the substitution could be made.

David Hay had a particularly fine tournament, coming close to scoring from long-range against Brazil, but almost immediately upon his return to Scotland he was transferred to Chelsea for a fee of around £250,000. In the previous season, Hay (who had some training in accountancy) had been involved in an on-going dispute about payment for players unavailable through injury, and it did not require a Mensa-type IQ to realise that the player and his manager 'enjoyed' an uneasy relationship.

Hay had been a valuable player for Celtic and a versatile performer. His great contribution was his ability to obey instructions perfectly, operating efficiently and comfortably within the parameters of his manager's orders. He was at his best latterly as a 'ball-winning mid-fielder' but his skills were vastly superior to most players described in that manner. Many Celtic followers believe that the club experienced problems for several seasons in replacing this man. Some claimed that, with the Hay's transfer, Celtic in reality lost two players, as George Connelly went on to have a poor season and continued his decline into football oblivion. Hay had been Connelly's closest friend at Celtic Park, and when his mentor suddenly disappeared, Connelly found it difficult to cope.

The glamour of the World Cup – and Scotland's ill-luck in it – gave domestic football a sense of anticlimax but there should have been an incentive for all the top clubs. As from the start of 1975–76, the Premier League (comprising only ten clubs) would be in operation, and how teams performed in 1974–75 would determine their status. In effect, it meant that eight out of the 18 sides in the top division would be relegated at the end of the season.

Celtic made a reasonable start to the campaign but the warning signs were in evidence. In the League Cup section, matched with Motherwell, Dundee United and Ayr United, they qualified comfortably enough in the end but went down surprisingly to Ayr United by 3–2 at Somerset Park on 14 August, despite a long-range goal from George Connelly. In a nervous semi-final, watched by a meagre 19,332, a single goal from Steve Murray in 62 minutes was all that separated Celtic from lowly Airdrie.

In the championship itself, setting out to win ten titles in a row, Celtic's form stuttered and it was clear that problems now existed in defence. Early in the season, Stein used both Denis Connaghan and Alistair Hunter in goal. Clearly, the manager was not too happy about the last line of defence and, before the season's end, would introduce Graham Barclay for one Scottish Cup tie and then sign Peter Latchford from West Bromwich Albion.

Another problem was emerging. Throughout 1974–75 Billy McNeill's form was inconsistent by his own exacting standards, the captain and sheet-anchor in defence having lost at least half a step from his speed. Most days, McNeill would be his usual self, exuding confidence and encouraging his team to even greater efforts; now, however, when a striker took him on individually and without fear, McNeill would sometimes appear uncomfortable. In the past, a sweeper like John Clark could compensate for any slight deficiency in McNeill's play on the ground by dint of telepathy, and Jim Brogan could use his natural briskness and speed in the seasons that followed. In 1974–75, however, Billy McNeill's partner in defence was usually George Connelly and the Fifer lacked mobility. The captain, who had made his competitive début against Clyde back in August 1958, was approaching the end of a most remarkable and successful career with Celtic.

The one league match lost was a crucial one, namely the Old Firm clash at Celtic Park on 14 September, played before 60,000 spectators. Although Celtic blamed the referee, Rangers deserved to win 2–1 based on their second-half comeback. The match official had a dismal afternoon, denying Celtic a clear penalty in the opening minute when Dalglish was pushed off the ball by Forsyth and later ordering off Brogan when the Celt, trying to take a throw-in rightly awarded to Celtic, was obstructed by Derek Parlane. The fact that Parlane was also dismissed some 30 minutes later was of little consolation to Celtic. Ian Archer, writing in the *Glasgow Herald* about this 'nasty, brutish game', singled out Derek Parlane for particular censure: 'His attitude was essentially unsporting as he kicked at players when the ball was away, refused to retreat ten yards when ordered, contested balls when they were out of play, and made mock gestures of trying to butt Celtic goalkeeper Connaghan when he had the ball in his hands.'

Still, a Celtic defence with Billy McNeill in form should have been able to cope with the 'rummle-them-up' tactics of Parlane . . . and Connaghan, equally distracted, was at fault for both Rangers' goals.

The middle of September was a bad time for Celtic as the shock defeat by Rangers was followed by a poor performance against Olympiakos of Greece in the European Cup. Jimmy Johnstone was deployed for this match but, once the Greeks had reacted to his presence by double-marking him, Celtic had little idea of how to break down their opponents' organised defence. Celtic's own defenders were not fully prepared for the simple breakaway and Viera put the visitors in front after 36 minutes. Despite all Celtic's frantic efforts, it took until the 81st minute for Paul Wilson to equalise. A 1–1 draw at home in a European match is a poor result, and the silence of the 40,000 fans at the end told its own story. The Celtic of the recent past would not have had to employ the hysterical power-game to overcome European visitors, nor should an unfancied Greek side leave Celtic Park with honours shared.

George Connelly missed the European tie against Olympiakos and was dropped again for the Old Firm match. Rumours of his intention to quit football altogether were sweeping Glasgow before and after the Rangers match. In the past he had been 'posted missing', and Stein had called his bluff by placing him on the transfer-list during 1973–74 – but, according to the manager, there had been no serious bidders. His problems were not just emotional ones; against Basle in the European Cup, he had sustained a broken ankle and that injury had kept him out of the game for some months at the latter part of 1973–74.

Jock Stein and Sean Fallon, on the surface hard, grim men, tried every tactic to persuade the player into resuming training. After one such success they made a point of asking every regular member of the Celtic squad to be 'understanding' about George's emotional difficulties. Connelly duly reappeared in the dressing-room, somewhat abashed and ill-at-ease at the sudden, awkward silence which greeted him. Jimmy Johnstone, with the best intentions in the world, welcomed him back to the fold: 'Hello George, good to see you again . . . but remember, George, it's me that's supposed to be the daft one an' no' you!'

The humour was rough-and-ready but not unkind. On one coach journey to an away fixture some players, recalling Connelly's stated desire to be a long-distance lorry-driver, pointed out the better and more elaborate models on the road: 'George, how do you fancy that one?' Connelly seemed more at ease, smiling at the banter, and during the early weeks of 1974–75 was playing well . . . until his bewildering decision to quit football completely.

For the most part, under Jock Stein, Celtic won the important fixtures, the so-called 'crunch games'. The defeat by Rangers at Parkhead – the Ibrox club's first victory there since 1968 – had caused some doubts to creep in, and the lacklustre draw with Olympiakos provoked more anxiety. But the second leg at Athens on 2 October answered a few questions. Within three minutes Celtic were reeling as a Greek striker slipped into a clear position at a free-kick to glance a header past the helpless Connaghan; with 20 minutes played Celtic gave away another free-kick, and the fierce shot was deflected past Connaghan. The visitors tried hard but lacked conviction. For the first time in seven seasons they had fallen at the first European hurdle and to a side who, no matter how well disciplined, would not have withstood sterner Celtic teams.

The optimists within Celtic's support would be reassured by the continuing domination of the domestic scene, despite the occasional stutter. More encouraging was the fact that Celtic, having won the League Cup with a vintage attacking performance against Hibernian in late October, were showing signs of a return to form, as witnessed by the 6–0 rout of Airdrie at Celtic Park on 16 November, and a similar result against Dundee at Dens Park on 14 December.

Approaching the New Year, Celtic appeared to be in a strong position: their form was improving, they held a two-point lead over Rangers at the top of the table at exactly the halfway stage in the campaign, and they went on to feast on Clyde by 5–1 on 1 January 1975 – a result which increased Celtic's advantage in goal average over their rivals.

And then the wheels came off.

On 4 January, Celtic went to Ibrox and gave up an early goal to

Derek Johnstone but the champions looked irresistible in the opening stages; both Hood and Dalglish had missed clear-cut chances on the heavy pitch before Rangers scored, and Paul Wilson was rampant on the wing. Rangers' keeper Kennedy made a series of outstanding saves, some of them brave dives at Celtic feet, and even at half-time on a sodden Ibrox pitch with the rain pouring down Celtic still looked a good bet. In the second half, Rangers thrived on the muddy conditions and a second goal in 50 minutes ended Celtic's challenge. Increasingly, the lightweight Celtic midfielders and forwards were becoming bogged down and Rangers, growing in confidence by the minute, scored again in 74 minutes. Celtic had no answer.

Later on, this result was viewed as a turning point but it need not have been one. The two clubs were level at the top, but Rangers now had a slight advantage in goal average; they had also received a tremendous boost in morale. In fact, 11 January was a more critical day for Celtic than the overblown tribal encounter of the previous week; Motherwell, fighting for a place in the Premier League, came to Celtic Park and won by 3–2 before a shell-shocked crowd of 26,000. For the second time in succession, Celtic's defence had given up three goals, and Billy McNeill looked very uncomfortable in trying to cope with Willie Pettigrew.

In February, Celtic's grip on the championship was weakening further: a draw at Arbroath (2–2) on 8 February was followed by a midweek draw against Dumbarton at Celtic Park and on the 22nd by a loss (2–1) to Hibernian at Easter Road. The Edinburgh ground, scene of so many triumphs, was the end of the road for Celtic's title hopes in 1974–75. Playing with a lack of confidence, they continued to struggle in the championship and eventually slumped to a third-place finish, behind Rangers and Hibernian.

Twenty-three years later, Billy McNeill still finds it hard to believe: 'Looking back, it's still difficult to put your finger on a specific problem . . . there's no doubt we still had outstanding players . . . there was a nagging kind of mystery about how things went for us after the Ne'erday game; we had the players, and we had the incentive, but . . . I don't recall there being an acceptance among the boys that it was over; too many of us there simply would not have allowed that to happen. It underlines the value of the right result in the Old Firm match at New Year.'

Ironically, as Celtic struggled to regain form, Rangers too were stuttering. It would not have taken much more to mount a successful defence of the championship but the will was not there. Fatigue had set in and staleness; like blowing out a candle, the magic had gone.

Celtic's form, after the 2–1 loss at Easter Road on 22 February, went into a tailspin; at least the end would be mercifully quick. Defeats came from Aberdeen at Pittodrie (3–2) from Dundee United at Celtic Park (1–0) and from Airdrie at Broomfield (1–0). Celtic had gone full-circle with this last defeat; weaker Celtic sides – before Stein took over – had stumbled there regularly. Some players had not performed as well as the supporters had expected them to: Billy McNeill had shaded off into a perceptible decline while Kenny Dalglish had reached a plateau on his rise to greatness, and Harry Hood and Dixie Deans had been inconsistent.

Not too surprisingly, some fingers were pointed in Stein's direction. For once, the changes made regularly by the manager to 'freshen things up' had led to unrest among players and supporters. And yet 'failure' is scarcely the word to apply to a season in which the side finished third in the championship, the Drybrough Cup had been won, the League Cup gained . . . and the Scottish Cup remained within reach. Progress to Hampden Park and the final on 3 May had not been easy or spectacular. The first tie had sent Celtic to Easter Road on 25 January and 36,821 watched a tense affair; Deans gave Celtic the lead in 12 minutes and the result was in doubt until Steve Murray's goal ten minutes from the end. Celtic then had the prospect of a comfortable home tie against Clydebank on 15 February and Stein 'rested' Billy McNeill for this match, won 4–1 after having given up the first goal in 26 minutes. However, they struggled against lowly Dumbarton at Boghead before scraping through by 2–1 and were indebted to new goalkeeper Peter Latchford for some courageous saves.

The latter stages of the Scottish Cup produced more typical Celtic performances. On Wednesday, 2 April, Celtic faced Dundee yet again in a semi-final; this time the Taysiders' hopes were high as Celtic had yielded the league championship to Rangers only four days earlier. Tommy Gemmell, an expert in psychological warfare, expressed the opinion that Celtic would be at a low ebb; it was his mistake, however, that led to Ronnie Glavin dispossessing him to score the game's only goal in 59 minutes.

Celtic's opponents in the final were unfashionable Airdrieonians who had fallen just short of gaining a place in the following season's Premier Division. In the Hampden sunshine a crowd of 75,457 gathered to watch Billy McNeill's last match for Celtic – although only the manager and his team-mates knew this prior to kick-off. As always, he played a captain's part in steadying the defence when Airdrie, stung by Paul Wilson's header in 14 minutes, applied sustained pressure.

Airdrie did equalise in 42 minutes, but a minute later Wilson headed a second goal for Celtic from Lennox's corner-kick. Shortly after the interval Pat McCluskey decided the outcome by converting a penalty after Lennox had been tripped.

Billy McNeill went up to receive the trophy yet again and was borne aloft by his players; Jock Stein looked reasonably happy with life; the supporters were optimistic, assuming that 'the Big Man' would be planning next season's campaign already, and that the championship would be recovered.

*

On 5 July 1975, while returning from Manchester Airport after a holiday in Spain, Jock Stein was seriously injured in a car accident on the A74 near Lockerbie. He was lucky to survive the crash, and required the whole year to recuperate. His assistant, Sean Fallon, took over as the caretaker manager for the 1975–76 season.

Chapter 11

The Last Hurrah

This was to be a season to savour. Jock Stein returned to Parkhead and, to the delight of every Celtic follower, appeared to be recovering from the dreadful accident which had forced his absence from the ground during the last season. His performance was a masterpiece – not in the flamboyant, riotous colours of his early seasons but rather in subdued, subtle tones. In artistic terms, a Rembrandt rather than a Van Gogh.

His return meant other changes at Celtic Park. After being in charge for 1975–76 and having to cope with the unexpected crisis, Sean Fallon was given a new post – that of the man in charge of youth development – and it was clear that any further advancement within the hierarchy at Celtic Park was now out of the question for the likeable Irishman. Fallon had worked hard as a caretaker manager in a most difficult, thankless season, and had been a shade unlucky on the football field. In a larger sense, he had been most unfortunate in the timing and circumstances of his promotion because, when the accident occurred, Sean Fallon was 54 years of age, three months older than Jock Stein.

It was not the best of times to take over as the thoughts of everyone at Celtic Park were with the injured Jock Stein and gossip was rife about the prospects of his return.

Sean Fallon's position as Jock Stein's assistant was given to Dave McParland, Partick Thistle's manager. This was another surprise move, and there were rumours that the former Jag was now being groomed as Stein's eventual successor. During the season this idea gained a wider credence when Stein himself expressed considerable satisfaction with his new assistant's performance while in charge of the training.

The League Cup campaign started promisingly with successive wins against Dundee United (1–0), Dumbarton (3–0) and Arbroath (5–0) in the sectional play but in the return fixtures Stein could see clearly that defensive frailties would have to be remedied soon. A 3–3 draw at Boghead against Dumbarton, exciting as it was for the spectators, could not be tolerated, and goals were given up late in the game against Arbroath (2–1) and Dundee United (1–1). Celtic had advanced reasonably comfortably but Jock Stein, recognising the problem, was already working on the solution. Billy McNeill was still being missed and Roddie MacDonald was occasionally being caught out through his inexperience; Joannes Edvaldsson, four years older than MacDonald, was more than competent as his partner but was lacking in pace.

On 1 September, Jock Stein announced a foray into the transfer market . . . and it was a shock. The manager persuaded Pat Stanton to move from Hibernian to Celtic, somehow convincing the Edinburgh side to exchange him for Jackie McNamara.[1] Stanton, capped 16 times for Scotland, was an accomplished defender, always cool under pressure, but he had been a fixture at Easter Road and seemingly as rooted to the capital as the castle rock.

Some Celtic supporters doubted the wisdom of such a transfer as Stanton was now 32 years of age and entering the veteran stage of his career. Stein had no doubts whatsoever. He had been in charge of Stanton when he managed Hibernian and had monitored the player's career ever since. He knew what he was getting: a skilled player, a resolute defender and a good professional who might give three seasons' service if employed wisely.

Pat Stanton may have longed for the relative peace and quiet of Edinburgh very quickly for his début came at Celtic Park in the opening league fixture of the season and the opponents were Rangers. In the turbulent atmosphere of an Old Firm clash Stanton's skills took time to emerge, and by half-time Celtic were two goals down to their rivals, apparently more fired up than ever. Both goals came about through errors caused by defenders failing to read each other's intentions. The second half was a great improvement: Celtic took the game to Rangers, and Stanton slotted in beside MacDonald in the heart of defence to allow the more attack-minded Ronnie Glavin to move forward and enable Celtic to dictate the play. Ten minutes after the interval Paul Wilson shot for Rangers' goal, but mishit; fortunately, his effort had enough force to cross the line and put Celtic back into contention. The pressure continued relentlessly on Rangers' goal, but chances were not taken and the fans had started to reconcile themselves to yet another moral victory when Tommy Burns released Wilson again. The winger raced through and finished the move crisply to equalise with only three minutes left to play.

A draw against Rangers is normally an acceptable result but Celtic's form was still unsettled. The team visited Tannadice again but this time went down weakly to an early goal from Gordon Wallace and an out-of-form Kenny Dalglish was singled out for some barracking by a segment of the disappointed travelling support. At Parkhead on the following Wednesday, Celtic faced Wisla Krakow in the UEFA Cup. The Poles were a typical Eastern European side, competent and technically highly skilled – an ideal litmus-test for any club with serious aspirations in Europe. Celtic were not ready for such an examination, and struggled to gain a scarcely deserved 2–2 draw, Dalglish's equaliser coming in injury time. The defence, without Stanton who had been signed too late for this round's deadline, were at sixes and sevens when the visitors scored twice in the second half.

Once again Stein ventured into the transfer market, this time for a forward. Possibly on the recommendation of Dave McParland, familiar with the player from his time at Firhill, Stein picked up Joe Craig of Partick Thistle for £60,000. Unlike most of Stein's strikers, Craig was tall and gangly, loose-limbed, but a regular goalscorer who would add to Jock Stein's reputation as a fine judge of strikers. Craig made his début against Hearts but failed to score in a close-fought 2–2 draw at Celtic Park although his former Thistle colleague Glavin opened the scoring for Celtic. Ronnie Glavin was clearly relishing the attacking opportunities that the transfer of Pat Stanton had opened up; the midfielder would eventually end up as Celtic's leading goalscorer in the 1976–77 campaign.

The end of September usually provides a chance for appraisal . . . and Celtic's report-card was mixed. In Europe, the review had to be a poor one as a competent Wisla Krakow had dismissed Celtic from the UEFA Cup in the first round with a 2–2 draw at Celtic Park and a comfortable 2–0 win in Poland. Celtic were not ready to compete with the top European sides, and their summary dismissal was probably valuable in that they could now concentrate exclusively on the domestic scene.

The league campaign, always Jock Stein's basic target as the springboard for Europe, had got off to a shaky start but the indications were that the players were settling down. At Kilmarnock on 25 September the team had looked very comfortable romping to a 4–0 victory over the home side with newcomer Joe Craig scoring his first goal for Celtic.

The League Cup was considered a barometer of Celtic's fortunes for the season. They had qualified from a section which included Dundee United and the solid Taysiders were now in serious contention for pole-position in the league. The customary hiccough had come against inferior opposition in the shape of Albion Rovers at Cliftonhill where Celtic had scraped through by 1–0 in the first leg of the quarter-finals. The ground, like its owners, had seen better days, although prosperity had never been in vogue at Coatbridge, in one of the most deprived areas in industrial Scotland . . . and a traditional Celtic stronghold. Celtic now looked certain to qualify for the semi-finals (which they duly did after beating the visitors by 5–0 at Celtic Park after a sporting reception for Albion Rovers from the Parkhead crowd).

The manager? He looked well but seemed more subdued. Jim Farrell, always observant, notes that he was quieter, frequently lapsing into uncharacteristic silence – so different from his easy mastery of small-talk and patter. However, the important thing was that he was back in charge. The supporters welcomed the impression of decisiveness that emanated from him and which was shown in the capture of Stanton and Craig. Both newcomers were settling in nicely and looked excellent prospects for the rest of the season, and both seemed in the tradition of other Stein swoops in the past.

October showed the manager as returning to his former self. On the pitch, the players were gelling into a formidable side. The results clearly indicated the improvement with victories over Ayr United and Motherwell by an identical 2–0 score and an impressive 5–1 rout of Dundee United at Parkhead on 20 October.

However, it was the individual performances of players which excited the supporters: Danny McGrain was an excellent right-back, on the verge of great things in the game; he did not have the flamboyance of a Tommy Gemmell but he was reliability personified, a calm, competent defender who read the match well and could transform the situation with an accurate long pass to a Celtic forward lurking in the midfield. Kenny Dalglish, fully recovered from his sluggish start to the season, took the breath away with his talents and enthusiasm; a constant danger when playing behind the other strikers, he was a menace when leading from the front. He could chest the ball down, hold it and create space while waiting for help to arrive, and he knew or sensed when to distribute the ball with the maximum effect. He could also score goals. Two other young men were also breaking through: Roy Aitken was showing signs of becoming a most accomplished player, his basic skills matching his strength and energy; while Tommy Burns, unmistakable with his flaming red hair, seemed in the long tradition of Celtic players. Both had skill in abundance, and hearts as big as Celtic Park.

At long last, Jock Stein and the club finally reached a definite conclusion to the George Connelly affair. Everything possible had been tried to prolong this player's career, Stein showing unusual patience in dealing with him and his on-off relationship with the club. At last, Connelly was given a free transfer on 18 October 1976 with Celtic reluctantly abandoning any lingering hopes about resurrecting his career. It was a loss for everybody but at least one source of dressing-room discord had finally been removed. Several members of the Celtic squad quite naturally resented the amount of attention lavished on George Connelly and his too-frequent absences, and were privately relieved at his departure as he could well have been a contender for several different positions within the team.

The Premier League had achieved the major task envisioned for it as no one team had yet established a clear-cut supremacy over the others in the title race. Dundee United and Aberdeen jousted with Celtic for first place throughout the first quarter of the campaign while Partick Thistle and Hibernian hovered in close contention. One side was missing from the leaders and that was Rangers. The champions of the previous season had got off to a miserable start and, although they would improve later, no real challenge came from Ibrox.

In late October, Rangers were dealt two blows in quick succession. The first took place in England when they went down to the Midlands to fulfil a pointless friendly match against Birmingham; before, during and after the game their fans indulged in an orgy of hooliganism. The newspapers, north and south of the border, made a major issue of the rioting and, practically as a consequence of the criticism, the Ibrox club made a classic misjudgement in public relations by stating that they would now field players who were Catholic. What they had done was to admit in effect that up to that time the club had been practising a sectarian policy. Till October 1976 the issue had been shrouded in evasion. The obvious connection between sectarianism and hooliganism, especially in the west of Scotland, had also been established by the timing of Rangers' switch in policy.

The other blow landed in the semi-final of the League Cup when Aberdeen humiliated Rangers by 5–1, and sent a warning shot across Celtic's bows for the final which was to be held on 6 November at Hampden Park.

That match was a frustrating experience. Celtic started strongly before the 69,707 crowd and it came as no surprise when Dalglish scored after only 12 minutes. As he had done against Albion Rovers in the quarter-final, and against Hearts in the semi-final, Celtic's captain did against Aberdeen by scoring in his patented cool manner from the penalty spot after being hauled down inside the penalty area. Aberdeen fought back to equalise after 25 minutes but, from then on, the attacking football came only from Celtic. Despite all their pressure and near misses from Lennox (a second-half substitute for Burns), Doyle and Wilson, Aberdeen held out till the end. The decisive goal came within two minutes of the start of extra-time when Robb scored, squeezing the ball past Latchford from the narrowest of angles.

Stein, so often incandescent with rage at unexpected failure in League Cup finals, was philosophical about this defeat. He knew, as did every neutral, that Celtic had outplayed Aberdeen, and that luck had been an important part in the Dons' victory. He knew also that the absence of Stanton and Craig – ineligible to turn out for Celtic in the competition – had momentarily disrupted the rhythm of a settled team.

Aberdeen were ecstatic at their reprieve and ultimate triumph, and nobody more so than their manager Ally MacLeod. He refused to acknowledge the good fortune his side had enjoyed throughout a one-sided contest and did not quarrel with the description of himself as 'the miracle-worker'. It came as no surprise that MacLeod was appointed Scotland team manager when the post became available the following summer.

Because of international commitments Celtic had two weeks to recover from the Hampden disappointment and on 20 November lined up against Hearts at Tynecastle in a most vital fixture for both clubs. The outcome was a classic Hearts v Celtic confrontation: twice Hearts went into a two-goal lead, and led by 3–2 at the interval; in the second half Celtic stormed into attack and drew level with Dalglish's goal in 60 minutes, but Hearts were always dangerous on the break, in particular their striker Gibson who had scored all three of their goals. Three minutes from the end of a pulsating contest Ronnie Glavin struck to give Celtic a memorable 4–3 victory. It proved to be a turning-point in the season for both sides. Hearts started to decline rapidly and were plunged into a fight to avoid relegation; Celtic, on the other hand, were revived in full and, with a settled line-up, started to make up ground in the championship.

Four days later, on 24 November, they visited Ibrox Park. It looked ominous for the visitors after only 12 minutes when Lennox was tackled crudely in the penalty area by Greig; the referee immediately awarded a penalty-kick but was persuaded to consult his linesman. At that point, the official changed his mind and denied Celtic the award. Lennox, a thorn in John Greig's flesh for the best part of a decade, was carried off with what turned out to be a broken ankle.

After 36 minutes Joe Craig scored a memorable goal when he wheeled suddenly just outside the area and surprised the Rangers defenders with a venomous shot. The ball simply flew past the keeper to the delight of the Celtic fans crammed into the terracing behind him. From then on, Celtic coped with all Rangers' attempts to get back into the match with the defence – perhaps rebuked by Stein for conceding three goals at Tynecastle – giving away nothing. Those two victories within a few days did a great deal to encourage Celtic and their supporters. That raw, misty night at Ibrox was the occasion for all the songs of triumph as the supporters made their way home, making light of a Glasgow Corporation bus strike.

After the euphoria, the home fixture against Kilmarnock was an anticlimax. The visitors, doomed to finish last in the Premier League, were expected to put up a determined but futile resistance, but they surprised everybody, and perhaps themselves, by scoring in only five minutes. Celtic struggled to rouse themselves and, as half-time approached, still trailed by 1–0. Anybody who decided early to join the long queues at Celtic Park's primitive facilities for a pie and Bovril that cold afternoon missed all the excitement as the home side scored twice in the minute before the interval through Joe Craig and Paul Wilson. The second half was as dreich as the weather with neither side looking as if they could provide any more goals.

The weather continued to be miserable throughout December with Celtic playing only two matches. In fact, the pitch did not look playable for the visit of Ayr United on 18 December but the referee ruled otherwise. Celtic stormed into attack to score three goals within the opening 20 minutes to settle the outcome; they eased up after that start and won by 3–0. More importantly, the victory meant that they now joined Aberdeen and Dundee United at the top of the table but had eased into first place thanks to a slightly better goal average than Aberdeen.

The next fixture was a critical one – the Boxing Day clash with Aberdeen at Celtic Park, watched by a crowd of 47,000 (a figure surpassed at the ground that season only by the two matches against Rangers). Aberdeen were keen to prove that the League Cup triumph was no fluke and took the lead twice before half-time with goals from Drew Jarvie . . . but each time Joe Craig equalised. The score was 2–2 at half-time and, despite scares at both ends, a splendid match finished with no further scoring.

The bad weather caused the postponement of matches against Motherwell and Rangers at the New Year. However, the fixture at

Tannadice on 8 January went ahead with 16,000 crammed into the ground. A tight, tense match looked as if it would be decided by Kenny Dalglish's goal in 13 minutes, but United's tall striker Tom McAdam equalised with 15 minutes left. Celtic retaliated by storming into attack and their efforts were rewarded when Johnny Doyle scored the decisive goal four minutes from the end.

Three days later the postponed fixture against Rangers was played at Parkhead but there had been considerable doubt about this match starting. Celtic's traditional remedy of straw spread on the pitch in copious quantities looked to have saved the day yet again but, even as the straw was being lifted, the temperature was dipping fast. The kick-off was delayed for ten minutes while some 30 volunteers under the direction of Celtic groundstaff worked feverishly to prepare the surface before the referee Ian Foote (wearing a thick overcoat over his black uniform) would give a reluctant go-ahead.

It proved less than a classic contest, as both sets of players moved tentatively on the slippery pitch and the referee clamped down effectively on any rash challenges for the ball. The only goal of a poorish game came in the 75th minute after a short corner-kick when Roddy MacDonald's header for goal was diverted by Rangers' defender Colin Jackson past his own keeper. Rangers fought back gamely and two minutes from the end McLean's clever header from the edge of the penalty area deceived the stranded Latchford, but Roy Aitken raced back to scramble the ball clear before it could cross the line.

These results at the turn of the year in matches against their closest challengers did much to help Celtic regain the title. Wins over Rangers and Dundee United and a draw with Aberdeen served notice to the rest of the league that Celtic were now back in business.

Aberdeen appeared to be still in contention but their hopes nose-dived on 12 January with a dropped point in a home draw with Partick Thistle and the suggestion of a bribery scandal at Pittodrie. There seemed little to it but the affair started with a telephone call from a public call-box partly overheard by a local journalist. The press made a great deal of it and Grampian Police were called in to investigate . . . but absolutely nothing was ever found to incriminate anyone of taking or offering bribes or of betting against their own team. Yet such things do distract and undermine players' confidence. Some poor performances followed from Aberdeen in which points were squandered in drawn matches which should have been won easily, and their threat in the championship was diminished.

The weather continued to wreak havoc with the fixture list and

Celtic played only one league match in January. However, the game at Kilmarnock resulted in a fine 3–1 victory and the sustaining of Celtic's drive towards the championship. Once again, lowly Kilmarnock scored first but Ronnie Glavin equalised ten minutes later; after Paul Wilson had put Celtic in front early in the second half, Glavin settled the match by scoring from the penalty spot.

The championship would be won if Celtic continued to play steadily. The loss of the league title the previous season was now acting as a spur to the side and there was no danger of complacency creeping in with the winning-post in sight.

The Scottish Cup created problems, however. On 29 January Celtic travelled to Broomfield and struggled to find their touch on the poor surface and within the narrow confines of the pitch. Airdrie scored first, but Doyle largely ended any speculation of an upset by responding quickly with the equaliser. The replay was a much simpler matter; Celtic led by 4–0 at half-time and ran out winners by 5–0 with Joe Craig scoring four times in the rout. On 27 February Ayr United came to Parkhead in the next round and attracted a splendid crowd of 38,000. Ronnie Glavin scored in 63 minutes and Celtic looked in complete control of the situation; but with only two minutes remaining Cramond stole an equaliser to earn a lucrative replay for Ayr United. Again, the scenario was a familiar one as a more determined Celtic gave a competent performance in the rematch at Somerset Park. Johnny Doyle, formerly of Ayr United, and Roy Aitken, a native of those parts, scored the two goals in the second half to give Celtic a comfortable 3–1 win.

The major talking-point in Scottish football that day was not Celtic's victory (which was expected) but their signing of a new player because the deal involved no ordinary transfer, and no ordinary player. Alfie Conn of Tottenham Hotspur had not really settled during his stay in England. There were several disquieting aspects to the player and the more critical among the support suggested the following: he could be a disappointing under-achiever on occasion; he might be considered injury-prone; at times, loss of temper had led to a disciplinary record; and rumour had it that he might be a troublemaker in the dressing-room.

The most significant factor in the whole equation, however, was the fact that Alfie Conn was a former Rangers player . . . and Stein's paying out of £65,000 for him has to be viewed in the larger context of Rangers' continuing travails in 1976–77. Alfie Conn provided Stein with another opportunity to wrong-foot Rangers. Celtic's manager also knew that Rangers, in view of their struggling form, were thinking about moving for Conn. However, the Ibrox management vacillated and, while they did, Jock Stein struck; on 1 March 1977 Alfie Conn became a Celtic player. It was a public-relations master-stroke.

Back in October, Rangers had made the announcement that they would be prepared to sign Roman Catholics . . . and things had got worse for them. On the field they were a mediocre side, trailing in the league championship and crushed by Aberdeen in the League Cup. They had only the Scottish Cup to play for, and their followers were not confident about the prospects in that competition. The newspapers, eager to be in on an easy kill, pointed out the fact that attendances at Ibrox had dropped considerably since the fatal announcement and suggested that much more than disappointing form had been the cause. The journalists were also quick to indicate that, so far, Rangers had failed to sign any Catholic player, prominent or otherwise. The club had lost a great deal of credibility.

Jock Stein knew that one of the hardest battles to be won involved the on-going struggle for football supremacy in Glasgow, and he rarely missed an opportunity to 'keep Rangers off the back pages'. One journalist, Ken Robertson of the *Daily Express,* recalls dropping in frequently at Celtic Park and being grilled by Stein about news or rumours from Ibrox. Stein would appraise the item of information, and would then get to work on the journalist: 'That's very interesting . . . but I can give you something better than that for your paper.'

Only one minor detail had to be completed, and that was up to Alfie Conn on the pitch and 'playing in the hoops': he came on as a substitute at Pittodrie on 5 March, and had little opportunity to make an impression as Celtic went down by 2–0. He played against Partick Thistle at Celtic Park on 9 March, and just before half-time scored a splendid goal to give Celtic the lead and the fans a new hero. Jock Stein was delighted at the end of this match; the gamble, if it were a gamble, had paid off almost immediately.

Any lingering doubts about the allegiance of the new Celt were dispelled at Ibrox on 19 March in an old-fashioned thriller. Rangers were determined to salvage something from the season, and also to gain some momentum for their appearance in the Scottish Cup semi-final. Conn was given a torrid reception by the Rangers supporters who hurled a barrage of verbal abuse every time he moved towards the ball; the player responded with an impish grin, as if enjoying the treatment, infuriating the Rangers fans all the more. However, the Celtic player could scarcely have enjoyed the gratuitous elbow in the face delivered within seconds of the kick-off by one of his former colleagues as he moved upfield.

Apart from that one incident, the behaviour of the players was impeccable as they concentrated on the game. Celtic opened much more positively and Roy Aitken, playing wide on the right side of midfield, opened the scoring from close range in 12 minutes. Shortly afterwards, Conn hit the post with a viciously curling shot from 20 yards but Parlane equalised for Rangers before half-time with a snap-shot from the edge of the penalty area. The game swung from end to end. With only eleven minutes left, Parlane again scored for Rangers after a clever dummy from Derek Johnstone . . . and trouble broke out on the terracing at the Celtic end of the ground.

Play was held up while the situation was sorted out: hundreds of spectators had spilled on to the area behind the goal in an attempt to avoid the rain of cans and bottles from further back. The police kept them from encroaching on to the pitch, while others attempted to quell the fighting between what appeared to be two rival gangs. Stein, in a light raincoat, lumbered from the Celtic dugout to help, ushering intruders away from the field and taking time to tend his goalkeeper who had picked up a leg injury in attempting to save Parlane's shot. With order partly restored, Stein could be seen barking out instructions to his players as he limped off the field.

Whatever he said must have worked because, within five minutes of the goal, Celtic were level with a memorable counterblast from Roy Aitken. Doyle, racing down the right wing, was obstructed and then fouled near the corner flag; he took the free-kick himself and placed it perfectly for 'Aitken about five yards out. Aitken met the ball on the volley, and the ball seemed to explode into the back of Rangers' net. The TV cameras caught the moment perfectly: the Rangers supporters behind the goal were still in exultant mood; the backdrop was a red-white-and-blue rainbow of scarves and banners held aloft in triumph – until Roy Aitken connected with the cross. The triumphalism was replaced by a sullen, angry introspection.

The point earned at Ibrox made Celtic overwhelming favourites to regain the championship and suggested that Jock Stein had returned with a vengeance. Celtic had played Rangers four times in the Premier League and had avoided defeat each time with a draw and a victory at both Parkhead and Ibrox, an indication of Stein's hand on the tiller.

On 26 March Celtic disposed of Dundee United's faltering challenge in a 2–0 home win with 37,000 in attendance. Latchford would be sidelined for almost a month with his injured leg, and Stein called upon Roy Baines to replace him. Baines, like Latchford, was an Englishman; he had 'enjoyed' an anonymous career with Derby County, Hibernian and Morton although he had had a trial period with Celtic in 1968. Stein was impressed enough by him to recommend his services to Bob Shankly at Hibernian. Back in October 1976, Roy Baines finally became a Celtic player, being transferred from Morton to Celtic Park in exchange for Andy Ritchie.

It was an eventful day for the big goalkeeper and his moment of glory came in the first half when Dundee United were awarded a penalty-kick. Hamish McAlpine, United's veteran keeper, came up to take the kick and give his team the lead . . . but Baines guessed correctly and dived to save the shot. Celtic took command after that incident and Joe Craig scored, accepting an incisive through-ball from Conn to beat McAlpine.

Three excursions to Edinburgh in quick succession did a great deal to ensure Celtic's 30th league championship, though the two visits to Easter Road were shrouded in controversy. On 30 March Celtic faced Hibernian and approached the rearranged fixture with a certain reluctance. Celtic had preferred a different date, but Hibs disagreed and the matter was settled by the Scottish League in favour of the Edinburgh side. The match was played and produced a dull draw before a poor crowd (11,841). On 2 April, the following Saturday, Celtic made the same journey to the capital and disposed of Hearts comfortably by 3–0 and almost ensured that the Tynecastle squad would be faced with the spectre of relegation. On 16 April Celtic returned to Easter Road, this time hoping to clinch the league title . . . but controversy was in the air once more.

Relations between the two sets of directors had cooled because of the dispute over the scheduling of the recent match. Although aware that this game could be an important occasion for Celtic – and one of the highlights of the Scottish football season – the Hibernian board of directors, largely at the instigation of the chairman Tom Hart, refused to allow TV cameras into the ground. Celtic won the match 1–0 through Joe Craig's close-in shot but their supporters – apart from those present in the 22,306 crowd at Easter Road – were denied the sight of the goal and the subsequent celebrations on television that night. Thus, in a situation pervaded with irony, Pat Stanton, one of Hibernian's greatest players, won his only league championship medal at Easter Road – but playing for Celtic.

Celtic now had to prepare for the Scottish Cup final on 7 May 1977 against a Rangers side which had shown every indication in the recent

Ibrox clash that they had recovered their usual efficiency. In fact, their form had improved so much that they would finish second in the league table, although a distant nine points behind Celtic.

Ten days before the cup final, four Celtic players were chosen to play for Scotland against Sweden in a friendly international at Hampden Park, though Stein was not happy about that situation in view of the forthcoming Old Firm clash. Danny McGrain and Kenny Dalglish performed quite brilliantly, replicating the form they had shown for Celtic all season. Joe Craig, outstanding in his first season at Parkhead, came on as a late substitute and immediately went into the history books by scoring for his country on his début with his first touch of the ball. The fears of Celtic's manager were realised in the early stages of the match when Ronnie Glavin had to limp off with an ankle injury; as was soon confirmed, he would be unable to participate in the Scottish Cup final against Rangers.

The final was a tense affair, played out on a cold, windswept Hampden lashed by rain and watched by only 54,252 spectators, the crowd being reduced dramatically by the miserable weather and the live television coverage.

Once again in a match against Rangers, Jock Stein proved himself as a master tactician. With Glavin unavailable, he called upon Paul Wilson to pose problems for the Ibrox side; Wilson, an unpredictable player, had to be watched closely and he had been a regular scorer against Rangers. They could not ignore this threat, and Stein sensed that they would have to make some adjustments in order to deal with him.

Rangers' striking partnership of Parlane and Johnstone would be a handful physically for the Celtic defence and Stein made a switch to counter that threat. He brought in the Icelander Joannes Edvaldsson to play alongside Roddie MacDonald: Edvaldsson was a burly, no-nonsense type of defender, admirably equipped to deal with Derek Johnstone in the air. Roddie MacDonald, reassured by his cohorts Edvaldsson and the ever-watchful Pat Stanton, would have to cope with Derek Parlane (who had scored both Rangers' goals in the recent league match at Ibrox).

Stein had elected to fight a tactical battle and had chosen to contest a low-scoring match with no flowing, attacking football. Rather, this Scottish Cup final would be a war of attrition with Celtic opting for depth in defence and speed on the counter-attack.

The outcome was decided in the 20th minute following a controversial decision by the referee, R.B. Valentine. Celtic's corner on the left was taken by Conn; MacDonald headed the ball back across the face of the goal and his effort was only partially cleared. Edvaldsson reached it first and got the ball past Rangers' goalkeeper Kennedy; Johnstone was stationed on the line and scrambled the ball away at the post, but handled it in the process. Mr Valentine, in an excellent position, awarded a penalty-kick immediately, and every Rangers player converged upon him in an attempt to make him change his mind.

Was it a penalty? Repeated TV showings of the incident are inconclusive, but were taken from an angle which provided a worse view than that enjoyed by the referee. What was obvious was that Johnstone at first felt his only option was to handle the ball; in the split-second before the ball reached him he made as if to raise his knee and draw his hand away . . . but failed to do so. In any match other than a Scottish Cup final (and in any match other than an Old Firm clash) it would have been a penalty-kick . . . and the matter would have ended at that point.

While the Rangers players argued with Mr Valentine, the Celts were having discussions among themselves, and obviously the topic of discussion concerned the man chosen to take the penalty. First of all, Glavin was missing from the line-up and the most obvious replacement was Kenny Dalglish, who had scored seven times from penalties in the campaign and who, as captain, might have chosen to bear the responsibility.

To the astonishment of the supporters, it was Andy Lynch who stepped forward. It emerged that Lynch had volunteered at the last moment to take the vital kick . . . and it also was revealed later that the player had taken only two penalties in his career when playing with Hearts and missed both times. Probably, nobody in the ground that day knew these facts but the tension was almost unbearable as the player approached the ball with the Rangers fans baying in derision behind the goal. A second or so later the ball was nestling in the goalkeeper's left-hand corner, stroked along the ground by the Celtic defender just outside the keeper's reach.

Perhaps Andy Lynch had a point to prove because, only a few weeks earlier, he had denied Celtic the chance to clinch the league title at Fir Park against Motherwell. On that occasion, with Celtic trailing 1–0 but pressing furiously with five minutes left, Lynch had scored an embarrassing own-goal and had repeated the performance in the very last minute. Roy Baines, it was reported, confessed to being relieved to hear the final whistle because he thought that Lynch fancied a hat-trick! All that was now forgotten in the euphoria of an early lead against Rangers in the Scottish Cup final.

The rest of the match went according to plan – Stein's plan.

Rangers had no answer to Celtic's strength in the heart of defence, and both Parlane and Johnstone were snuffed out of the match. Edvaldsson, who had never played in a winning Celtic side against Rangers, was imperturbable and did not give Johnstone an inch, and Roddie MacDonald was immense in marking Parlane into invisibility and causing problems at the other end when he moved forward for set-pieces. As Stein had ordained, Celtic attacked mainly on the break and should have scored twice near the end as Rangers abandoned their customary caution.

It was a match without flair as various joustings on the pitch succeeded only in removing players from the action: Sandy Jardine fought a 90-minute duel with Alfie Conn and kept a tight rein on the Celt, but had to remove himself as an attacking threat in order to do so. Similarly, Celtic's attacking full-back Danny McGrain found that Rangers had delegated Alex MacDonald to block any of his advances down the right. McGrain might have been frustrated offensively but MacDonald, so often a threat to Celtic in the past, had sacrificed himself as a goalscorer. With Celtic enjoying that vital one-goal lead from the 20th minute, these duels continued to work in favour of the Parkhead club.

A tactical victory, orchestrated by a master, but a triumph in a minor key. There was an element of the autumnal about that day at Hampden . . . and that was a contemporary view, not one derived from the vantage of hindsight.

Comparisons were made with other recent victories achieved by Celtic over Rangers in Scottish Cup finals: on 26 April 1969, before a crowd of 132,870 packed into Hampden Park, Celtic gave an awesome display of skill and power to thrash a strong Rangers side by 4–0; on 12 May 1971, 103,332 crowded into Hampden for the replay won 2–1 by Celtic after the Parkhead club had dominated the first half with some sparkling football; but now, on 7 May 1977, only 54,252 were inside Hampden for a drab encounter between the old rivals.

Some might consider the 1976–77 season as one of Jock Stein's major accomplishments. He had returned to one of the most demanding jobs in football after a long absence and he had had to prove himself all over again, at an older age and at a time when his health was still suffering from the after-effects of the car accident.

Simply speaking, he did everything right that season. He remedied the weaknesses apparent in the previous campaign with the purchase of Pat Stanton and Joe Craig; he utilised the mature talents of Danny

McGrain and Kenny Dalglish to the best effect; alongside them, he nurtured the burgeoning talents of youngsters like Tommy Burns and Roy Aitken, destined to become Celtic heroes; and he realised clearly that there could be no place for George Connelly at Celtic Park any more.

He did a great deal to restore morale at Celtic Park after the shakiness so obvious there as 1975–76 drew to a close. Once again, Celtic were winning the close-fought matches, and getting something out of fixtures in which they had played with less than their usual panache. They had revived the habit of winning, and nowhere was this clearer than in the clashes with Rangers: five meetings, and no defeats. In Glasgow's long-running version of civil war, he had won every battle and, with the audacious capture of Alfie Conn, he had seized the high ground in the public-relations struggle.

Years later, John Greig, Rangers' formidable captain, would admit in a radio programme that Jock Stein was always figuring in the minds of the Ibrox men: 'We would get into the dressing-room at half-time, and know that we had done well, but we all knew that Jock Stein was in there next door and was already speaking to his men . . . We felt that we were playing against 12 players . . . and I can pay no greater compliment than that to any manager.'

Despite all that, there was a touch of sadness about the massive brooding presence in Celtic's dugout as Stein sat Buddha-like watching the action unfold on the pitch.

Notes

1. McNamara later became assistant manager at Hibernian, and his son, also Jackie, now plays for Celtic

Chapter 12

The Final Curtain

It is painful to recall the events of the 1977–78 season, a campaign which started to unravel with the loss of the team's most outstanding player and the club's captain. On 10 August 1977 Kenny Dalglish was transferred to Liverpool for a fee of £440,000, and the money – a record amount for a Scottish player at that time – was of no consolation whatsoever. Nothing could compensate for the loss of such a talent as Dalglish, recognised as the player who had been carrying Celtic for some time.

Dalglish had wanted away to test himself in the larger and more competitive arena of the English First Division, and had made more than one request for a transfer in the past. While Jock Stein had been in hospital, and Celtic in turmoil as a consequence, the player had withdrawn his request and soldiered on out of a sense of loyalty, but rumours persisted about his restlessness. The supporters had been partially reassured back in May when he had re-signed for Celtic prior to the Scottish Cup final against Rangers, but he had made it very clear privately within the club and to the manager that he wanted away.

During the summer Celtic went on a close-season tour of the Far East, visiting Singapore and Australia, but Dalglish did not travel with the party which left on 8 July. On 31 July Celtic faced Red Star (Belgrade) at the Olympic Park, Melbourne, and triumphed by 2–0 over the highly sophisticated and powerful Slavs in the World of Soccer Cup.

The news was greeted with misplaced euphoria back in Scotland but one can only wonder how Celtic supporters might have reacted had they realised that Kenny Dalglish would be transferred in the very near future, that Pat Stanton would never complete another competitive match for Celtic, and that under Jock Stein the club would never win another trophy.

Dalglish repeated his request for a transfer and Stein attempted to talk him out of it, but the player was determined to go. When he realised that the move was inevitable, Stein contacted Bob Paisley, the manager of Liverpool, to inform him of the development. Since the halcyon days of the Liverpool-Celtic rivalry under Stein and Shankly, the two clubs had been close, and an informal agreement existed between them that they would inform each other of possible deals. Unfortunately, the subservience of Scottish football clubs to market forces meant that the traffic in exceptional players was one way.

The transfer negotiations lasted a couple of days amid a deepening sense of gloom. Liverpool were desperate to sign Dalglish and Celtic were unable to hold on to him, despite last-minute impassioned pleas from Stein and Desmond White (if the stories were to be believed). The Celtic board were prepared to accept Liverpool's derisory opening offer, but Stein knew that Liverpool wanted the player to replace Kevin Keegan, recently transferred to SV Hamburg, and he managed to get the Liverpool negotiators to up their bid to £440,000. Significantly, both sets of directors were astonished at the final amount: Celtic's in jubilation at the size of the cheque, and Liverpool's in astonishment at signing Kenny Dalglish while still having close to £300,000 left after the sale of Keegan.

The departure of Kenny Dalglish marked another watershed in Celtic's history. The most important factor behind the transfer was more simple but unpalatable for Celtic supporters. Dalglish was leaving his one senior club after seven years of exemplary service to go to another which he perceived to be bigger, better and more ambitious. Sadly for Celtic followers, he was right. It was yet another indication – following the transfers of Lou Macari and David Hay – that the club could not hold on to their star players.

It was a move Dalglish was entitled to make, and which proved to be a major stepping-stone in a most remarkable career. At the time, Celtic did not seem too perturbed at his loss, the directors feeling confident that Dalglish could be replaced. But the effect on Jock Stein was more profound, and he later pointed out: 'I agree that £400,000 is a lot of money, but where do you buy another player like Dalglish?'

Jock Stein was gutted by the loss. Back in 1970 he had made a conscious decision to break up the side that had won the European Cup. That decision required courage and nerve, and boundless energy in effecting the transition. It was a move by the manager sustained by the conviction that the next outstanding Celtic team was already in place at Parkhead. In those intervening seven years, few of those earmarked for greatness at Parkhead remained as Celtic players: Dalglish, Macari and Hay had moved elsewhere; Davidson had never fulfilled his earlier promise; McLaughlin's career in the top flight had been thwarted by injury; and Connelly's had ended because of emotional problems. Of all the promising young men of 'the Quality Street Kids', only Danny McGrain was still playing for Celtic. The manager was now facing his hardest challenge at a time when he was least prepared physically and emotionally to deal with it.

What were Stein's options in 1977?

Instead of money for Dalglish, Celtic could have insisted on a player-swap with Liverpool in part-payment. The English side had a large squad, some of whom might well have relished the prospect of first-team duty under the guidance of a legendary manager like Jock Stein. But that option was not really considered . . .

Players have always been available in Scotland if the price is right, and back in 1977 the sum of £440,000 was a considerable one. Paul Sturrock of Dundee United had broken through for the Tayside club, and he was a thoughtful and talented player; young Frank McGarvey of St Mirren was showing promise, and would have been delighted to come to Celtic Park. But the weeks were passing, and there were no signs of action . . .

The directors were puzzled particularly in view of the manager's performance at a board meeting. Apparently, Stein had entered the room briskly and gave every impression of being the vibrant personality of old, positive and cheerful and radiating confidence. He informed the directors that he had been rethinking matters after the departure of Dalglish and that he was considering buying three players from Scottish clubs. One director at that meeting, Kevin Kelly, recalls being delighted with the announcement: all three named were 'outstanding performers, exciting players', men who could do much to reconcile the fans to the loss of Dalglish. The board wholeheartedly approved the manager's wishes and gave permission for the negotiations to proceed.

Weeks passed . . . but there was no movement on the transfer front. Kevin Kelly remembers coming back from a holiday and phoning another director to ask about progress; the other man told him that there had been no further word about the transfers.

In 1973 Stein could cope with the loss of such an outstanding talent as Lou Macari, but the Stein of 1977 was no longer the same man. It was not just the passing of four more years but the accumulation of seasons of stress and the very real effects of that dreadful car accident.

Dundee United visited Celtic Park on 13 August for the first league game of the season and, despite the sunshine and the promise of a new season, the visitors gave their customary 'Dundee-United-in-Glasgow' performance. They came prepared to defend in depth and to hit occasionally on the break. The result was an all too predictable tedious 0–0 draw.

Much worse than the result for Celtic was the further loss of two players, both of whom important figures for this vital season. Alfie Conn, Jock Stein's impudent capture from Tottenham Hotspur, was carried off just before half-time with a knee injury, and Pat Stanton, the veteran defender, had to be helped off the pitch near the end. Both injuries looked serious at the time, and indeed they were. The following day Jock Stein had to face the fact that Celtic would have to play the 1977–78 campaign without the best forward in Britain (Kenny Dalglish) and the best defender in Scotland (Pat Stanton). Alfie Conn – who had played well throughout the Far East tour, giving every indication that his purchase was much more than a propaganda coup – was able to resume his career with Celtic but his cartilage problem ensured that his return would be short-lived and ineffective. Pat Stanton was never able to play football again.

Surely, it was time for Celtic to act decisively on the transfer front. But there was an ominous silence from the manager's office.

Celtic travelled to Somerset Park to face Ayr United the following week in what should have been a routine collection of two points but an element of farce intruded. Johnny Doyle, an ex-Ayr United player, was determined to do well against his former club despite some barracking from the home support. Near the end, he failed to hear a whistle and his cross/shot felled the referee. When the official recovered after treatment from the trainers, he ordered Doyle off. The match finished quietly enough a few minutes later but Celtic had lost two valuable points needlessly. Afterwards, the incident was smoothed over and the general agreement was that an honest mistake had been made and that nothing more could be done. The media treated the matter with a certain amount of levity and laughter which did nothing to help morale at Celtic Park.

Worse was to befall the club in the next few weeks of the new season. Motherwell came to Glasgow, endured a fair amount of pressure and stole away ten minutes from the end to score the only goal of an uninspiring contest. The scorer was Vic Davidson, an ex-Celt and a player considered by many supporters to have been released too soon by Celtic.

At Ibrox on 8 September Celtic led by 2–0 at the interval with two goals from Joannes Edvaldsson and looked very comfortable. The supporters were reassuring themselves with the thought that a convincing win over Rangers at Ibrox was exactly the sort of result that can turn a season around. Rangers readjusted their side at the interval and in the second half produced all the football while their opponents were reduced to hanging on grimly to salvage something from the match. Celtic failed, and Rangers were worthy winners by 3–2.

It was a sobering experience and Celtic were now a club in crisis. A draw on the opening day of the season followed by three successive defeats – including a traumatic loss at the hands of their greatest rivals – confirmed the growing impression that this campaign would be a disaster. Even worse for Celtic was the fact that the second half of the fixture at Ibrox became the springboard for Rangers' success in 1977–78.

Stein was ultra-sensitive to the criticism of that match, responding ferociously to suggestions that Celtic had opted merely to contain Rangers after the interval and had thus given the home side the opportunity to claw themselves back into a contest that should have been beyond them. The diatribe attributed to Celtic's manager in the club newspaper was remarkably unconvincing. Increasingly, his performance was coming under public scrutiny, and for the first time in recent seasons the evaluations were relatively objective. Journalists, previously intimidated by the force of Stein's personality and energy, had conspired in fostering the belief that Celtic and Jock Stein were still at the height of their powers. Now, even they were aware that the situation had changed; it was not too often that Stein had been out-thought by Jock Wallace, as seemed to have happened during that match at Ibrox.

The vibrancy which had characterised Stein was no longer so apparent, and the growing fear was that those gifts might never return. Outwardly, he appeared as calm and confident as ever – maybe too calm. The Jock Stein of the past would never have tolerated the apathetic displays of his players without losing his temper. The Stein of the past would never have endured such mediocrity without doing something about it. Physically, he seemed heavier and was walking more slowly; it was noted that the limp from an injury sustained in a match against Rangers back in 1955 was more pronounced. Those supporters who habitually stationed themselves behind the Celtic dugout spoke frequently about how less animated he now was; Jim Craig, one of his more thoughtful former players, commented: 'He was different, changed. He looked like a man *watching* a football match.'

Several things had contributed to the decline in his powers. For one thing, the greatest manager in the history of Scottish football was now 55 years old, the age at which he had always contemplated retirement. A proud man, Jock Stein could never find it easy to accept less than the best from himself, and he recognised that his powers were waning. More than anybody else, Jock Stein recognised that years of tension and stress can have an accumulating effect on the body and the mind. Failure can be a grinding-down of the spirit, but success can be equally stressful.

As a revolutionary manager, one who had changed the whole concept of the manager-coach in Scotland, a man who wanted to put his own ideas and thoughts into practice, Stein had worked harder than anybody else in the game, perhaps even obsessively for too many years. An enthusiast, he had stayed behind to help youngsters work on their game, always patient with them, always encouraging. Danny McGrain remembers how Stein had been intrigued to watch Kenny Dalglish and himself, both teenagers at the time, put in some extra practice on an overlapping procedure; Stein watched intently, offered some suggestions, and stayed with them for half an hour or so until they had perfected it – and this after the regular practice and training session was over. The same Danny McGrain, somewhat older and recovering from a fractured skull, remembers the hours of heading practice with his manager as they worked day after day trying to restore the player's confidence: 'All I needed was somebody to throw the ball to me and anybody on the groundstaff could have done that, but Mr Stein undertook that himself away from the attention of other people.'[1]

Secondly, the effects of the car crash near Lockerbie must not be underestimated. Physically, the accident took a fierce toll of his body. He required months of recuperation. Some accounts suggest that he never did recover fully, that pain and discomfort were constant companions, and that 'he never had a good night's sleep after'. Emotionally, it is more difficult to evaluate but there is no doubt that any traumatic incident such as a car crash can have devastating effects on the psyche, no matter how sensible or resilient the victim is. The authors put Jock Stein's scenario to an eminent psychologist, a man unconnected with football, asking him to comment informally. The expert took pains to explain the background of a traumatic and life-threatening incident. 'In a situation like this the victim is brought face to face starkly with the fact of his own mortality. For months or years afterwards, consciously or subconsciously, the victim is forced to realise that he was within seconds or inches from his own death. That realisation can change everything for the rest of his life.'

Consider Stein prior to the accident: a man in good health, confident and capable, enjoying the respect and adulation of his peers, and entirely secure in his position. Suddenly, with no warning at all, and without a chance to do anything to avert disaster, he has a horrific car crash on a familiar road. The realisation that the collision was somebody else's fault entirely, the tragic accumulation of a series of random occurrences, and that he was no longer in control of his own fate, might well make matters worse from the victim's perspective.[2]

Stein had always been realistic, at times even fatalistic. From childhood days he knew that a miner's employment could be ended abruptly by an accident in the pit, and that a miner's life, plagued by illness, might well be cut short. A footballer's career – an escape from such an existence – could be terminated just as suddenly.

As the son of a miner, he could see the effects of life underground on an older generation. Too many of his father's contemporaries had ended their days suffering from lung disease; too many had been forced to quit working because of injuries sustained in conditions which would be condemned later as unsafe.

Football – even football with Albion Rovers – had come as an escape from that sort of life. Signing for Celtic and playing in a successful side must have struck even the pragmatic Stein as a dream come true. But on 31 August 1955 Celtic played Rangers in a League Cup tie; ten minutes before half-time Jock Stein went down in a tackle and had to be helped from the field with an ankle injury. In those pre-substitute days he resumed as a 'passenger' on the left wing for the second half and finished the match, but the injury proved stubborn and his career was virtually over.

Stein never forgot the fragility of success and worked ferociously hard to ensure he won it. The crash – for which he was entirely blameless – must have wakened some of the insecurities of his earlier days, and perhaps that is why he returned to work at Celtic Park too soon for his own good, and against the advice of his chairman. Desmond White, concerned about the effects on the manager's health, counselled Stein against returning too quickly to one of the most demanding jobs in football. As an accountant, furthermore, he advised against a premature return to work because that would adversely affect Stein's settlement with his insurance company.

The blows that Celtic sustained with the loss of Dalglish early in August, followed by Stanton and Conn within the first 90 minutes of the league campaign, must have done much to convince Stein that the season would be a disaster. Since the accident – and even during the successful 1976–77 campaign, now seen as a last hurrah – Stein had made noises to his board about stepping aside but had been coaxed into continuing with the reassurance from Desmond White in particular that he was still doing the job better than anybody else could. Perhaps Stein's earlier overtures showed a need for such reassurance, but when he started to sound out his employers in 1977–78, the endorsement was not so clear-cut.

Stein had to make things happen in order to turn Celtic around as they slipped lower and lower in the league table. With £440,000 in the bank from the transfer of Kenny Dalglish, it was apparent that Celtic needed to buy quality players and everybody waited for Stein to make some dramatic moves. The outcome was disappointing throughout the season as the manager's Midas touch seemed to have deserted him. Consider the signings and remember that they were designed to cover the loss of Dalglish (and Stanton): Ian McWilliam came from Queen's Park, and Roy Kay from Hearts on a free transfer; in the days before the Ibrox match Jock Stein had made two more signings, Tom McAdam from Dundee United for £60,000 and John Dowie from Fulham for £25,000; in October the manager signed on Frank Munro from Wolverhampton Wanderers originally on a month's trial; and in November, Joe Filippi came from Ayr United in an exchange deal.

Stein had earned the reputation of a man who could pick and inspire players. One observer put it admirably: 'He could turn the average player into a good player . . . and the good player into a great player.' But not in 1977–78.

What went wrong? His judgement may have failed him; perhaps the players he bought were simply not good enough for Celtic – and, based on their performances, that is a valid comment. Some have suggested a fatal touch of hubris – Jock Stein believed he could still weave his magic and transform these average players. This latter scenario suggests that Stein was determined to prove to himself and others that he still had the ability which made him such a great manager for so long, and that he was stubborn enough to attempt the task with inferior materials.

A recurring – and maddening – *leitmotif* was provided by TV. During that winter it seemed that every time Celtic lost, Kenny Dalglish was seen starring for Liverpool, his neon smile lighting up the screen as he celebrated goal after goal. Stein was decidedly curt with an English-based BBC interviewer, commenting acidly: 'At least now they have to admit in England that he has developed into a world-class player.'

The newcomers struggled at Celtic Park. Ian McWilliam deserves a footnote in the club's history as probably its tallest player (six foot five inches) but the giant defender made no impression; Roy Kay, perhaps worth mentioning as the bearer of one of the shortest names in football, left Celtic at the season's end exactly as he had come – on a free transfer; John Dowie made his début against Rangers and was substituted long before the end; but the most bizarre situation involved Frank Munro . . .

Although he had won nine caps for Scotland as a central defender, Munro had never fully lived up to his potential during spells at Chelsea, Dundee United, Aberdeen and Wolves. The player was a few days short of his 30th birthday and perhaps winding down his career when Stein signed him to provide stability and experience for a much-changed defence. It backfired horribly. Munro made his début against St Mirren at Parkhead on 15 October, taking the place of the injured Andy Lynch as a player and as captain. The idea of making a loan-player the captain of the side after less than 24 hours at Celtic Park was a strange one, unprecedented at the club. Admittedly, the man was experienced and had been emotionally committed to Celtic since his boyhood days in Dundee, but this decision by Stein served only to send odd signals to the other members of the team.

After leading out the side, Frank Munro, looking unfit and overweight, made an unfortunate start to his Celtic career. After 59 minutes of a boring match, he attempted to clear a harmless ball from the wing but diverted it past Peter Latchford amid stunned silence. The match finished in a surprise 2–1 victory for the visitors, gained when Billy Stark nipped in past a static Celtic defence.

After nine league fixtures Celtic were at the foot of the table; in fact, last season's champions looked like candidates for relegation. The newspapers were in a quandary over Celtic's sudden decline and in particular over the performance of the manager. For so long he had been the outstanding personality in Scottish football but the journalists could see the deterioration. So often Jock Stein had continued to win trophies with Celtic sides which could not match his teams of the mid-1960s; and for so long he had been the source of minor scoops and stories on a quiet day in football. Accordingly, the journalists continued to give Jock Stein the respect accorded to a man who could still prove them all wrong.

Only one player turned out to be a success in the long run and that was Tom McAdam, signed from Dundee United as a striker just before the defeat at Ibrox. Ironically, he went on to have a very useful Celtic career as a central defender – although he was by no means a failure as a forward – but significantly the switch back to defence was made by Jock Stein's successor.

Very little was going right for Celtic on the pitch and the decline was most apparent in the European theatre, so often the scene of triumph. After disposing of the amateur Luxembourg outfit Jeunesse d'Esch by an 11–1 aggregate, Celtic faced SWW Innsbruck of Austria and the tie offered an opportunity to kick-start the season after its dismal opening. The first leg took place in Glasgow on 19 October and Celtic's performance was disappointing despite a 2–1 win. A smallish crowd of almost 30,000 watched their team struggle to make chances which were squandered. Shortly after Joe Craig had opened the scoring in 49 minutes, the defence slipped up to allow the unmarked Kreiss a free header past Latchford. Tommy Burns put Celtic in front again 12 minutes from time with a fierce shot after an earlier effort had been blocked. This match should have been won much more comfortably, and the vital away goal should not have been surrendered.

Before the second leg in Austria, Celtic gave flickering signs of revival: a narrow win eked out at Tannadice by 2–1 after the home side had scored first in only two minutes; and an uncomfortable 3–2 win over Ayr United at Parkhead after trailing by 2–1 at half-time. And Celtic continued to progress in the League Cup, scraping past Stirling Albion on a 3–2 aggregate with only 12,000 present for the second leg (1–1) at Celtic Park.

The return leg of that European Cup tie in Austria shattered the illusion, however, and provided a miserable end to Jock Stein's exploits in Europe with Celtic. This match was played on UEFA instructions at Salzburg rather than at Innsbruck because of previous crowd trouble, and it proved a disaster for Celtic. The Glasgow side, virtually sleepwalking, were simply mugged by reality. Within 27 minutes Innsbruck had scored three times, punishing their opponents' defensive frailty; the Austrians had opened strongly, tackling ferociously for every ball and running hard at Celtic. The Scottish champions had little answer to the onslaught, beaten to every ball and in danger of being humiliated both physically and technically. The saddest thing was the awareness that Innsbruck were little more than an average side.

Back at the hotel in the Tyrolean hills after the match, the Scottish journalists accompanying the Celtic party were astonished to find that Jock Stein quickly made his excuses and went to bed. Normally on the European trips, Stein, a poor sleeper at the best of times, would hold court in the team's hotel, drinking cups of tea and regaling the press with his views on football. Many of the journalists, exhausted after their exertions, would be longing for their bed but unwilling to leave in case Stein would casually allow some information to be imparted to the others. But not this time . . . the manager looked tired and acted tired.

The purchase of Joe Fillipi, a journeyman full-back from Ayr United, indicated that Celtic were worried about the fitness of Danny McGrain who had limped off against Hibernian at Celtic Park on 1 October, having helped his side to an encouraging 3–1 win. Astonishingly, that harmless-looking ankle-knock led to his absence from Celtic's side for almost 18 months. The absence of McGrain – a world-class player – was a severe blow to the struggling team as his injury mysteriously refused to clear up despite a variety of treatments from doctors and specialists. It was scarcely fair to expect that Filippi could replace a player of the calibre of Danny McGrain in the affection of the supporters – and so it proved.

The signings made by Stein continued to puzzle Scottish football. The brilliance of Dalglish, the polish of Stanton and the class of McGrain was being replaced by the workmanlike skills of players generally considered as no more than ordinary or reliable. Stein was unlucky in that he did not get the performances from his more established men that season but that was yet another indication of the sea-change in the manager.

Celtic's form continued to improve slowly, however, and the fans could take some consolation in the team's progress through the League Cup after the hiccough against Stirling Albion. In November Celtic won both legs of the quarter-final against St Mirren – and that was an accomplishment in 1977–78 as in the league campaign the Parkhead men could draw only one match and lose the other three against the Buddies. A crowd of 18,101 at Paisley saw Celtic storm into a three-goal lead after 50 minutes before St Mirren, managed by a young Alex Ferguson, scored one goal to restore some confidence for the visit to Parkhead; another disappointing crowd at Celtic Park (17,000) on 19 November one week later saw Celtic win comfortably enough by 2–0, Paul Wilson and Johnny Doyle netting early in the second half to give their side a 5–1 aggregate victory.

The Old Firm clash on 12 November was inconclusive. Rangers started the match more confidently and deserved a half-time lead of 1–0, but the home crowd of 56,000 was in an uproar throughout the second half as Celtic piled on the pressure. Within five minutes of the restart Tom McAdam had equalised with a typical goal; the newcomer Fillipi made space for himself down the right and crossed a tempting

ball for Craig who nodded it down for McAdam to lash home. Fou
minutes later Parkhead erupted again when McAdam netted ... but the
referee disallowed it and marched back into Celtic's half of the field to
award them a free-kick. Worse was to follow for Celtic after another ten
minutes of sustained pressure: Joe Craig, breaking through on goal, was
dragged down in the penalty area by Forsyth in the most blatant of
tackles but this time the official did apply the advantage rule in some
form or another. The ball had broken to Tom McAdam, but the Celtic
striker – like every other player in the vicinity – had stopped in his
tracks. It was a most curious decision, especially in view of his earlier
one, and the constant replaying of it on TV did very little to show the
referee in anything other than a foolish light. Celtic were unable to
break through for a decisive goal and the match finished 1–1, any
consolation lying in the knowledge that, despite their lead in the
championship, Rangers were not a better team.

The mini-revival continued with some spirited performances: Billy
McNeill was cheered to the rafters by the 27,000 crowd when he took
his place in the Aberdeen dugout a week later and Celtic beat his team
by 3–2; Partick Thistle came to Parkhead next and were summarily
dismissed by a 3–0 scoreline; at Love Street, Celtic rallied from 3–1
down to St Mirren to take advantage of an ordering-off and scored
twice within the last ten minutes to snatch one point. For the third
match in a row Andy Lynch had scored from the spot but the cynics
pointed out that the claims for the most important penalty of all had
been rejected by a referee.

Dundee United came to Celtic Park on Christmas Eve in their
customary Ebeneezer Scrooge guise and left unlamented, defeated by
Edvaldsson's goal with only eight minutes left to play. The crowd of
21,000, frustrated by the visitors' defensive tactics, had started to
become alarmed as United knocked the ball around with some
confidence just prior to Celtic's goal. Still, a win was a win and Celtic
had caught up with United in the standings with a game in hand. Now
in fifth place, virtually the best position they had attained since the
opening of the season, the club were in a better position to mount a
challenge of sorts.

The league campaign collapsed for Celtic over the New Year period,
that critical period when the title is so often decided in the mud, rain
and sleet of Scottish midwinter.

At Somerset Park on Hogmanay, they went down weakly 2–1 to a
hardworking Ayr United. It was a disappointment and a serious setback,
but worse was to follow at home against Motherwell on 2 January.

Celtic outplayed the Lanarkshire side but could not find the net; and Motherwell broke away to score the vital goal in 24 minutes. Celtic redoubled their efforts, and were denied two valid-looking claims for penalty-kicks by the referee, David Syme, an official fated to cross swords with Celtic repeatedly in the future.[3]

The stage was set for another Old Firm clash at Ibrox on 7 January, and the mood of resentment among the Celtic support was tangible. Every omen in that luckless season pointed to yet another moral victory for Celtic . . . but two points for Rangers in their quest for the championship. For some supporters that might have been bearable – almost. However, the events at Ibrox simply beggared belief, and the controversy was initiated by the refereeing of the match official, J.R.P. Gordon.

Rangers took the lead with an exceptional goal from Gordon Smith, but Celtic had had the better of the opening and were continuing to play positively, pressing Rangers hard immediately. A cross floated across Rangers' goalmouth and Joe Craig was rising at the back post to head in the equaliser until he was pushed by Colin Jackson, opting to give away a penalty-kick rather than a certain goal. At first the players scarcely bothered to appeal for the award, so blatant and clear-cut was it, and the Celtic fans were in an uproar, anticipating the equaliser from the spot. But the referee hesitated and started to turn away.

The bedlam started at that point.

More than half the Celtic team started to appeal furiously to Gordon and he remained undecided. Finally, he started to trot over to the linesman on the stand side with several Celtic players in close attendance. In a most bizarre fashion, but with a sudden rush of decisiveness, Gordon – only ten yards away from his assistant – suddenly wheeled sharply upfield.

Meanwhile, Rangers' goalkeeper had retrieved the ball from behind the goal-line and, without waiting for a whistle or acknowledgement from the referee (who was running towards the linesman), tapped the ball forward. As Gordon wheeled upfield, he saw that the game had restarted and that Rangers were moving upfield; incredibly, he waved play on, as if using the advantage rule. Only two Celtic players, one of whom was the goalkeeper, were in any position to defend against this situation . . . and Rangers scored through John Greig. The scorer, a veteran defender at that stage, was scarcely the sort of player likely to turn up in the opposition's penalty area seconds after a Rangers goal-kick.

To the disbelief of the Celtic players, the goal was allowed to stand, a disbelief which turned to outrage immediately with the realisation that within seconds the referee had turned down the most obvious of penalty-kicks and had awarded a goal to their opponents. In the stands, the mood was turning ugly and several hotheads among the supporters came over the walls, but were quickly ushered away.

The mayhem was not over. The Celtic players were furious, convinced to a man that they were being cheated; the Rangers players stood back, talking to themselves, and at least a couple of them, originally mystified but now embarrassed, looked over at their rivals and shrugged in some form of sympathy. It looked as though the Celtic players were about to walk off the pitch in protest at the proceedings. Some headed towards the main stand, either on their way off the field or to get instructions from the dugout; others continued jostling and arguing with the referee; yet others stood in confusion. The manager, although thoroughly aggrieved, gestured to his players to restart the game, and the trainers, Bob Rooney and Neil Mochan, rushed on to the pitch, clearly asking for calm and encouraging them to continue.

Eventually, the game – up to that stage, ironically, one of the best Old Firm matches for a long time – resumed and was played out in an unreal atmosphere. To their credit, Celtic continued to make a contest of it and most press accounts catalogue their ill luck in the second half: another penalty – this time for 'hands' – denied and an Aitken shot which rebounded from the post. The match finished up 3–1 for Rangers but the controversy continued in the streets and in the pubs, fuelled by TV evidence. The cameras had captured the affair and endless reruns simply failed to see any rationale behind the referee's decisions.

For once, the papers were united about the calibre of refereeing. The chief correspondent of the *Glasgow Herald* had his match report headlined 'Five Questions for Old Firm Referee' – and followed that up with a series of questions, virtually a cross-examination, concerning the one incident, described by the reporter as 'two minutes of mayhem'. The whole episode had a touch of the surreal about it ... and to the devotees of the theatre of the absurd it appeared entirely logical and natural that Mr Gordon should be appointed as one of the European referees for the World Cup held in the Argentine in 1978.[4]

Refereeing had played a part in Celtic's decline throughout 1977–78 but the question of officiating only highlighted the waning of Jock Stein's powers. Throughout his career as a manager Stein had always been able to intimidate match officials with his forceful personality and imposing presence; one former Celtic director described this ability memorably: 'He cowed them into fairness.' The increasing frequency of doubtful decisions against Celtic suggested that the manager's legendary influence was fading away, and Stein seemed resigned to the fact.

In the recent past, any harsh or dubious decision could be overcome by the talents of the Celtic players, but that collective talent or attitude was no longer there. Their league form was in a downward spiral; in a miserable coincidence, Celtic's performance matched almost exactly the disastrous start to the season with losses to Ayr United, Motherwell, Rangers to be followed by defeats from Aberdeen and St Mirren.

Jock Stein's position was by now untenable. Several times over the past 12 months he had already offered to go, and had gone as far as nominating Billy McNeill as the best possible replacement to the directors. Previously, Desmond White had resisted the manager's repeated suggestion, but now the chairman was prepared to act. After a couple of meetings the general scenario was mapped out: the manager would continue in full charge until the end of the season, after which he would be invited to join the board of directors; the chairman would contact his counterpart at Aberdeen in order to initiate negotiations with the heir-apparent; Jock Stein would be in frequent communication with McNeill prior to the takeover

Meanwhile, Celtic's week-to-week task would be to see through 1977–78 and perhaps end it with some success in the League Cup or the Scottish Cup. The bad weather throughout the winter had caused a delay in playing the League Cup final against Rangers but, before that, Celtic had to face Kilmarnock of the First Division, who visited Parkhead on Scottish Cup business and put up a most determined resistance. Despite all the Celtic pressure, after Kilmarnock scored, the visitors held out until six minutes from the end when Roddie MacDonald equalised from close range. It was a disappointing performance, but the supporters consoled themselves with the club's admirable record in Scottish Cup replays. But in 1977–78 tradition meant very little.

At Rugby Park, Celtic lost 1–0 to Kilmarnock when McDicken scored a late goal; Roy Aitken, still a relatively young player, was appointed captain for the night but may have taken his responsibilities too seriously as he was ordered off for two very physical challenges on opponents. One reporter, Rodger Baillie, described the return of the Celtic supporters' buses across Fenwick Moor with a touch of hyperbole: 'Napoleon's retreat from Moscow could not have been any gloomier.'

The League Cup final, at Hampden Park on 18 March, loomed as Celtic's last chance for glory that season, and it was generally felt that with a little luck they could beat Rangers. Absolutely no luck was available for Celtic in 1977–78 and the 60,168 crowd watched a tense match fought out on a bright spring afternoon. Rangers scored first in 38 minutes when Davie Cooper netted after fine work by Smith. Basically, it was a dour war of attrition fought out in midfield, a stalemate in which neither side looked too likely to score again. However, with only five minutes left young Alan Sneddon – only a month in Celtic's first team – advanced up the right to cross high into the area, where Joannes Edvaldsson rose to head the ball into Rangers' net for an equaliser. During extra-time there were close things at each end. Inevitably, the end came with a sickening thud and the tinge of controversy when, with three minutes left, Celtic's goalkeeper Latchford and MacDonald of Rangers clashed when going for a cross and the ball bounced out for an alert Smith to score by diving to head home. Noting the collision between goalkeeper and forward, some referees might well have automatically awarded a free-kick to the keeper ... but David Syme allowed the goal without a moment's hesitation.

There was little else for Celtic to play for that season, although they managed to thrash Rangers at Parkhead a week later by 2–0 in the last Old Firm league fixture. The remaining matches were played out before smallish crowds and little excitement as Jock Stein's tenure drew to a close.

Behind the scenes at Celtic Park, everybody knew that the great man's days were numbered: directors, staff and players. Despite the rumours, few actually realised that the league fixture against St Mirren at Paisley on 29 April 1978 would be Stein's last match in charge of the club that he had transformed. There was something at stake as a win for Celtic would have earned them a place in Europe, albeit only in the UEFA Cup, but the side caved in and went down 3–1 in a display described as 'spineless'.

Alex Ferguson, St Mirren's manager, accepted Stein's congratulations and strode into the whitewashed tunnel; Jock Stein nodded to the referee and linesmen, took a last look at the Celtic supporters heading for the exits at Love Street, and limped into the darkness of the tunnel ...

Notes

1. Danny McGrain was in such awe of his manager that he always referred to him as 'Mr Stein'.
2. The accident occurred on the notorious A74 when a car being driven down the wrong side of the dual carriageway crashed

into Stein's vehicle. It emerged later that some locals had been in the habit of using 'wrong-way' stretches of the motorway as a shortcut.

3. Like his father before him, Syme had several run-ins with Celtic managers. Allegedly, after one performance at Celtic Park, the younger Syme, aware that he had had a bad day, was greeted by Jock Stein's sarcastic congratulations: 'Well done . . . your father would have been proud of you.' Curiously, his grandfather, another David Syme, played for Celtic a couple of times in goal during the 1918–19 season.

4. Controversy continued to dog this referee as he was involved years later in a gift-taking scandal prior to a European Cup tie.

Epilogue

The record of Jock Stein's accomplishment speaks for itself: a European Cup, ten championships, eight Scottish Cups and six League Cups. Achievement is satisfying, but the true magnificence of his years at Celtic Park lay in his teams – and it should be remembered that Stein, in his 13 years at Parkhead, was in charge of three quite distinct teams. The more erudite commentators use words like 'brio' and 'gusto' and 'flair' to capture the essence of those sides; our postman, a lifelong Hibs supporter, is more down-to-earth: 'Celtic? Whit a team that wis! Whit a team!'

The difficulty in writing about those days is to separate the truth from the myth, the man from the legend. Research can be enjoyable: reading the old newspapers yellowing in libraries or on microfilm, studying the TV clips and videos, interviewing former players and managers, talking to journalists and 'football men', sitting in the pub blethering to the old-timers. Memories can be faulty, understandably so – high on emotion, low on reason. So, the writer has to steer a difficult course. It would be easy to describe every player as a 'star', every goal as 'spectacular', every performance as 'brilliant'. Easy, but not fair to supporters who deserve the truth in a book about their club and its heroes.

This is not a true biography about Jock Stein in the sense of laying his whole life bare; rather, it is an account of his public life as Celtic's manager, attempting to give a picture of a man at the height of his considerable powers. The authors feel that Jock Stein was the greatest manager in the history of Scottish football and are filled with admiration for his accomplishments and personality. Admiration, but not hero-worship, and not idolatry.

All careers decline – as do all men, inevitably. Football is for the young, and ageing can be cruel. This book is a football life, and ideally the story of such a man would end with the capture of a European Cup to crown a career; instead . . . Frequently, life does not imitate art. A proud man, Stein fought hard to retain a great and deserved reputation and resisted the advance of age with every resource, especially cunning. It was a brave fight, but one doomed to end in failure. In Stein's case, the failure is surely a relative term.

As a performer, Jock Stein was a late bloomer and achieved success only in the last phase, as a veteran player with Celtic. His affection for the club and its supporters was a belated but genuine one, and he admitted later that he had stayed on too long as Celtic's manager out of 'a misplaced sense of loyalty'. He recognised the problem of the older manager: 'You are still saying all the right things . . . but they're not listening as much.'

Archie Macpherson was asked by us to list Stein's qualities as a manager. He started with 'presence'. Jock Stein had the ability both to reassure and to intimidate. We have seen numerous examples of his authority over players, but his forceful personality had an effect on others, too, most notably the media.

In his early days, Stein did not trust the BBC to cover Celtic fairly, and was quick to voice his criticisms. Peter Thomson, more or less the supremo of Scottish football broadcasting, was terrified of Stein, so much so that it was believed that he never went to Celtic Park after Stein's arrival, fearing the man who dubbed him 'Blue Peter'. Relationships between Celtic's manager and the BBC declined rapidly, the attitude of the Corporation (or Thomson) being that 'Celtic would need us first'. The club's astounding success changed all that, and eventually that august body was begging for interviews, but Stein was slow to forgive and frequently remained 'difficult' with those who had offended him.

Stein read all the newspapers, and studied the clippings; frequently, he would phone up the reporter responsible and, if the article had been offensive or derogatory, he would be furious. One editor described the effect of such a call: 'Your ear would feel like a seared pork chop after he finished with you.' At press conferences, he would often pick on individual journalists in a savage manner and the feeling persisted that he was establishing a psychological hold over them, to be used in the future, as required.

Stein was quick-witted and had a caustic turn of phrase. In a post-match interview, minutes after Celtic had beaten Rangers 2–1, narrowly but very convincingly, in a Scottish Cup final replay, he blandly agreed with the interviewer: 'Yes, a good result . . . ' A pause, and then he added, '. . . for Rangers.'

At other times, Stein could be more conciliatory. Defending a player, he would point out: 'Did you not notice that Dundee had two men marking him all night? You can't criticise a player for being outnumbered, can you?' One of the authors remembers clearly speaking to him for an hour in the lobby of the Royal York Hotel in Toronto: relaxed and at ease, he sat in an armchair, his back to the wall in a position that commanded a view of the whole foyer. He missed nothing, as his eyes watched the comings and goings of his players. The author asked him how the traditional formations would fare against the modern variations he was experimenting with. He looked astonished at first, before realising that it was a genuine question, born out of ignorance. His answer was gentle: 'You've spent too long in Canada, Tom. The old system just couldn't cope . . . they would always be outnumbered in the vital areas of the pitch. The old way was static and predictable; the new systems are fluid . . .'

He was not well educated in a strictly formal sense, but he had a natural intelligence. Bob Crampsey, a former headmaster, considers him as 'the finest possible advertisement for the existence of the Scottish junior secondary school'. Billy McNeill, when told by us that the last section of this book was titled 'The Old Fox', smiled and said, 'Big Jock was always a fox.'

Stein was quick to size up situations. Kevin Kelly remembers one of his ploys with referees: the official would knock on the dressing-room door about 30 minutes before kick-off to ask for the team sheet. Stein would explain his delay: 'One of the players is a bit nervous. He's in the toilet right now, throwing up. I don't know if he can play; I'll see how he's getting on. Can we have another couple of minutes? By the way, is that the other team sheet in your hand? Could I have a wee look?' Kelly was convinced that a quick glance at the opponents' list told Stein exactly how the other side would attempt to play and give him time to counter it. He was also certain that Stein was careful to attempt this gambit with the same referee only once.

Jimmy Farrell, a director at Parkhead throughout Stein's tenure, noted: 'He was always asking questions . . . he wanted information about things.' For Farrell, it indicated an inquisitive mind and an interest in affairs from which a lack of education had excluded him.

He would talk tirelessly about football. After Celtic's visit to Deventer in 1965, Dr Fitzsimons, Jimmy Farrell and Stein went to a restaurant in the Dutch city. The night wore on into the small hours, as did the arguments. Finally, Farrell and Fitzsimons pleaded weariness and went to their hotel room. Thirty minutes later, Stein knocked on the door and entered, ready to resume the discussion. Dr Fitzsimons' eyes closed and he nodded off . . . Stein poked him in the chest and 'patted' him on the cheek: 'Don't you go to sleep on me, I've not finished yet . . .'

Socially, he was a man who could mix relatively easily. He had the gift of small-talk and enjoyed the patter with football types. Much of his *bonhomie* was on the outside, however, as he was cautious about revealing too much of his private self except to trusted friends of long standing. Crampsey again found the best description: 'a very private public man'. He spent long hours working on Celtic's behalf, too many long hours, but he valued his home life. Cyril Horne told us: 'He insisted on privacy at home and he was very proud of his family – his wife Jean and children Ray and George. They were a close-knit family.'

He was not strictly a teetotaller; he enjoyed the occasional glass of wine but frowned on his players over-indulging – a typical trait in a traditional manager. Wisely, he (and Fallon and Mochan) knew when to make themselves scarce, sensing those times his players needed to let their hair down. Ronnie Simpson insists that Celtic were not noted as a hard-drinking club, 'not in the same league as others I have known'. Bobby Murdoch has a clear picture in his mind of the day before Stein's car accident, when he was on holiday in Minorca. He and his wife had joined up with the Steins at the hotel and, after ordering another beer, was told by Stein, 'You shouldn't be drinking that stuff.' Murdoch shakes his head in some disbelief: 'I was over 30 years of age . . . I was on my holidays . . . and I didn't even play for Celtic then.'

That accident on the A74 in July 1975 has to be viewed as a major turning-point in Jock Stein's career as Celtic's manager. After that, despite reasonable success, his edge had gone – that abrasive driving ambition that had taken him so far. He moved more slowly and his periods of silence were longer; at times, he appeared lost in private thought. We have tried to resist the trend in modern biography to branch into psychiatry, but it is clear that Jock Stein was never again the same man.

Until the accident, Stein was not a man who thought much about money. He was happy enough with his salary at Celtic Park although he appears disgracefully underpaid in comparison with others in Britain. He enjoyed the trust of his chairmen in the matter of expenses; he was a manager who put in long days at Glasgow and then travelled frequently to England to attend a match – not just to watch it but to learn and listen.

Archie Macpherson remembers the number of times he was joined by Stein for 'Football Nights' up and down the country: 'He never let you down . . . he would be there as he promised, no matter how crowded his schedule. He never once asked for a red cent – and he could have been given a lot.'

After the accident, Stein was forced to think about providing for his family in the event of his absence; the man he engaged as his accountant was appalled at the haphazard state of his finances, and by the relatively low salary paid to such a prominent manager.

His 'gambling' was a matter of speculation. It seems that it was a form of relaxation, an attempt to match his wits against bookmakers . . . and to celebrate the occasional win. Tony Queen, the Glasgow bookmaker and passenger in the car, was a close friend and he has stated that he would never have accepted a wager from Stein: 'I would have chased him if he had tried.' Incidentally, before and after he became 'Sir Robert', Bob Kelly was a more compulsive gambler than Stein – a fact which contributed to the bond between the men.

Managers have been known to profit by the transfer of players and, in the arcane world of football finances, this was relatively easy to do. Jimmy Farrell stated Stein's position clearly enough: 'I have never heard of Jock Stein being associated with that sort of activity . . . but I know of other managers who have. Stein was never an avaricious man.'

What remains clear is that Stein never weakened Celtic in order to benefit personally, directly or indirectly, from a transfer fee; those who left were expendable, or wanted to go. Jock Stein was accused of breaking up the Lisbon Lions too soon, and perhaps this is true. He had a group of exceptional young players waiting to take their place, however, and he seemed to welcome the challenge of creating his own side rather than developing the team he had largely inherited in 1965.

Jock Stein could manipulate crowds and he was a politician in the best sense of the word, with the politician's talent for gesture, but it was not mere tokenism. He never forgot his roots, nor did he lose any affection for the mining communities. During the miners' strike in 1984 he was reported as having stuffed 'several notes of various denominations' into the collection-box of a NUM representative outside a football ground. Similarly, he had the statesman's ability to deliver the telling phrase, an ability which meant that conversations in the pubs stopped whenever his familiar, broad face appeared on the TV screen.

He was not afraid to take risks either physically or psychologically. On at least two occasions (at Stirling and Ibrox) he left the dugout to wade into Celtic supporters to help sort out disturbances. That required physical courage.

He was a man entirely comfortable with the power that a football manager wields. Clubs in those days virtually owned the services of their players through the terms of harsh contracts; Stein was at ease with that system and understood it perfectly. Frequently his players complained about a low basic wage, but they could not argue with the bonuses that success brought. They complained often about the training gear, the rough and uncomfortable tops which left a rash, but Stein could brush that aside with the observation that football was a form of manual labour, shaming his players with descriptions of working conditions in the pits. Like his counterpart at Liverpool, he hated to see players in the treatment room, preferring his men to work their way through the pain. He could be brutal at times and some of his players hated him. One famous ex-Celt, walking towards a supporters' function, expressed his frustration: 'How could we ever tell these people [the supporters] just what a bastard he was?'

Growing up in industrial Lanarkshire as the son of a miner, Jock Stein was a Labour man through and through. He was no revolutionary, however. He accepted in general terms the structure of society and was happy to see improvements and a fairer share for those deprived. Like many Labour voters of that generation, there was a strong streak of conservatism in his make-up; rapid change was not to be trusted too much . . .

He was Scottish through and through. Some journalists have suggested that he was the family member most unwilling to move to England when the 'invitations' started to come from top clubs; the most erudite of them said simply: 'Jock got home-sick after he passed the traffic lights at Baillieston.'

He was refreshingly free of the taint of sectarianism which scars much of the west of Scotland, and thought he had ruined his chances of becoming Dunfermline's manager in 1960 with his forthright answer to a question about his beliefs. At Celtic Park, a club with a Catholic ambience, he simply did not allow his religion to become an issue; his sense of humour allowed him to see some of the 'discrepancies' in his position, and he relished that.

As a football man, however, Jock Stein was an international figure. He was a man who wanted to learn, and he went to school everywhere: a visit to Helenio Herrera in Italy, matches in England and the Continent, lectures and demonstrations at Lilleshall, dropping in to chat with European sides at their hotels in Scotland . . . He may not have been a genuine innovator, a man who totally changed the way we look at football, but he had the marvellous ability to see what was happening in the football world and the strength of will to adapt it successfully to his Scottish sides. His mind, despite his homespun Scottishness, was sophisticated in football matters.

He was – and remains – the greatest Scottish manager of them all.

★

The last word belongs to a Catholic priest in a recent conversation with the authors: 'Have you heard about the Celtic supporter who died and went to Heaven? St Peter saw his jersey and told him he was just in time for the game against Rangers. The supporter went along to the ground and joined 50,000 other Tims. Truly he was in Heaven: Rangers were denied a penalty and had two players sent off before half-time, and Celtic led 3–0. Oddly enough, the Celtic supporter was a wee bit bored and his attention wandered. He noticed some commotion in the Celtic dugout and asked his neighbour about it. "You mean the old yin with the white beard and hair? Don't worry – that's just God and sometimes he gets carried away and thinks he's Jock Stein."'

Index